Max Bygraves

IN HIS OWN WORDS

Max Bygraves
IN HIS OWN WORDS

The Breedon Books
Publishing Company
Derby

First published in Great Britain by
The Breedon Books Publishing Company Limited
Breedon House, 44 Friar Gate, Derby, DE1 1DA.
1997

ISBN 1 85983 079 X

Printed and bound by Butler & Tanner Ltd., Selwood Printing Works, Caxton Road, Frome,
Somerset.

Colour separations by RPS Ltd, Leicester.

Jackets and gold-blocking by Lawrence-Allen Colour Printers, Weston-super-Mare, Avon.

Contents

WORDS

Words …Words …Words
Can say so much, or nothing at all.
They can be the making of you,
Or equally, your downfall.

Words can tell of love and truth,
Of violence, hate and greed.
They can persuade and encourage you,
Or they can deceive and mislead.

Words can be very beautiful,
Or ugly and unkind.
They can be eyes to a blind man
And can ease a troubled mind.

Words can be simple, or very involved,
They can be spoken lightly or seriously,
But always think before you use them
Words last for ever …choose them carefully.

Devina Symes

Foreword

AS a theatre show producer I have known Max for many years. He is, without doubt, one of the finest entertainers that Britain has produced, yet he remains a very humble and nice man, a gentleman who is a good friend and a great family man.

When you are in his company he soon makes you forget that he is a living legend. He is one of the most successful recording stars Britain has ever known and he is constantly in demand to appear in Australia, New Zealand and the USA.

He is an icon in British showbusiness. His audiences are not just of the older generation either. He is fast becoming a cult figure among the young. It is amazing to see large numbers of students queuing to buy tickets for his shows. They enjoy his act along with the rest of us. During his marvellous summer season in Bournemouth in 1996 it was often remarked to me how many young people were really keen to see Max.

It is no surprise really, because he has spanned the years so well and he is such a great performer. I have produced and watched him countless times, yet I am still drawn to watch his performance again and again. He is a master of showbusiness technique, a great raconteur who achieves an instant rapport with his audience. He can tell an old gag and effortlessly make it appear to be brand new. No matter how big the stage or auditorium he reduces it to the size of a living room, and you just cannot help enjoying his company because he is always a mate and never a big time star.

I first became aware of Max Bygraves when I listened to *Educating Archie* on the radio when I was a boy. I became a fan instantly and I am still a fan. He is not only a marvellous entertainer but a great ambassador for showbusiness.

Thank you, Max.

JOHNNY MANS
SUMMER 1997

CHAPTER ONE

The Good Old Days

*I*T'S VERY easy to tell when you are knocking on a bit. Kids keep asking what you did, rather than what you do. What did you do in the war? You don't know if they mean the Gulf, Falklands, World War Two, World War One, Boer, Crimean or Napoleonic! Neither do they! That's when I decided to put quill to paper and tell you a story — the story of Max Bygraves who was born in the good old days and has been enjoying those good old days ever since. Today I'm in my very sprightly 70s — still singing, dancing, telling a few gags and enjoying myself in theatres all over the world. I don't have to do it but I like to enjoy myself, and I do it in the best way I know how, by sharing my pleasure with others.

Some of those good old days are a bit more gooder than others. Yes, that's right, English was never my favourite subject at school. I've since learned the value of a good education — it must be valuable because it costs the earth.

Let's travel in time together, back to the good old days of my childhood. I come from one of the most exotic locations in Britain — Rotherhithe! It's a wonderful hamlet in East London alongside the Thames, and I used to spend many happy hours gazing into the flowing water counting the dead cats — and worse things — that floated by. To kids like myself the driftwood could be anything from a Spanish galleon to the wreckage of the Titanic, or, indeed, a pirate ship plundering and pillaging its way to Bermondsey.

Imagine the scene. Rotherhithe on the afternoon of October 16th 1922. Amid a warren of abodes that even the most imaginative of estate agents could hardly describe better than by using the word 'slums', is the two-roomed council flat which served as the castle of one Henry Bygraves, his young wife, Lily, and their 18-month-old son Henry junior. Most of the men from that labyrinth of a couple of hundred council flats worked at the Surrey Docks. Well some of them worked there, others just went along to see if anything had happened to fall off the back of a crane.

Henry Bygraves was a bit different. He had another identity. On that particular afternoon in October, he was on his way to The Ring in Blackfriars, a short tram-ride from Rotherhithe and a mecca for the boxing and wrestling fraternity. In one session there would be the smell of blood and sweat as the boxers slugged it out to the accompanying roar of the crowd; and in the next, that same crowd would be baying as exotically-named, and even more exotically-dressed, wrestlers attempted to maim each other for life. Such genteel words of encouragement as, "Rip 'is bloomin' arm orf!" and "'it 'im wiv the soggy end!" would fill the smoke-laden air, and a good time would be had by all.

Anyway, Henry Bygraves got on the tram to Blackfriars. When he got off at the other end, he was no longer Henry Bygraves. He had become Battling Tom Smith and was one of the gladiators scheduled to duck between the ropes that afternoon. The name-change was simply because he thought it would look better on the posters.

That afternoon he lived up to his title and battled away for six rounds before finally losing on points. He collected 30 bob — £1.50 if you prefer (or probably half an ECU) — and packed his gear back into his brown carrier bag. He didn't hang about because he was due to fight again that night at Stepney, and he had to nip home to Rotherhithe first for a news bulletin.

That was when we first met. He looked down at me and heard that I had just weighed in at 9lbs 6ozs. I would have returned his gaze but I found it impossible to keep my eyes open as I had just fought a few rounds of my own to get into the world. He smiled at me, gave my mum a kiss, and was gone. He left the 30 bob behind and caught a bus to Stepney where he had a celebration all of his own. He beat his opponent and pocketed a tenner, returning home straight away. Not for him the wetting of the baby's head in the local alehouse, he wanted to be home with his family.

Let me put you in the picture about the family background. Before deciding to become a professional boxer, my dad had been in the Army.

Although his name was Henry, he was called Harry, not an uncommon practice and one that was passed on to my brother Harry ...er Henry. Dad lived off his army pay until it ran out, and that was when he decided to become a paid scrapper. He married my mother, Lily, in 1919 when he was 23 and she was just 18. My grandfather had been a seaman and was affectionately known by all as 'Captain'. He used to be very popular in the local, where he would tell tales of the sea and sing shanties. He enjoyed himself because his glass never seemed to be empty and the landlord reaped the benefit of all the willing buyers. He met my grandmother in America where she had emigrated with her family who hailed from Limerick.

When times got a bit difficult for the Captain and Harriet, his wife, they did what many others did in those times, they went to the pawn-shop. They did not have a lot in the way of valuables, but they did have false teeth, which were considered to be fair currency in that area in those days. You could tell when times were hard because everyone gritted their gums and decided *not* to grin and bear it!

As one of six kids, my dad was brought up a good Catholic, which is probably why he had six kids of his own. Thinking back, I wonder why it never occurred to him that the priests who encourage such large families, never themselves have to change nappies, or stay awake night after night rocking a pink crying machine.

Yes, after I was born, Harry and Lily created another four kids, all girls. There was Lily, Patricia, Kathleen and Maureen. You can see the Irish influence in the choice of names. Me? No, I was not named Max! I was named Walter William. I'll explain how Max came about a little later on. I wonder if I would have been accepted as an entertainer with a name like Walter Bygraves? Sounds a bit like a doctor or a solicitor. Wally Bygraves sounds more like an insult so I think I'll stick with Max. It hasn't done me any harm so far.

As I was saying earlier, we lived in Swan Lane Buildings in Rotherhithe Street, along with more than 200 other families. If ever you sneezed, there was a chorus of "Bless You" and it was what you might call 'intimate'. It could have been named 'The Whispering Gallery', because you were able to hear everything that went on, and you could tell if anyone was having a lean time of it simply by looking at their dustbin. The rat-race there was a nightly event and took place around the bins in the court-yard. Swan Lane Buildings kept the nit-nurse in business, but it was almost a no-go area for 'Scrag' the cat-meat man — he used to get mugged by the local toms.

The environment was quite cultural. There was the gas-works at one end of the street and the glue factory nearby. Fishers Wharf was pretty close, too, and just about anything and everything was unloaded there. As kids we used to amuse ourselves by tormenting the neighbours or the many salesman who attempted to sell a wide range of goods, from fish to carpets. Our parents tried to exercise some sort of control but, secretly I think, they enjoyed having us around as a line of defence against the rent-man, the police, and anyone else who the local residents regarded as an alien.

As you will have gathered, it was a pretty poor area with some pretty poor people, although, every dog has its day and most families experienced the occasional bit of luck, usually when the money went on the right horse for a change! We were not too badly off by comparison with others. True, the flat was small and Harry and I had to share a bed, as did all the girls, but my dad earned quite well from his boxing and I never remember going short of something on the table.

Looking at me, you might get the impression that my dad was probably a heavyweight. Nothing could be further from the truth. He was a fly-weight and stood about 5ft 4ins. He packed a punch, though, and, if he had had the right manager and was fighting today, Battling Tom Smith would probably have been championship material. He was a dedicated family man and when he took his rests from boxing he still sought casual labour work at the docks to make sure that there would be no shortage at home. Of course, the day finally came when he spent more time on his backside than on his feet and so he called it a day, retired from boxing and relied totally on labouring at the docks.

As I grew up I went through all the stages that other kids experience. Friday night was bath night, which meant that a great galvanised tub was taken down from the wall and dragged into the kitchen. The girls had their baths first, then Harry, and finally me. You can imagine what it was like. If we had all been playing down by the river, we always brought a bit of silt home with us, especially if we had removed our shoes and socks and had a paddle. Going for a 'dip' in the river at Rotherhithe wasn't quite the same as everywhere else. The 'dip' was short for diphtheria! It's a wonder that any of us survived when you look at it through the eyes of present-day health visitors and social workers.

Anyway, by the time I got into the bath you could practically walk on the water. It would probably cost you a fortune to get a bath like that in a health spa today. Sometimes I would get into the water white, then come out looking like a vicar, completely black with a white ring around my neck. You think that I'm exaggerating? I can tell you this, by the time that we had all finished in the bath you could have sold the water to the local ink factory!

I still don't know how my parents managed with six of us. Having finished with boxing, my dad would sometimes go for weeks without work and would have to go on the dole, which meant that he could have a pound a week from the government. You could do quite a lot with that in those days but it was still well below the bread line, and so it was my mother's expertise in getting a lot from very little which was the thing which kept us going. There was always some Irish stew simmering in a cauldron on the stove, and into it went anything that we could lay our hands on. Careful shopping at the end of a day meant that suspect fruit and veg and oddments of meat could be bought quite cheaply, and this kept the pot boiling.

I was five when I first went to school. I remember it well because I remember the look of joy on my mother's face as she waved me goodbye — and the look of horror on the teacher's face as she welcomed another Bygraves. School was a strange experience. I had never had to sit still before. We were given a slate and some chalk — which puzzled me because I could not see what was wrong with scrawling on the pavement as we usually did. Years later I thought of becoming a pavement artist but I was put off when someone pointed out that not many people would buy pictures of pavements!

The name of my school was — are you sitting down? — St Joseph's Paradise Street. Yes really! With a block of flats much the same as where we lived, an iron foundry, a sawmill, a couple of shops, five pubs, a Catholic church and a police station in the same road, and the Rotherhithe aroma wafting through the air, it completely wrecked my concept of Paradise.

I learned a lot at school. How to fiddle the milk-money, how to look thoughtful as you gazed out of a window, how to pull the plaits of the girls and make it look as though someone else had done it, how to scarper with the velocity of a bullet if you broke a window playing football, how to look as if butter wouldn't melt in your mouth as you held a stolen apple behind your back. Now that's what I call an education.

There's been a lot of talk over the last couple of years about tests with which to assess both pupils and teachers. It's a good job they didn't test us. I would have gained an 'O' level in skiving and the school would have been closed down. I learned the three 'R's, though, and by today's standards that would have meant that I qualified for university!

My father was fair. We knew that he was the boss but he was never any sort of tyrant. I could count with the fingers of one hand the number of times he took his belt to me. I deserved it each time because I had committed one of the worst sins in his book: dishonesty. He taught me a few sharp lessons and I have to admit that it is something I strongly believe in today. There is no point in telling lies, stealing, or making promises that you cannot possibly keep. It doesn't impress anyone really and it is guaranteed to backfire. I learned that lesson the hard way and I can still feel the sting of my dad's educational strap.

One of my favourite things at home was our gramophone. It was a huge thing with a large horn that looked like an ear trumpet for an elephant. We used to buy records from Petticoat Lane at a penny each, and often had musical soirees with popular bands playing the hits of the day. I would singalonga records even then, although I had no idea at that stage that one day I would have a collection of platinum, gold and silver discs of my own.

Despite the environment I enjoyed my childhood days. They were formative and I am grateful to all the characters that figured in my life in those times. I learned something from each of them and I can still recall the experiences, conversations and events of those days in Rotherhithe. It was a tough neighbourhood, living in tough times, but it taught you how to appreciate the good things when they came and, most of all, it taught you to survive. Many's the time that I've thanked Swan Lane Buildings, Paradise Street, Albion Street Market, and all my other haunts for the lessons they taught me.

I had loving parents and that meant a lot to me. I hope that I have, even in a small way, been the same to my own children. My dad was almost always cheerful. He used to sing a lot and had quite a good voice too. Spirits were rarely low in our home. There was always an air of optimism, a sense that something better was just around the corner. And do you know what? It always was!

At the age of ten I got my first job when I became a milkman's assistant. If I told you that I was already dreaming of a career in showbusiness I would be telling you a lie. Such a thing had never entered my head at this stage. I was a schoolboy who wanted to earn a few bob and, although I knew that school wasn't for ever, it was still something with which I would be involved tomorrow, and that was far enough ahead for me to contemplate.

Mr Dowsett gave me two shillings a week to help with deliveries before I went to school and pick up empties at lunch-time. I learned from my mum and dad that life was all about earning a few bob here and there. My mother, for instance, had a little part-time job at one of the nearby wharves, where she used to sort butter-beans, chucking out the bad ones from the tons of good ones.

I've told you that I had never thought about a career in showbusiness but I suppose at the age of ten I already had one. I used to sing songs and do impersonations at parties. It was mostly for fun but I discovered that I could earn a bob or two when there was a whip-round after I had finished. One of my most popular numbers was *Melancholy Baby*, even though I thought that melancholy was a type of fruit-cum-vegetable you got at posh greengrocers.

Since I performed the same repertoire to the same people at all the local 'do's', the novelty of the Bygraves kid doing a 'turn' soon wore off, but that bit of extra cash came in handy. Money was very tight during the depression days of the 1920s and '30s and every little helped. My brother also worked on a milk round and in the evenings I would add to the coffers with a paper round. It was all-hands-on-deck in those days. Every member of every family did something toward the cause, and then, if a neighbour was in need, everyone would do what they could to help.

At the age of 12 I decided that some extra education might not be a bad idea, so I started going to evening classes and became very interested in shoe-repairing as I guessed that it would be a trade that was always in demand. Although I say it myself, I became quite good at it and I managed to get hold of some tools and a couple of lasts and set to work. I saved the family a bit in shoe repairs and took in five or six pairs a week for other people. It all worked quite well considering. I earned some extra cash and had a trade. The only problem was that I could only work in the evenings and my only workshop was the loo. Needless to say, I was interrupted fairly frequently, and the atmosphere in my 'workshop' was not what you might call healthy.

From being fairly well-off when my dad was boxing, we had gradually moved into the realms of being truly poor. We were still living in the little flat and now, of course, there were nine of us — my parents, me, my brother and four sisters and my mother's father who had come to live with us as he needed looking after. No wonder everyone in the family was encouraged to do whatever they could to add something to the family kitty.

Let me just tell you a few things about the family when we were kids. You have already met my parents and my brother, Harry, but now let me introduce my sisters. We all got on very well. Let's face it, when you're sleeping head to toe with your brothers and sisters, you daren't have any serious argument with them. Lily was something of a tomboy and tried to outdo Harry and me at everything a boy could do. If we played cricket, she had to play cricket. If we played football, she had to play football. We always beat her at one thing, though — that's if we could find a convenient wall!

Patricia had a different quest in life. She was a provider. She would run errands for people and, as well as getting a few coppers for them, she was forever getting cast-offs, not only for herself, but for the rest of the family as well. I remember my mother working hard for ages in order to let some trousers down that Patricia had brought home, only to realise in the end that they were plus-fours! Then there were the strange boots that she brought home, no soles, no heels, no toes. I thought they were great, something really different. I wore them for a week before realising that they were spats!

Kath had a problem. Did I say Kath had a problem? What I really meant was that we kids had a problem that was created by Kath. It happened most nights. We would be in the bed doing our famous family sardines impression when there would be this warm sensation, trickling beneath our legs. Harry would turn to me and say: "Tide's in again!" Yes, Kath was a bed-wetter and I never let her forget it.

Maureen was the youngest and protected by us all. While the rest of us were running wild in Rotherhithe, she was still under mum's wing. She grew up to be just like my mother and other sisters — lovely.

I forget what it is that they say is the mother of invention, but in our home it was desperation. As an example, if my dad invested in a copy of the *News Chronicle*, he wasn't just getting the biggest newspaper for the cheapest price, oh, no! First of all there were the benefits of keeping abreast of the really important things of the day, the runners and riders and so on. Then the reading of the newspaper was just the start. A couple of sheets of it would make a very interesting tablecloth. Since so many people appear to like to read while they are eating, I have never understood why the newspaper tablecloth has never been marketed properly! Another sheet of the paper could be folded into shape as inner soles for shoes, while still another one could be used as a firelighter. The remainder was carefully torn into squares and became our loo roll. Not an ounce of that paper was ever wasted.

My dad was a clever bloke really. He once came up with the great idea of putting a torch in life-jackets to help in the rescue of people from the sea at night. He made a prototype and I went with him as he tried to flog the idea to Lloyds. A commissionaire stopped him at the door, listened to the idea, and then told him that no-one would see him without a previous appointment. He told him to write in and send the prototype for someone to consider. My dad didn't bother, partly because he could not afford the postage. It was about a year later when we read in the paper of an almost identical invention being put into operation. We often wondered if my dad had helped a commissionaire to become a wealthy man.

I haven't said much about my grandad, my mother's father, who had come to live with us. He was an interesting bloke, always well-groomed, and very popular with the ladies without even trying. He was a gentleman and by trade was a leather currier. He worked for a firm called Connolly's, whose chief claim to fame was that they supplied the leather upholstery for Rolls-Royce cars. It's a nice feeling to know that the leather in my own Rolls was made by the firm for which my grandfather worked. Although his presence made it even more crowded in our flat, we were enriched by his being there because he always had a tale to tell and played a large part in our education.

Education was high on my dad's list of priorities for us. Not only did he want us to make the most of our official schooling but he was also keen that we should get as much grounding as possible in life itself, which is another reason why we were encouraged to get little jobs and learn the art of survival. There was even more to it than that. He used to use the children's crossword in the evening paper to quiz us in general knowledge, and he even gave us French lessons! He had spent four years in France while he was with the Army, and spoke the language like a native. By the time he had finished with us we knew a bit more than 'la plume de ma tante' and, in his own amazing way, my dad gave us an education that money would have been unable to buy.

Naturally enough, the family were eagerly awaiting the day when both Harry and I would leave school and go to work. At the time, it seemed to me that the day was never going to dawn, yet when I look back it seems that my schooldays were over all too quickly. The day finally came when I had to roll up my sleeves properly and get on with earning a living.

Harry's job landed him in hot water with both the law and our dad. He was helping with a hauliers, horse and cart style, and was told to unload a stack of boxes of Oxo-cubes from one cart to another. The upshot of it was that he had unwittingly become involved in a racket to steal 18,000 Oxo cubes. The police were on to it straight away and took Harry to the station before sending a copper round to our place to tell my dad.

You can imagine the shock to my mum and dad when they heard the news. Harry had been arrested and was obviously involved, even though he had been set up. At the end of the day he was put on probation for two years and the bloke who had organised it went into Wormwood Scrubs for three months. By far the worst part of it all was when my dad went to Tower Bridge police station to collect Harry. As they left the premises, my dad punched Harry and knocked him down the flight of stone steps to the pavement below. Harry picked himself up and ran all the way home. When he got there he dived into bed alongside me, crying his eyes out. I put my arms around him and cried with him, even though I was not at all involved. Next day, Harry's face became really swollen and when he was taken down to the hospital, it was discovered that he had a broken jaw. My father cried when he realised what he had done and it was the very last time that he ever hit any of us.

I realised that as my time for starting work drew ever closer, I had better watch my step and I probably enjoyed the remainder of my schooldays better than at any other time. My schoolwork got better and I did do very well at English. But there was another side to my schooling which was to help me much later in my career. I was picked for the school choir.

Miss Murray was our music teacher and she was a lady with a mission. She wanted the school to win the 'Best School Choir in South London' competition, which would have meant that we would be presented with a rather fine trophy, not quite the FA Cup but worth much more in Miss Murray's eyes. She was so taken with my voice that she decided that I would be the soloist at a special concert in Westminster Cathedral, which was a pretty tough piece to conquer, singing *Jesu Joy of Man's Desiring*. The intrepid Miss Murray kept me after school for night after night in order to perfect the piece. I had to come in when she nodded her head and, after a couple of months, we had got it off to a fine art — she nodded and I sang.

The Saturday of the competition arrived and I was just managing to keep the butterflies under control. At last it was our turn and Miss Murray took her place at the piano. That was when I nearly went into panic overdrive — I couldn't see her! I wouldn't know when she nodded. I don't know how white I went but nobody would have been surprised to hear that the competition was being sponsored by Home-Pride. The rules clearly stated that you had to sing from where you were, but I knew that there was no way I would be able to sing without seeing Miss Murray. As she went into the intro, everyone was watching her and so I quietly walked toward the piano, almost unnoticed. I stopped as soon as I could see her and did my stuff. It went really well and once I had finished I slid back to my place. The judges did not even notice that I had broken the rules.

Yes, we won. Miss Murray was thrilled to bits to receive the trophy she had so coveted. On the tram home she asked me why I had left my place. I told her that a voice inside me had told me that I mustn't let the school down. She didn't believe a word of it, of course, but she didn't press me to tell the truth, which was that the voice had actually said: "If you don't do something pretty quick Wally, you're going to look a right twerp!"

There was one other incident from my schooldays that played a part in my life — I got worms! Yes really! They were pretty active, too and, as a result I lost a lot of weight and my so-called friends began to call me 'Skinny Wally'. Eventually I was put into hospital and became a sort of guinea-pig as various cures were tried to rid me of the worm safari park. I can still taste some of the things that they gave me, ugh! Eventually the hospital won the battle and I was sent for three months convalescence in a nursing home in Ramsgate. It was called the Convent of the Holy Cross and was run by nuns. I became good pals with another lad from my area, Denis O'Connor. He was recovering from jaundice and looked like an anaemic lemon.

That three months was good for me. Not only did I make a full recovery but I had a great time by the seaside, and fell in love with Nurse McNally. Everyone fell in love with Nurse McNally. She was a schoolboy's dream. I don't know if it was her looks or the smell of her disinfectant, but she certainly had an effect that had never before experienced by those of us who were 12 and over. As a result we all became perfect gentlemen whenever she was around and, when I returned home to Rotherhithe, I found myself saying 'please,' and 'thankyou,' all the time, even opening doors for my mum and sisters. My dad gave me one of 'those' looks and asked me quite candidly, "Have you become a 'nancy-boy' while you've been away?"

I hadn't of course, and within a week or so I was back to my usual self. I gained more weight and strength and, as I approached my 14th birthday, I was strong and fit and ready to leave school, hopefully to get a job on the docks. I was grateful to my teachers for the education that I had received, and all the more so when I see the state of teachers today!

Soon the great day arrived, my last day at school. I took a last lingering look over my shoulder as I walked out of the gates of St Joseph's, and then turned to look ahead. I knew that there was an adventure awaiting me, but I had no idea what it was.

What a wonderful adventure it has turned out to be!

CHAPTER TWO

Earning A Living

*I*T'S amazing how quickly you can grow up when you have to. I had already seen a fair bit of life from all angles before I left school, but that was nothing when compared with what the world had in store for me in the years to come. I believe in school education but there is no better teacher than life itself.

Like most people of my age, my first stop after leaving school was the Labour Exchange. I've always thought that was a very strange name for a place like that. I can understand Stock Exchange, and even Corn Exchange where all the best gags come from, but Labour Exchange? It sounds more like a maternity hospital.

Anyway, off I went to the Labour Exchange — Job Centre, if you are too young to know what I am talking about — and, sure enough, they had just the job for me. I was to be a page-boy at the Savoy Hotel in The Strand. The fact that I was rather tall for my age, and most page-boys were supposed to be short enough to have to jump to see over a suitcase, didn't seem to register with the people at the LE.

I turned up for the job interview looking pretty smart. I had on a suit with long trousers! There was so much Vaseline on my hair that if a fly had tried to land it would have slipped off my head. As I stood outside the hotel, watching the posh world of the West End go by, a lady was having some trouble getting out of a taxi. I helped her and she gave me a ninepence tip, not bad considering that I hadn't even got the job yet!

A commissionaire, very tall and military looking, had been watching this little event and, as far as he was concerned, I had just done him out of ninepence. He was not a happy chap! When I told him that I'd come for a job he jerked a thumb over his shoulder and hissed, "Round the back!" through his teeth. I didn't wait to discuss it further but made my way round to the back entrance of the hotel where I found a gargantuan man who seemed to take great delight in interspersing his sentences by breaking wind and making quite a performance out of it so that it was impossible to overlook what he was doing.

I handed him the card that the Labour Exchange had given me and he guffawed with laughter, while attempting to talk and fart all at the same time. The result was something that sounded like a hoarse walrus with flatulence. I gathered that he was highly amused by the fact that I was so tall and had still been sent for the job of page-boy. Within minutes I had met a commissionaire and a timekeeper — for that was this man's prime occupation — both of whom I would have loved to punch on the nose. I didn't normally go around wanting to punch people on the nose, so I supposed I was just having a bad day.

Eventually the walrus phoned through to someone else who came out to see me. Judging by his countenance I would have guessed him to be the local undertaker or someone obsessed with doing Buster Keaton impersonations. Whatever he was, he looked me up and down as if I was something that had stuck to his shoe, demanded the Labour Exchange card, scribbled something on it and handed it back to me without saying a word. I looked at the card, looked back at him and he had gone. Added to the card were just two words: 'Too tall'. The timekeeper told me that he had told me so and I made my exit.

In case I forget, I have to tell you that about 30 years later I drew up outside that same hotel in my Rolls-Royce — MB1 — half expecting to see that same commissionaire. Of course, I didn't but the uniform was much the same. He opened the door for me and said: "Hello Mr Bygraves. What are you doing here?"

"I'm working here," I replied. "I'm your cabaret for the next three weeks."

"Oh good!" came the reply, then he jerked his thumb over his shoulder and said: "Round the back!"

Different bloke, same job.

The timekeeper? He wasn't there. He probably went to Hollywood to star in *Gone With The Wind*.

The Labour Exchange did not seem too interested in my adventure at the Savoy but promptly gave me another potential job. This was with an advertising agency in High Holborn, almost adjoining the Holborn Empire. The firm was W.S.Crawford, a busy agency who needed a fresh pair of legs. You didn't need to have a brain, just a pair of legs. Needless to say I filled the bill and got the job.

I soon found out why the legs were so important as I spent most of my working day running backwards and forwards to Fleet Street and London Wall to deliver advertising copy to the various newspaper offices. I worked from nine in the morning until six in the evening and had a full hour for lunch, which I spent mostly on my own, eating my sandwiches in nearby Lincoln's Inn Fields which was, and still is, a park near the Law Courts.

One of my delights was to look at the photographs outside the Holborn Empire to see who was appearing there. I found myself drawn toward the theatre on most days, even if I had already looked at the photographs the day before. Somehow, being near the theatre felt like being at home, although I didn't fully realise it at the time.

A perk of the job was that I used to get tips for delivering copy quickly and I used to spend some of my extra cash by going to the Holborn Empire after work at least once a week. I used to buy the cheapest ticket and sit high up in 'the gods'. I loved everything that I saw and it didn't matter to me that I was on my own. Little did I know then that I would one day appear with some of those same people that I applauded on that Holborn Empire stage.

Going to the theatre gave me a very unwelcome experience as well. I used to have to get a copy of the *Daily Telegraph* every day from a news vendor near the office. It was for Sir William Crawford himself, so I never missed buying it. Gradually I got on conversation terms with the news vendor and, after disclosing my love of visiting the theatre, he told me that he was also fascin-ated by it and suggested that we go together some time.

Since I was quite delighted to find someone who shared my love of entertainment I had no hesitation in agreeing and, sure enough, we went along one evening. It was a good show and I was enjoying myself and my smiles conveyed that to my new-found pal. He was also smiling a lot but grad-ually I realised that he wasn't looking at the stage very much, he seemed much more interested in me. When he put his hand on my leg, my worst fears were confirmed.

It's a different world today and many young people have sacrificed innocence for wisdom. A 14-year-old today would know how to cope when a bloke starts to make advances to him, but I just froze. Yes, I had heard all about 'nancy-boys', but I didn't know much about them and I certainly had not expected this weather-beaten news vendor to be one. I didn't know how to escape and just sat there trying to position myself in as repellent a way as possible. When the show ended I tried to plot my escape. I didn't want to turn nasty because he was older than me and could probably have turned a lot nastier.

When we left the theatre he hooked his arm through mine like a bloke hanging on to a woman. He told me that we could go and have a 'nice cup of cocoa' at his place in Lambeth. Then he started telling me what a handsome young man I was. The alarm bells in my head sounded more like air-raid sirens but I still didn't know what to do. Almost before I knew it we were on a tram heading for Lambeth. I kept up a polite conversation while my mind raced along in top gear trying to find an escape route.

The tram stopped at Westminster Bridge for a short time and there were some men walking past. I could see them in the light from the tram and, to my utter amazement and relief, I suddenly saw a very familiar face indeed.

"Dad!" I shouted, and before my 'friend' could say anything, I wrestled free and jumped off the tram. Needless to say, the news vendor and I were pals no longer. As for my dad, well, I grabbed his arm and would not let go until we were safely home, despite his protests of: "Don't do that, people will think you're a 'nancy-boy'!"

I continued to go to the theatre, but I was very careful who sat alongside me and for years afterwards I was particularly suspicious of news vendors.

I didn't just go to the theatre for my entertainment. There were the picture-houses too, where our temperatures would run high every time Jessie Matthews started dancing. I fell in love with Jean Harlow time and time again, and always fancied myself as a Humphrey Bogart or James Cagney in gangster roles, although probably I would have had my card marked as 'Too tall'!

Visiting newspaper offices was wonderful. In those days of ink and paper there was a great atmosphere in Fleet Street. It was exciting. You always felt that something major had just happened, was just happening, or was just about to happen. I was quite taken with it and felt a part of the bustling world of the press. It is all a bit different today. There are no longer the vast offices of clattering typewriters, clouds of smoke and half-empty cups of coffee. The computer age has taken the heart out of Fleet Street as well.

But in my messenger days it was a very lively place to be and there were some lively characters as well. There were also lots of different sidelines and schemes being run by many of those lively characters. One of them was in charge of the *Daily Herald's* insurance promotion. If you took the *Daily Herald* every day, the newspaper would insure you, free of charge, against injury, death and all sorts of other daily risks.

The man in charge of this scheme was one of the characters I regularly visited as part of my job. One day he asked me if my dad took the *Daily Herald* and when I told him that he did sometimes, he gave me a form and said that I should get my dad to commit himself to the *Herald* and take advantage of the insurance scheme. The whole family would then be insured.

My dad thought it was a fair deal and filled in all the appropriate details. The very next day I returned it to my man at the *Herald*, whom I had nick-named 'Fagin' because he both looked and sounded like my idea of that infamous Dickens character, and after glancing through the form, he patted me on the back and said: "Well done, from this moment you and your family are safely insured."

No, there was no catch to it. The scheme was absolutely genuine. I left the office feeling quite pleased with what I had done for the family and, not looking where I was going, I walked straight into a bike that another messenger had left in the way. I somersaulted over it, landed badly, and broke my arm. A gentleman helped me to get to hospital where my arm was put in a sling.

I was concerned that my family would be a bit distressed about my accident when I got home, but I should have known better. Delete sympathy and write in sarcasm. I suffered an evening of jokes at my expense, even from my mother! But I had the last laugh. The next day I went back to see Fagin, showed him my arm and claimed insurance. His face was a picture. A few weeks later I received a fiver from the insurance company and I treated myself — to a bike!

Talking of characters, I must tell you about a friend of my dad who was also into boxing. His name was Harry Lewis, the son of a Jewish tailor with a place in Petticoat Lane. Harry and my dad served in the Army together and were the best of mates. Harry and his dad did the tailoring work together and they had a wonderful scam going. Outside the shop they would have a row of ten bob suits with no prices on. Harry used to prowl around them whilst wearing a very obvious hearing-aid.

When a punter stopped to take a look, Harry would speak to him making it abundantly clear that he was 'deaf' by asking the potential victim to keep on repeating himself. Finally, when the punter asked how much the suits were, Harry would yell into the shop to ask his dad. Loudly his dad called back, "Thirty shillings."

"How much?" Harry would demand again.

"Thirty shillings!" his dad would roar back.

Harry would then turn quietly to the punter and say, "Thirteen shillings!"

The customer would not be able to get the money out of his pocket quickly enough. It hardly ever failed and Harry and his dad chuckled all the way to the bank with a pretty good weekly profit on those ten bob suits. Who said boxers were thick?

Talking about lolly, I used to give up 12 bob a week to my mum and dad toward the family budget, and I lost another shilling in tax and stamp, so I had two bob a week to myself out of my wages and supplemented that with the various tips that I picked up. It wasn't exactly a fortune and I had my skint weeks the same as everyone else, but I was happy.

I was 15 in 1937 and life was treating me fairly well, even though the storm clouds of war were gathering in Europe and we were all still feeling the pangs of the depression years. The charm of life was in its simplicity. Our expectations were much less than those of today and, as a result, we were not disappointed so much. We also took our delights in a much more simple way. The pleasures for me were things like 'going down the lane' on a Sunday morning to jostle, and be jostled by, the throngs who gathered around Petticoat and Brick Lane to pick up bargains.

You could buy anything there in those days. I've seen goats and monkeys for sale alongside jellied eels, bundles of clothes, rusting fire-grates and homing pigeons. Yes, homing pigeons! I don't know how they got away with that either. I'm sure I saw the same birds being sold week after week, probably to the same customers too!

Having a bike meant that I could get out a bit more and I used to like to cycle out into the Kent countryside with friends, and sometimes we would even stay out for the whole weekend, camping out. At home we were still living in the same flat but now that we were all working, space seemed even less. Camping out was like having a giant bedroom and I loved it.

The pictures, fun-fairs, circuses, the theatre and the dance halls were all on our entertainment list, and, of course, we liked a game of football as well. Most of us were into keeping fit and used to do exercises and swim. One thing that we didn't do was to sit in front of a television at every opportunity, which is why we were fitter and had more time to enjoy ourselves in the more meaningful way that I've just described.

I had a shock when I was 15 because I suddenly noticed that I had hair sprouting in places where I would never have expected it. I went to my dad, rather pale-faced, to seek his advice. I lifted up my arm to show him just a part of the sprouting phenomenon, and told him that it was happening in other places too! Very gravely my father looked me in the eye.

"That's God, punishing you for all your misdeeds, he's turning you into a coconut!"

While all this was going on, I was still repairing shoes, going to woodwork evening classes and, without knowing it, I was embarking on a career that, as yet, I knew nothing about. The woodwork was very interesting but it was not an earner like the shoe repairs. I used to make 'useful things' which I gave away as gifts. Among those things were a pipe-rack for my dad and a pastry-board for my mum. I completely overlooked the fact that my mum never made pastry and that my dad did not smoke, so the 'usefulness' of my creations left a lot to be desired. The thought was there, though!

The career? Well, I mentioned in the last chapter about my success in the singing competition and I used to do a party-piece with a couple of numbers at local social events. I didn't sing the ecclesiastical stuff but some well-known songs and ditties. Before long, people were knocking at the door and inviting my mum to their parties, with the instruction not to forget to bring me. I was expected to provide a bit of a cabaret and, to be honest, I enjoyed it, especially when, at the end, I was given a bit of cash for my trouble. At the very least I received my supper, so it was well worth singing for.

If you had asked me at this point whether I wanted to be a professional entertainer, I would probably have looked rather blank as I had never had such a thought. We lived day-by-day and, when I appeared at these various 'do's', I was simply doing something for that moment. The word 'tomorrow' had not yet entered my vocabulary. On reflection it is obvious that I was getting a good grounding for the years to come. My audiences ranged from women and kids to ham-forearmed dockers, and they all seemed to enjoy my comedy songs as much as I enjoyed singing them.

Annie Johnson is a name that might not mean much to you but she played a part in my education when I was a lad. Annie was my first kiss! She had been telling me for quite a while that every time we were together her glasses steamed up. I thought she was complaining about something but, since I didn't know what I was doing wrong, I could hardly be expected to know how to put things right and you don't really like to ask about things like that, do you?

We were discussing movie stars one day and Annie got on to the subject of who was the best kisser. I argued that I was better than any of the stars she mentioned until, finally, she challenged me to prove it. Of course, I didn't have a clue, but she did! I thought she was trying to nick my chewing-gum! Years later, Annie came to see one of my shows and re-introduced herself to me. I discovered that she was now married and had nine kids. I didn't have the heart to suggest that she might have been sponsored by Wrigleys — she might have given me the rough edge of her tongue this time!

By now, girls had been added to my list of interests and had earned themselves a spot high in the charts. They were, in fact, vying neck and neck for my affections with my bike. Alton Towers, fine though it is, has nothing to compare with cycling in London during the 1930s. If your tyres were not inflated enough you experienced all the bone-rattling of a fairground ride, and if you overdid it the inner-tube was prone to exploding and acting as a laxative for days.

If that was not enough excitement there were the thrill rides. A gang of us used to go to the top of Shooter's Hill in South London and cycle down the main road. At the bottom was a set of traffic lights and the thrill of the ride was to hurtle down the hill at speeds in excess of 30 mph and test your nerve or your brakes as the lights changed in front of you. Would they change to green before you reached the bottom? Would your brakes save you as they changed to red? Would you dare shoot the lights and end up careering through oncoming traffic as you dodged the ultimate hazard, the tram-lines, which could bring your front wheel to a dead stop while the rest of you carried on? It was all good fun, honest it was!

I was once fined for cycling without lights after lighting-up time. It cost me five bob and some nightmares. I thought that I would have my picture on wanted posters all over town and bring disgrace to my family. To this day I'm not sure if that fine gave me a police record.

So there I was at 15. My dad was working all hours and my mother had a job in a factory making gas masks. There were still two kids at school but the rest of us were working. I was quite happy with my job at Crawford's and my prospects were to stay there, save a few bob if I could, get married and settle down to a life that would bring me my own family and a continuation of the cycle.

My mother was not making gas masks for fun. Those clouds that were gathering over Europe were getting blacker, and the fact that my father had so much work was further evidence that more and more of the able-bodied were being recruited as the designs of Adolf Hitler became ever-increasingly apparent.

I was learning some of the trade when I was at Crawford's. Nobody actually taught me anything but it was impossible not to pick things up. As I hurried from office to office I would often look at the copy I was carrying to see how the advertisements were constructed to get the best effect. It taught me a lot about the psychology of advertising and generally getting the message across. It was another string to my bow which was later to prove so helpful as I needed to be 'media aware' when I entered showbusiness.

Another aspect of my daily visits to Fleet Street was that it was impossible to ignore the news. You felt that you wanted to know what was going on, and preferably before it happened! Talk of war was constant, with the press full of the latest developments abroad and how it might effect us in Britain. I was still naive enough not to allow such a minor affair as a world war get in the way of my enjoyment of life, but I still found myself avidly reading the daily bulletins with increasing fascination.

My trips to the theatre continued and I saw such stars as Wee Georgie Wood, the brilliant Max Miller and Albert Whelan, who had one of the most unusual acts that I have ever seen. He used to walk on to the stage whistling the same tune as the band. Still whistling he would remove his top-hat and then his gloves. The music stopped and he told a few gags. Then the music started again and he whistled along while putting on his gloves and hat before strolling off again.

My theatre haunts were the Holborn Empire and the New Cross Empire, but on a Saturday night you would probably find me at the Palais de Danse at the top of Deptford High Street. A group of us used to go there every week. It was a typical Palais with a large dance-hall and obligatory mirror-ball in the centre. It was a mecca for both romantics and those of us who had not yet made the metamorphosis from creatures of lust to creatures of love.

There were two things to take into account once you had charmed the lady off her feet with your opening, "D'yer come 'ere offen?" Her looks had to be acceptable, but where she lived was of paramount importance. If she was not on the same bus route then you were wasting your time. If she lived in the right direction you would try to see her home, usually to be sent packing by her gorilla of a dad! Later you would meet up with your mates at a 24-hour tea-stall near Rotherhithe Tunnel. They had usually also been seeing girls home so you could gather together over a cup of tea and a hot pie and swap lies about how your evening had gone.

As I was growing up and getting more interested in social activities than in going to Mass, my mother became increasingly concerned for my spiritual welfare. I no longer enjoyed sitting through these religious services, and said so. My mother was hurt but I could not be a hypocrite. Like most teenagers, I was far too interested in enjoying myself.

My elder brother, Harry, was into keeping fit in a big way and used to spend a lot of time in the gym. He was now quite a bit bigger than my dad and would often spar with him. The sparring would sometimes become quite serious and one day it reached boiling point when my dad decided that he needed to remind Harry of the order of things. It ended with Harry suffering serious injuries which my dad deeply regretted, and we were all sworn to secrecy about it, in case anyone got the wrong idea and thought my dad was into child abuse.

My father and Harry reached an understanding after that incident. It taught Harry a lesson and the two became much closer, which was the way things should be. My dad liked the idea that Harry and I might follow his footsteps into the boxing ring but, as the 1930s reached their end, it was obvious that a very different kind of fighting was going to be required from us. With Adolf on the march in Europe, our fighting was not going to be for a belt and a few bob. It was going to be a matter of life and death.

CHAPTER THREE

The War

THE newspapers, the radio and general conversation talked of little else but the situation in Europe, where Hitler's army appeared to be walking around as if they owned the place and were causing the most horrific suffering, although none of us knew just how horrific those sufferings were until after the war had ended. Mr Chamberlain went to Munich for a word with Herr Hitler and came back with that famous piece of paper which said that we were going to continue to enjoy peace. The optimism in all of us wanted to believe him but when we saw more and more gas masks being made in our factories and saw the German Army moving ever closer to Poland, a country Britain had vowed to defend, the more practical side of our characters knew that there was bound to be trouble ahead.

On September 3rd 1939, at 11am, everyone gathered around their radios to hear Mr Chamberlain broadcast to the nation. We were at war with Germany! It is difficult to describe what that meant exactly. Everybody knew that it was grave news but, at the same time, there was the instant demonstration of the sort of spirit that the British people keep stored up for just such an occasion. There was this mixture of fear, determination, anger and resolve, coupled with the belief that the situation would only last six months at the most.

In one way or another the entire nation was affected by the news. My brother Harry enlisted immediately and joined the Royal Engineers. After some heavy training he went off to France to fight. I was still only 17 and so under the age for recruitment, much to my mother's relief. My dad remained as docker, but a government decree meant that dockers became a specialised trade and, as such, could be moved about the country to wherever the need was greatest. During those war years he went to Liverpool, Cardiff and Glasgow, as well as working in London.

I also lost my job. I hadn't done anything wrong but the firm closed once hostilities were announced. Newspapers were soon cut down to single broadsheets, and there was no longer the advertising space to necessitate the use of an advertising agency. Crawford's, like many other advertising agencies, went out of business. I went to Paddock Wood in Kent for three weeks and earned a bit of cash by hop-picking. It was good fun, a healthy occupation, and you got paid for it. Whitbreads owned the farm and we were looked after. Sadly, when the harvest was over, we all had to 'hop it' back to London.

Because I could make pipe-racks and pastry-boards I became a carpenter's apprentice and worked in the building trade. I worked for a company called F.G. Minter who paid me twice as much as I had been earning at Crawford's, which was pretty useful since we no longer had the contribution from Harry. One of my first jobs was helping to put up air-raid shelters at Crosse and Blackwell's soup factory in Bermondsey, so, if anyone remembers taking refuge in those shelters, yours truly had a hand in them.

I was only an apprentice, of course, and, since air-raid shelters did not require pipe-racks or pastry-boards, there was a limit to the expression of my obvious talents. The experienced carpenters took me under their wing and gave me the opportunity to do what I was really good at. I swept up, sharpened their chisels and made sure that there was always a bucket of tea on the go. Yes, a bucket of tea! We thought hygiene was something you would shout in greeting to a girl of that name!

The tea was obtained from a local cafe, until I came to an arrangement with an aunt of mine who lived nearby. Between us we made a small profit, not much but enough to make it worthwhile doing. The deal ended when we moved to another area to work but it was an interesting enterprise while it lasted.

I was more than a little keen to join up but I was still not old enough, so I continued with my job and became quite friendly with a carpenter by the name of Albert. He was heavily into entertainment and used to give charity performances with a little concert party that he had brought together. Albert did some comedy routines, there was another bloke who was a baritone, two female singers and an accordion player. They all did their own spots but also combined with comedy patter and usually finished their show by all taking part in a well-known routine called, "If I Were Not Upon The Stage …"

When Albert heard me singing and doing impressions at work he invited me to join the concert party and so, for a while, I went around with them after work visiting air-raid shelters and taking part in the show. Some nights the bombing was too severe to go home and we stayed in the shelter. Everyone mucked in. We did not get paid to entertain but being able to share in the tea and sandwiches and to take everyone's minds off the horrors of war was reward enough.

Some nights the bombing did not start until after we had left the shelter and were on our way home. I prayed a good many times when I was on my own and the drone of the German aircraft heralded the thudding and crashing of the bombs. At Rotherhithe we were an easy target because of the bend in the river and the dense area of homes and industry. The enemy pilots did not have to think about a target, the whole of Rotherhithe would do. I have never known anything so frightening in my life and I still cringe whenever I think about it. I'm sure that all of us who have experienced anything like that can never forget it.

The concert parties were good fun and I mostly did my impersonations as well as joining the others in the Finale routine. One of my best impersonations was of Arthur Tracy, who used to be billed as the 'Street Singer'. He was well known for singing *Marta* and my impersonation of him used to go down really well. I learned the lesson of organising your act and began to save Arthur until the end. Another of my more popular impersonations was Max Miller. I used to spend ten minutes doing him. I knew his routine by heart and did an exact repeat of him and his material. It went very well indeed. The foundations were still being put down for young Walter Bygraves to build for himself a solid career in showbusiness.

The bomb damage meant that it was all hands on deck to repair things as much and as quickly as possible. Even I was given hammer and nails and told to do my best. By the time that I had finished there were a number of homes all over South London that looked remarkably like pipe-racks. One day I was actually on a roof fixing a joist that had been damaged by a bomb blast the night before. It was morning, so when the air-raid siren went off I didn't take it too seriously, thinking that Adolf did the opposite of Red Indians and attacked only at night! When I looked up into the sky and saw the unmistakable outline of several German bombers, I began to take it all a lot more seriously.

No more than 100 yards away a bomb struck. The tremor shook the roof upon on which I was working and I slid down the tiles to the gutter, where I grabbed the top of my ladder with one hand to stop myself diving a straight 30 feet on to the concrete below. The ladder held firm for a split second and then began to topple, taking me with it. As it crashed to the ground, it catapulted me into a large privet hedge, which was altogether a better choice but still had the same effect as wrestling with a porcupine.

The woman who owned the house came trotting up to me, looked down at my crumpled position in her privet, adopted the classic pose of hand on hip and wagged her finger at me. "You should have been down the shelter!" she nagged.

I didn't know what to say — or rather I knew what I wanted to say but, after all, I had been brought up a gentleman!

I decided to take a lunch break and went to the local cafe. As I gazed out of the window I kept seeing buses go past with 'Yorkshire Grey' emblazoned on them. It sounds like a kind of tea but in fact was the name of a well-known pub in Eltham, and it had become even more well-known as the centre for medical examinations for volunteers to the armed forces. My experience on the roof had shown me that it was quite possible to get killed in wartime without even trying so my resolve to do something constructive became even stronger.

I finished my tea and jumped on the next bus to the 'Yorkshire Grey'. I passed the medical exam in A1 condition and three days later got my papers to report to RAF Cardington. I didn't have the heart to tell my mother so I left a note on the mantelpiece to both my parents telling them what I had done and assuring them that I loved them all and would take good care of myself. Much later, I was told that my mother had a good cry and then she hiccuped back the tears and said: "What is he doing in the RAF? He can't even drive a "plane!" Mums are wonderful aren't they?

Although I had been passed A1, there was a slight problem with my eyesight and that stopped me from joining air crew. Instead I joined the team of fitters on air-frames. My first evening in the RAF was to be something that I would never forget. How could I? It changed my entire life!

Not yet having been issued with uniforms we were still in civvies when we were ushered into the NAAFI for our first evening in the forces. My attention was drawn to a pianist who was struggling through a rendition of *In the Mood*. He wasn't so much tinkling the ivories as torturing them, and I'm sure that if Glenn Miller had walked in he would have shot himself. A sergeant walked on to the stage and addressed us. Behind his benign smile there was obviously a malignant spirit of sadism, but he hid it well. He told us what to expect from our first full day in the RAF and what we would be issued with, what life in future was going to be like, and just about everything else that we needed to know but would probably forget before too much time had passed.

My ears pricked up when he told us that would have to provide our own entertainment. Entertainment! Did somebody mention entertainment? He asked if any of us had been entertainers before the war started. One chap put up his hand and explained that he had been singing with the D'oyly Carte Opera Company. He was called on to the stage and gave us a rendering of *Bless This House* which was really very good and nobody doubted that he was a pro.

When the sergeant asked if there was anyone else who had done any entertaining I put up my hand and said I could an impersonation of Max Miller. Next thing I knew I was on the stage doing the Max Miller routine that I had performed back in Rotherhithe. It went very well and I was given a lot of applause and back-slapping as I returned to my seat. Several of the lads assumed that I was a professional and, I have to admit, that it made me glow with pride a little bit, especially when I thought back to all those stars that I'd seen at the Holborn Empire and realised that I was being put in the same category as them.

From that moment on, everyone started calling me Max, and that is what I have been called ever since. That's why that first evening at RAF Cardington was so significant — it was the birth of Max Bygraves!

I was Bygraves, Aircraftsman Second Class, number 1212094, and, not long after arriving at Cardington, I was sent together with the others for my initial square-bashing in Bridgnorth, that lovely town on the Shropshire border. To me it was the lap of luxury because I had my own bed, good food and a host of instant mates. I also had a most uncomfortable experience.

I was given an evening pass, which meant that I could go out into town for some entertainment, returning in a lorry provided for the purpose of bringing us all back at midnight. I made off on my own to have a look around the town, dutifully carrying my gas-mask, an immediate clue to other more experienced servicemen that I was a rookie. I didn't fancy the entertainment that was on offer because the cinema was closed and the pubs were all short of beer. The YMCA was not really my cup of tea so, after wandering around for a while, I decided to walk back to camp rather than wait for a few hours for the truck.

It was approaching dark when I left the town and I faced a walk of a couple of miles, which was not a problem because I was well used to Shanks's Pony. Seeing the camp lights in the distance, I suddenly had a brainstorm and decided that it would be much more sensible to cut across the fields than to follow the winding road. As I walked across one field all the lights in the camp suddenly went off — the black-out of course! I was forced to follow my nose. As I climbed the fence and ventured into the next field I gradually became aware of a presence. I didn't know what it was but there was definitely something else in the field. I froze!

Whatever it was came closer, and then suddenly the whole field turned into bedlam — I was among hundreds of free-range chickens! As soon as they became aware of my presence they took off in all directions, shrieking and squawking at the tops of their voices. Needless to say, I took off as well. They must have been pretty stupid chickens, I mean, do I look like a fox? Anyway, in my rush to get out of there I ended up by diving through a barbed wire fence, which made my hands, face and uniform look like shredded wheat. I ran all the way back to camp and slipped into bed as quietly as possible.

Next morning I was in absolute panic. How could I appear on parade in my condition and with my uniform in tatters? I tried to think of all different ways round it but, in the end, the inevitable happened. I stood there being looked at, up and down, by the man in charge, Flight-Sergeant English, who was actually a Welshman. He demanded an explanation in no uncertain terms and, after stammering and stuttering, I eventually came clean.

I began to tell my sorrowful tale about the previous night's events when I was interrupted by one of my new mates, Ben Slennet, who could sweet-talk a turkey into walking into the oven.

"Excuse me sir, but he's not telling the truth!" Ben went on to spin this yarn about how I had been accosted by about six soldiers and had taken exception to the way they were insulting the RAF. By the time he had finished I was a hero, Flight-Sergeant English was beaming at me and I was sent for medical treatment and a new uniform. All was forgiven just so long as I was defending the honour of his beloved RAF. Ben and I have met up quite a lot since then and always have a laugh about it. I hope Flight-Sergeant English did, too, when he eventually found out.

Just as a little diversion, if anyone reading this believes that they may have served with me in the RAF during that time, they have a 50/50 chance of being correct. You see there were two Walter William Bygraves knocking about, and we shared the same birthdate. In fact we shared the same birth certificate and the same mum and dad. Allow me to explain.

I mentioned that my brother Henry had joined the Army and gone to France. Well, he was among those who were evacuated from the beaches of Dunkirk and, when he arrived back in Britain, he didn't report to his unit. He came straight home, totally exhausted, and slept for a solid three days. When he started to get back into the land of the living he realised that he could not face another Dunkirk, so he 'borrowed' my name and birth certificate and joined the RAF. All the details were the same except that we had different numbers.

My mother received a letter saying that Henry was among those unaccounted for at Dunkirk and was told that the War Office would be in touch again when they had more news. She never heard any more. My father's sense of humour came to the fore when he heard that his two sons were now both in the RAF under the same name and details.

"I hope that, if one of you gets killed, they don't bury the other one!" he said.

Thanks dad!

Friendships develop in the Forces which are never forgotten. I have already mentioned Ben Slennet, but there was also Jimmy Cairns, a Scots lad from Greenock who had a problem with his adenoids and could not stop sniffing. One day the drill sergeant shouted at him: "Haven't you got a handkerchief Cairns?"

Quick as a flash, Jimmy replied: "Yes sir, but I don't lend it to strangers!"

Jimmy was sent to the cookhouse to do washing up duty and yours truly was sent with him for laughing. Jimmy and I became inseparable. Another pal was Harry Woods. We all knocked about together and went from Bridgnorth to Weston-Super-Mare for a crash course — no pun intended — on being fitters, before being transferred to Hornchurch in Essex, a lot closer to home for me. Harry decided to get married and asked me to be his best man. I was delighted and we got our passes sorted out for the trip to Liverpool where the lucky lady and Harry were to be wed.

Liverpool was like a foreign country to me. Bridgnorth had been the furthest north that I had ever travelled. I was unprepared for the Liverpudlian hospitality and a wedding reception that went on for several days. When we finally arrived back at the RAF camp we were well past our weekend pass deadline so, when we rolled in on the Tuesday night, we were in all sorts of trouble and were handed 14 days' detention, which meant a lot of running in full pack, loss of privileges, a solitary cell and loss of pay. It had been an expensive weekend but a lot of fun.

Ben Slennet became my agent in a way. I was just turning 18 and Ben was twice my age. He seemed to be dedicated to getting himself out of the RAF at the earliest opportunity and was excused just about everything that it was in his interests to be excused from. As I said before, he could charm the spikes off a cactus. In best Bilko fashion he arranged all sorts of jobs for himself, and always enlisted me as his assistant. He could make a half-hour lino-polishing job last all day and taught me the ropes with a crash course — yes, another one — on malingering. Ben was a master, but don't think that he was lazy, he wasn't. When he wanted to work he could work well and work fast, but he didn't believe in allowing life to push him around. Nowadays he would be referred to as a 'control freak'.

Having become his 'child protege' in the art of malingering, I then became his showbusiness client and he started to get me appearances at social functions. I can remember him arranging for me to do my stuff at a Buffaloes do. It reminds me of the kid who came home from school with some homework about animals and asked his dad: "How do buffaloes make love?" His dad shrugged and said: "It's no good asking me lad, I'm a Freemason!"

Anyway, Ben agreed a fee of £1 for me to do this Buffaloes event with his agent's fee deducted. It was good pay, much more than I was getting per week with the RAF. The only problem was how to get an evening pass. Ben saw to that. He went to the Orderly Officer and told him that I was going to do a charity show for the Buffs, with the proceeds going to the Red Cross. We got our passes and the evening was a success. The Buffs enjoyed it so much that they happily paid the fee and gave us a bottle of champagne as well. On the way home we split the fee and the champagne and arrived back at camp in good spirits. It was the start of a career move for me as Ben followed that with all kinds of other appearances. I don't know how he fixed half of them but I was getting paid to enjoy myself so I wasn't arguing. Not only did Ben keep the dates coming but he never failed to get us the passes either. He was a real pro.

Not all the gigs I did were paid ones, but those that were turned out to be pretty good. Whenever there was the chance of a weekend pass, Ben used to contact various pubs and arrange bookings. Even then I did not actually realise that I was being paid to perform and that I was now a professional entertainer. Being a bit dim I never gave it a second thought, other than the fact that we were getting a few bob on the side for having a bit of fun.

I used to go home and see the family whenever I could. Like most East Londoners they were in the front line of the bombing raids and it took its toll, with houses disappearing together with friends and neighbours. I caught my mother a little the worse for gin one night and it made me angry that I couldn't get her to come to her senses. I went off in a huff but, as I travelled back to camp I began to realise how selfish I had been. I was having an easy time in the RAF but, for people like my mum and her friends, the war was far from being a bit of fun. They had to have something to lean on at times. I silently wept and vowed that I would one day make it up to my mum for my selfishness. She had once held high hopes that I would become a priest. Instead her son was growing into an uncaring specimen who wanted everything to be the way that he wanted it to be. I chastised myself with my own thoughts and decided to sort myself out.

Performing for the RAF at various functions meant that I was backed by some really good musicians. I didn't just do impressions, I was also singing popular songs and that meant getting to know your musicians quite well. One of them was Ray Ellington, who became very famous indeed, both in his own right and as a regular on the legendary Goon Show. We worked together many times and for many years after first coming together in the RAF.

Yes of course, I took a healthy interest in the opposite sex. I wouldn't say that I was very likely to land the part as Casanova, but I knew what it was like to share a bag of chips and a pickled onion in a bus shelter. I suppose my initial chat-up lines lacked a little finesse but there was a war on, and offering to treat a girl to a saveloy and pease pudding was about as good as I got in trying to make the right impression.

There was one WAAF who I remember very well indeed. She used to cycle past at about five every morning. Who needed an alarm clock? Not me, this WAAF was worth staying awake all night for! I used to feel rotten all day if I didn't get a glimpse of her. But how to approach her? She was a class act and I just knew that if I managed to speak to her my mouth would dry up, my tongue would stick to the roof, and I would sound like an Oriental with a cleft palate. There can be nothing worse than when you have finally summoned up the courage to speak to a girl that you really fancy, and you have blurted out your rehearsed introduction, pathetic though it may be, and she says, "What?"

Luck was on my side though. I sang at a camp concert one night. Hang on a moment, I don't mean a 'camp' concert, the Danny La Rue sort, I mean a concert in the camp. The next morning I was hanging around waiting for my dream WAAF to cycle past when, suddenly, she stopped in front of me and actually spoke to me.

"Hello, you're the fellow who was singing with the band last night aren't you?"

I gulped and managed to nod. Then she asked me if I would write out the words to one of the songs, *If I Had My Way*. I said I would and off she cycled. The next morning I waited and she came past as usual. I gave her the paper with the words of the song and then gritted my teeth and put my head on the block.

" …Er, I was wondering …D'you think I could take you out one night?"

To my absolute astonishment and joy she agreed and we began to go out together regularly.

During the time that we were going out together she was promoted to corporal and then to sergeant and all the lads started calling me 'Crawler', because I was going out with a sergeant. I'll never forget that lovely girl because, you see, I married her.

Yes it was Blossom. We courted in the only way you could in those days. A quick kiss behind the bike shed, notes of endearment, and an intertwining of weekend passes.

She took me home to meet her mother, her only parent, and I'd like to say that we hit it off from the start. I'd like to say it but, in all truth, when her mum and I met it was dislike at first sight. I didn't mind her so much, but she didn't rate me at all. She wanted her daughter to get involved with the top brass, not the bloke who did the polishing. She wanted her daughter to have a future of silks and satins and suspected that I would be more likely to supply khaki and hessian.

I blotted my copybook on our first encounter when I discovered that she was a spiritualist. She asked me if I believed in the spirits and I joked, 'only out of a bottle'. She didn't think it was at all funny and Blossom didn't help. She was too uptight to laugh so she smiled with her eyes while her lovely mouth remained frozen. Blossom had three sisters and six brothers and they were all from Romford in Essex. I got on quite well with the rest of the family, but Mrs Murray was decidedly unimpressed with me.

Blossom's mum had told her kids that she was distantly related to royalty, but I never did find out if it was true. Most of the people that I knew who claimed a royal connection had a regular spot in the King's Head!

If the lads back at camp had called me 'Crawler' for going out with a sergeant, they would certainly have had a field day if they had seen me with Blossom's mum. I really put the charm on and continually told her how nice she looked in her new hat and all that stuff, hoping that it was not an old one that had been taken out of mothballs. Very gradually the ice turned to water and, although I don't think that I ever became her favourite person, she did put up with me.

Blossom had worked in the movie business before joining the RAF — she tore tickets at the local Roxy! She was madly in love with James Stewart and, if I wanted to get round her, I used to slip into an impersonation of him. She melted every time — I still do it if I'm in trouble!

One thing led to another and I eventually popped the question. To my utter relief she accepted, and I didn't even have to become James Stewart. We were married on September 12th 1942, we were both 19 and very much in love. I was in love with her and she was in love with my impersonation of James Stewart. We have never had a cross word since — I know when to keep my mouth shut!

The war was not getting any better. The six months that everyone had expected it to last had long gone and it was only the British spirit that kept everyone going. They were grim times but nobody wanted to give in. There were many laughs and lots of special songs and moments that put a fine gloss over the many wounds.

To my dismay I was posted to Scotland, to a place called Drem, which seemed to be in the middle of nowhere. Bloss stayed behind and we had to communicate by letter. I cherished every word that she wrote and, hopefully, my meagre offerings meant something to her too. It was awful being away from her. Every day seemed like a month. I had not been away for very long when she wrote me two of the most marvellous words that I've ever read: 'I'm pregnant'!

CHAPTER FOUR

Max The Family Man

I HAD never considered myself to be a family man. I'm not sure that I even knew what a family man was or what he was supposed to do. I was soon to find out! Christine was born the following May, the 3rd to be precise. It was 1943 — there, she can never lie about her age again! I took my new responsibilities very seriously though, and bought the lads a drink, oh yes, and some flowers for Blossom!

I had never thought of babies as being beautiful before then, but I saw it in Christine. She was lovely, just like her Mum. Bloss had been staying with her sister near Dagenham during her pregnancy, but when I was transferred for the umpteenth time, this time to Kew, we were able to find a place of our own. So, after Christine had come along, I was a family man and we all lived together as man, wife and noise.

I used to be able to bring home a bit of firewood from work, which was mostly spent in travelling all over East London trying to patch up bombed properties. Unfortunately, the wood didn't help much with the finances and it was a good job that I was able to continue earning a few bob by doing my 'act' around various London pubs. I hit a snag with that too: it was not as if I had an office job and could come and go as I pleased. To be off-duty you had to have a pass, and they were not so easy to come by as regularly as I needed them. I was advised to have a quiet word with the Flight-Sergeant and, sure enough, he was most interested in my sideline. He took me down to the Green Man pub in Leytonstone, still a well-known landmark, and watched me perform. I had worked there before and received a warm welcome. He was impressed and told me that he could fix me a pass any time I wanted one, for a small fee of course! Well, it began as a small fee but grew progressively as I went on. I had no option but to pay it since I was still making extra money to take care of my family.

I think that you need to have lived through the war years to fully understand them. The films rarely show what it was really like. The meekest of people turned out to be real heroes and, so often, those with the heroic image were the first to need a change of trousers. You got used to the drone of the aircraft and soon got to know whose they were by the different noise they made. You also got used to the thud of a falling bomb, the sharp cough of the anti-aircraft guns and the ominous and incessant ringing of the fire-engine and ambulance bells. One thing you never got used to was the devastation, the craters and heaps of rubble where there had once been family homes. Sometimes, amid the broken bricks and torn timbers, you could see the tattered tablecloth and smashed crockery that told you how a family had been sitting down to a meal together when the Luftwaffe struck.

The most frightening war-tool of that time was the V2 rocket. It was a terrible weapon that took you completely by surprise and had a devastating effect wherever it fell. I have sometimes wondered what sort of a mind it takes to create such weapons. I can understand a clenched fist, that is what I was brought up to understand. I can even understand a piece of wood, but intric-ate inventions of weaponry that are specifically designed to destroy life and cause untold horrors have always been a mystery to me.

Of course, the war years did have some things going for me. People in general were much more public spirited. There was camaraderie in the face of adversity, and a kind of trust that is so sadly lacking in these more modern times. Emotions ran high and the songs of the time meant so much. It was a terrible time that should never have happened but we made the best of it in true British style.

As the pace hotted up I was transferred, again! This time I went to Port Lympne near Folkestone. I think they were trying to get me nearer to the firing line. Blossom and Christine went back to Essex to stay with Bloss's sister, who helped look after Christine while Bloss worked as a telephonist.

She once told me that there were 'heavy-breathers' even in those days. One bloke, after her initial 'hello', proceeded to tell her what she wanted him to do to her. She waited for a pause and said: "You can tell all that just from me saying 'hello'?"

As well as doing my gigs on the side I had also been enlisted to take part in a concert organised by the RAF. It was called *Contact!*. Can you imagine a show with that title now? The show gave me some valuable experience as we played to quite a cross-section of people. Another show was called *Chocks Away*. All original stuff! Along the way I had been taught a few dance-steps by Vera Lynn's brother, Roger — the ukelele by Tony Sherwood — and how to get ripped off by all sorts of people. When I saw a talent contest advertised, I couldn't resist having a go and even made it to the final which was being held in Uxbridge over two nights. It needed two nights because there were 30 finalists. Among the judges were Ivor Novello, Elizabeth Allen and Freddie Carpenter. Trust me, Bygraves the chippie, to be judged by a Carpenter! I hope he liked what he sawed!

I gave it all I'd got in the final. I had increased my repertoire quite a bit and now included impressions of the Inkspots and a new young singer that everyone was raving about — Sinatra was his name. Wonder what happened to him? Sinatra was a little, skinny lad at that time and I used to put a lot of comedy into my impression of him, including his collapsing under the weight of the microphone. It all went down very well, so well in fact that I won the contest and took the trophy back to Port Lympne where I was greeted with all the enthusiasm of a new heavyweight champion of the world.

Suddenly there were lots of phone calls coming into Port Lympne asking me to appear in this RAF concert, or that charity do. There was one very well-spoken chap who called more often than most. It was through him that I had one of the most frightening experiences of my life up to then. He engaged me to do a special show at the Drury Lane Theatre. I was thrilled to accept but, when the big day came, my knees were doing a fair impression of a hungry woodpecker. Not only was this huge theatre renowned for its world stars, but the show was being played to a packed auditorium of 3,000 people, and I was being backed by a 35-piece orchestra!

All that and the best in sound and lighting was all a bit too much for this young lad from Rotherhithe. I managed to put the lid on my nerves, however, and did my act — and at the end came this wonderful noise of a huge audience clapping and cheering. I was ecstatic, and must have looked pretty stupid for the next few days as I went about my business with a sloppy grin on my face.

That well-spoken chap I mentioned was a Flight-Lieutenant who you may well have heard of. Harrison was his name, Rex Harrison!

Now you might think that I was a bit slow on the uptake, but it had still never occurred to me that I might be able to do this sort of thing for a living. It was a sort of hobby to me, a bit of fun which enabled me to earn a few extra bob now and then. After the war had turned in our favour, it became obvious that it was only a matter of time before the RAF would no longer have any need of my expertise. I assumed that I would go back into the building trade and thought little more of entertaining than what I was already doing.

Italy and Germany threw in the towel and then America bombed Japan. It was all over at last and tears of joy flooded the streets of Britain. Now we could get back to normal, that is, if we could remember what normal was like. I joined the ranks of the ex-servicemen and we all marched home in our demob suits. Christine was now two years old and we had to find somewhere to live again. A publican near Plumstead Common provided the answer by renting us a couple of rooms. Sid Carter was his name, an unspectacular bloke but a knight in shining armour to this young couple and their little girl.

I went back into the building trade and picked up just over a fiver for a 40-hour week. I was able to earn a bit extra by continuing to do my act in various places, and I even invested in a stage suit. It was actually a second-hand waiter's outfit but there is not much call for second-hand waiters. The suit was not particularly good but Bloss tarted it up a bit and, together with a shirt, bow-tie and shoes, I had made myself a stage costume for just £2 15s, or £2.75 in today's money. It was a good investment because I used it for the next three years.

As you might imagine, it was pretty tiring working by day, doing gigs at night and trying to fulfil your family commitments, and I was finding it hard going. The more I thought about it the more I came to realise that I was getting, near enough, the same for an evening's entertaining at a British Legion as I was for a whole week of slogging away in the building trade. The penny was beginning to drop. I knew that I had to launch myself more fully into my showbusiness interest and at least try to find out if I could make it. If I failed, I would go back to the carpentry, but I had to give it a try.

I'm not sure how I fiddled it but I managed to get myself into a show at the Grand Theatre in Clapham. I was paid. too. I received £11 for the week, twice my wages on the building site. The big bonus was that this theatre was regularly visited by top agents looking for new talent. One of these was a chap by the name of Gordon Norval. He didn't have a big agency but he knew the business and he booked me, there and then, to play six weeks at different theatres around the London area. They were not major venues and I was booked as second act on, performing for eight minutes only. At least it was regular work for a while and I dared to allow myself to feel just a little like a professional entertainer.

I was still a showbusiness fan and liked to go and see shows at the various theatres around London, which was why I was just about to walk into the London Palladium to pay my ninepence for a cheap seat when I was tapped on the shoulder by Flight-Lieutenant Landau. That was his title in the RAF, but in civvies he was a well-known London-based impresario who had been in charge of some of the Forces shows in which I'd appeared.

"What are you doing these days?" he asked.

When I told him, he screwed up his face and I'm not sure, to this day, whether it was because he was horrified by my having a part-time go at show-business, that I was still doing some chippie work, or that I was playing less-than-spectacular venues. However, the smile soon returned to his face.

"Here's a tip for you. The BBC are doing a new show called *They're Out*. It's for ex-servicemen with talent. Go and have a crack at it. They are auditioning this afternoon."

You couldn't see me for dust as I sprinted to the Aeolian Hall in Bond Street, the well-known BBC mausoleum of mirth and music. When I got there the waiting-room was packed with 20 or so others, all seeking a chance on this new show. One bloke looked more like his wife was about to give birth, he was so incredibly nervous. His eyes were mostly closed, his hands were constantly on the move between praying mode or wringing-out the laundry, and he appeared to be talking to himself, although there was no sound. He had no need to be nervous because his audition went like a dream and the rest of us were also-rans by comparison. Who was he? Would you believe, Frankie Howerd.

I came through as well and was told that I would be used on one of the shows — yet to be scheduled — and they would be in touch. It gave me renewed confidence and I went away with the thought that it would do my part-time showbiz career no harm at all and that, probably, some of the fellows I worked with on the building site would get a kick out of it too. Another thought was plaguing me at the time too.

While I was still in the RAF I had met a number of Australians, and several of them had spoken to me of the opportunities in their country, especially for entertainers of whom there were not nearly enough. Bloss and I talked about it and decided that, if we could get help from the £10 assisted travel scheme that was operating at the time, we would go for it. We went along to Australia House in Aldwych and joined a massive queue of would-be emigrants. Gradually the queue got shorter until there were only two couples ahead of us. We were quite excited by now so you can imagine how we felt when the door was suddenly closed and we were informed that we should come back the next day. Still, we were resolved to do just that — Bloss and I were not the sort to give up easily.

The post came before we set off for Australia House the next morning. I was already practising my Australian accent and asking Bloss if she thought she'd have any trouble in cooking kangaroo-tail soup. Australia, land of opportunity, you are about to be blessed with our presence, I was thinking. I chucked the mail on the table and called to ask Bloss if she was ready. She was, but as she came through the door my eye was drawn to one of the envelopes on the table. It was from the BBC.

'Dear Mr Bygraves,' it began. They used to call you Mister in those days. The secretaries even wore evening-gowns. Today when you go to the studios the receptionists say, "What do you want?" or "Who are you?" Even the commissionaire wears trainers! Anyway, the letter was asking me to go back for another audition. I had already realised that being accepted for a show that had yet to be scheduled was just another way of keeping you on the end of a string in case you were needed in the future. I didn't care about that. I had come to the notice of the BBC sufficiently for them to write to me. Then I hit the panic button — the return audition was for that very afternoon at 2.30pm. Australia suddenly disappeared from the map.

To cut a long story short, I was booked for the series along with Frankie Howerd, who I have already mentioned, and several others, including Benny Hill, Jimmy Edwards, Harry Secombe, and the amazing Spike Milligan. You can imagine what it was like when that lot were together. We were all a bit green, of course, and thrilled at the prospect of being heard by something like 30 million listeners. Yes, that was the average radio listening figures in the immediate post-war era.

I still didn't think of anything other than continuing as a chippie and earning a few extra bob as an entertainer. It still never really occurred to me that I might actually become a fully professional performer. Not just then anyway. I watched my daughter Christine growing into a beautiful young girl and I wanted to provide for both her and Bloss in the best way I knew how, and that meant being a carpenter who was also paid to entertain.

Among the vast army of radio listeners was Jack Payne, a bandleader who had turned impresario. He was about to tour a new show called *For the Fun of It*. Donald Peers was the star, and he was a big star too, singing all the songs the ladies liked to hear. Jack Payne had listened to the radio show and decided that Frankie Howerd and I would be useful support acts. The tour was to open in Sheffield and play Moss Empires for 16 weeks. I was offered £15 per week, of which I would have to pay ten per cent to Jack Payne's office, a common racket in those days, enabling promoters to get artistes at a reduced fee by claiming an agent's commission.

It was decision time. Only a short time previously, Bloss and I had been queuing with dreams of Australia. Now we decided to stay put and make do with life as it was. That radio broadcast had proved to be a major milestone in my life and we now had yet another big decision to make. If I was going to accept this offer it was going to mean a major upheaval. I could not possibly continue working in East London by day and then nip up to Sheffield, or any of the other provincial towns and cities on the tour, after work. When the tour ended there might be nothing else at the end of it and I could find myself back in London with no work at all.

Caution said forget it! Bloss said go for it! She was confident that if I finished up out of work at the end of the tour, it would not be for long. One thing that the East End teaches you is optimism based on the ability to live on your wits. She knew that I had been through enough scrapes to be able to find a way out for us if it all went wrong. So, with a vote of confidence from the missus, I accepted the offer.

Although Donald Peers was the star, running him a close second was Nosmo King, a great comic from whom other entertainers learned much about their craft. Yes, he had taken his name from a No Smoking sign but, corny as it may sound now, nobody forgot him. The tour was a real eye-opener for a couple of greenhorns like Frankie Howerd and me. We learned about digs and stage-struck landladies. There have been a million stories about them and most of them are true. They are a breed all of their own. They loved to tell you about the stars who had stayed with them but, at the same time, they had a certain innocence which could be quite charming. They go from the excessively generous to the incredibly mean. The joke about hanging a kipper on the wall for you to scrape your bread on for breakfast might be a slight exaggeration, but it is only a slight one!

Innocence? Yes, in some cases. How about the lady who had a drag act staying with her and thought he was ever such a nice man for bringing back a homeless sailor and allowing him to share his bed for the week. She never stopped telling us how kind the artiste was, and how patriotic for taking care of this poor sailor with nowhere to go. Hard to believe isn't it?

I would like to say that the tour was a brilliant success and that everyone was very happy. In some ways it was, but there were other drawbacks — not so much for me but certainly for Frankie and some of the others. Jack Payne lived up to his name and made life a perfect misery for just about anyone who worked for him. I kept a low profile most of the time, but Jack gave everyone else a hard time, including Donald Peers, the dancers, and anyone else who crossed his path. I don't think he had a kind word for anyone and poor Frankie, being of a nervous disposition, came in for more than his fair share of stick.

He didn't just get stick from Jack Payne either. One night in Sunderland he was on stage doing his stuff and not going too well. It wasn't that he was doing anything wrong, simply that the audience didn't understand his humour. Frankie was a very funny guy then, just as he was for the rest of his life, but that night in Sunderland they did not understand him at all and one clever so-and-so threw a large rivet at him. If it had hit him Frankie would have been in hospital at best, in his coffin at worst. There was no understanding or sympathy from Jack Payne — he wanted to tear up Frankie's contract! He didn't, though, and probably realised that he was on to a good thing because, within a couple of years, Frankie Howerd was a household name and Jack Payne's office was handling his affairs. At one stage, three-quarters of Frankie's income was going into Jack Payne's bank account as 'agency and management fees'! Stage entertainers have become a little wiser over the years and for the past few decades it has been the icons of pop music who have suffered in this way.

Blossom travelled to a few of the tour stops with Christine but she didn't enjoy it. Who could blame her? It was bad enough living in rooms that you called home, but to be living out of a suitcase wasn't much fun for a mother and her baby. Eventually the tour did come to an end, but not before Bloss discovered that she was pregnant again. Well, there was no night-time television in those days and you had to do something when you got home from the theatre.

We took rooms in Woolwich but it was probably the worst time we have ever had. The landlady wouldn't have children staying in the place, so my sister-in-law came to the rescue and looked after Christine at night. The place was freezing cold and there was never enough coal. I know that the winter of 1947 was one of the coldest on record, but even a polar bear would have left home if it had been asked to stay in one of those rooms. The little gas cooker leaked and you took your life in your hands every time you struck a match. Why did we put up with it? Simply because we had no other place to go.

At last our new baby arrived on February 22nd 1947. It was a wonderful son and he began life in the East End Maternity Home. I was thrilled, Bloss was thrilled and Christine had a brother. We decided to call him Anthony, and I know that many of you have since seen him with me on my stage and television shows. He began life as a chip off the old block, living in rooms. The landlady showed that she did have a heart after all by waiving her 'no children' rule for a month so that Bloss could get over the worst of her ordeal and we looked for somewhere else. To think that Anthony was on a month's notice from the day he was born still gives me a chuckle.

The clouds were certainly a bit black at that time as there was not much work about. With the pregnancy and the birth of Anthony, I was beginning to think that accepting that tour for Jack Payne had been a terrible mistake. Then the silver lining turned up.

His name was Jock Jacobsen. Like Jack Payne he was an impresario, manager, agent, you name it. We bumped into each other in Leicester Square one morning, a real coincidence since he had seen my act the previous night at Chelsea Palace. Jock was nothing like the archetypal agent. He was a genuinely nice man who saw any business relationship as one of mutual benefit and not simply a way of ripping someone off and making as much as possible out of them. He was in partnership with Norman Payne who had the same sort of character.

Jock turned out to be more than just a silver lining. He invited me to join his stable and become one of his acts. I agreed and it was the best business decision that I had ever taken. From that moment on I became a professional entertainer.

CHAPTER FIVE

I've Arrived, And To Prove It — I'm Here

THAT meeting with Jock Jacobsen proved to be more than a turning point for yours truly. Suddenly, things began to happen in a big way. My weekly income shot up to around £50. Jock took ten per cent but, to be honest, I'm sure that he spent a lot more than that on the telephone on my behalf. Out of nowhere I was getting a lot more club work. When I say clubs, I mean those places that have exotic-sounding names, like 'Blue Lagoon', 'Paradise', 'Flamingo' and other enticing titles in lights over their smart entrances. Call them what you will, most of them still resembled giant ashtrays. You had to share a dressing-room with a mop and a bucket and, quite often, you had to share your act with one or two drunks who had partaken of enough 'Dutch Courage' to shout over your punch-lines. Happy days!

They were not all like that, of course, and I was happy to work anywhere at that time. My diary was getting busier and busier and, amid those clubs, were a few theatre dates. Before long, Jock had also arranged for me to make a recording. It was with the Carrol Gibbons Band and on the Parlophone label. On the day of release, Jock and I bought a copy each, end of story!

Around that time I also became a film star, well, I got into films. Jock got me three films and I found the experience very beneficial indeed. My third was *Tom Brown's Schooldays*. I played the Schooldays — no! I was a coachman. Before that I was second lead to comic Hal Monty in a couple of Arthur Dent films. I received the princely sum of £50 a week for these films, enough to be able to buy a car — a Ford Anglia.

I was now a family man with two children, a fairly large rented house in Romford, and a car, the only one in the street in fact. Actually, that car could tell you a few stories. When I bought it, I didn't have a driving licence, so I took a test straight away and passed it first time. I think that the examiner's nerves were shot and he couldn't wait to get out of the car. I hadn't had the car for long before it was vandalised outside the house. It wasn't badly damaged, but scratched quite a bit, and obviously quite deliberately. I asked my brother, Harry, what he thought it was that would drive someone to do such a thing.

"They must have heard you sing!" Thanks a lot, Harry.

Life continued to be a little spartan during this time and we still had rationing on most things. If it hadn't been for the fact that you could see where you were going at night, you could be excused for thinking that there was still a war on. Entertainment, however, was booming. After all the anxieties and prohibitions of the conflict years, the VE and VJ parties lasted for years. Sport and showbusiness provided the entertainment. Huge crowds turned up to watch football, speedway and just about any other sporting event. Theatres and cinemas were packed and the radio was listened to by millions.

My wages increased to £60 a week when Jock booked me into a touring revue called *Fine Feathers Make Fine Birds*. I learned an invaluable lesson on that tour. You see, at that time I didn't have a bank account. I was paid in cash every show and put a bit under the mattress after sorting out the housekeeping and pocket money. I mentioned this to Ernie Payne, the producer. He was not related to Jack Payne by the way — this was another, quite different Payne! Ernie suggested that I should take just half my money each week and let him keep the rest in the bank, where it would be safe until the end of the ten-week tour. I would then have a pretty nice bundle to take back to my family.

You're ahead of me aren't you? Yes, Mr Payne disappeared during the last week, and with him went my savings. It was a hard lesson to take. I've heard people moan that showbiz folk are overpaid. Perhaps that is the case, but there are few people in showbusiness who could not tell you at least one story like that, and probably a lot more.

Life goes on and it wasn't the last time that I was to make or lose a few bob by following a variety of advice. I might as well give you a few examples. You're looking at the bloke who took advice from Andy Neatroux, a respected member of the Variety Club of Great Britain, who was working for John Bloom. Remember him? He was the washing machine tycoon. Andy gave me a tip-off about a share issue by Bloom and strongly advised that I take up the maximum option of 1,000 shares. The price was £1.40 per share. I took that advice and, within a week, Bloom had gone bust and the shares were worth threepence each!

Another time I was invited to take part in a legal tax-saving investment that involved 'straddling commodities'. The young executive, who sat at his desk in a plush office next door to the Ritz Hotel, was very convincing. I listened to what he had to say and decided that my £20,000 would be in safe hands. You know what they say about a fool and his money? Quite right, my money went the same way as the cash that I had entrusted to Ernie Payne!

That sort of thing has happened to me a number of times, but it would be unfair of me if I didn't also show you the other side of the coin. Some time after I had become established, a well-known song writer came to me and offered me the score to a musical he had created. He approached me because I had just had a big success with one of his numbers and he wanted to give me the chance to make something of this score. He warned me that someone else had already offered £300, but that if I could add another £50 to that it was all mine. I did, and it was a real winner. You'll see what I mean when I tell you that the man was Lionel Bart — and the score was for *Oliver*.

I had just enjoyed some success with *Fings Ain't What They Used To Be*, which is why Lionel came to me. I recorded *Consider Yourself*, and arranged for Shirley Bassey to record *As Long As He Needs Me*. They were both successes, and that score did very well for me as you may imagine. I later sold the rights as part of my company, Lakeview Music, to the American company, Essex Music. It had proved to be a very good investment.

But, back to the progress.

Jock continued to book me into some decent gigs and I still occasionally bumped into Frankie Howerd, who was, by now, a very big name. It was still only a few years after our first meeting but he had taken off very quickly. During one of our conversations he mentioned that much of his success was due to a young script-writer, who had kept him supplied with original material for his *Variety Band Box* show on the radio.

"He's about the same age as you — Sykes is his name," said Frankie. I had never heard of him, so Frankie invited me to the Camberwell Palace for the after-broadcast party that the BBC were throwing to mark the end of the series. Frankie thought that Sykes might be there and, if we met, it could be useful for both of us.

Blossom and I went along to the party but, to be honest, we felt a bit out of it. Frankie was constantly surrounded by people eager to congratulate him, and we saw no sign of this Sykes fellow, so we decided to leave. Before we jumped into the Anglia, Bloss thought that she had better visit the loo. I waited outside for her. She had no sooner gone in than she ran out again, looking a little shaken.

"There's a man being ill in there — he looks in a bad way!" she cried.

I was about to go in and see if there was anything that I could do, when the door burst open and this very white-faced bloke staggered out. I caught him just in time as he fell forward.

"Thanks mate!" he tried to grin and attempted an apologetic half-bow to Blossom. "My name's Sykes — Eric Sykes." Somehow he managed to write down his address on a scrap of paper and give it to me. We have been the best of pals ever since that day. He explained later, that he was so fed up with the poor pay that he had received from the BBC that he had tried to drink as much of their booze as possible, hence his pitiful condition.

Eric has written some brilliant stuff for me, as he has done for countless others like me. His material helped me no end. I can remember surviving the Glasgow Empire thanks to his help. Actually, I not only survived it, but I even got loud applause and whistles. That audience response reached the ears of Val Parnell, who was amazed that a comedian from London could not only live through a week at the Glasgow Empire but could actually win over those granite Scots.

The following week I was back in London, appearing at the Finsbury Park Empire. Ted Ray should have been appearing at the London Palladium, but there was a problem since he had another engagement which could not be altered. Jock Jacobsen overheard Val Parnell discussing the problem with Cissie Williams, who was responsible for booking acts for the Moss Empires.

Jock dived straight in and urged them to come up and see me at Finsbury Park. Val Parnell remembered what he had heard from Scotland and needed no second bidding. He came and watched me and then booked me straight away to fill in for Ted Ray.

It was May 1951 when I took to the stage of the London Palladium — and I was still appearing at Finsbury Park. My spots were staggered so that I could do both venues, and I was now doing my spot five times a day, shuttling back and forth between venues until Ted Ray was able to return. I cannot describe the excitement of it, but I was even more excited when Val Parnell engaged me to support nearly all his big American acts at the Palladium. Later I was to star there in my own right but, even as a chief support, it was thrilling.

By now, I was well known on the theatre circuit, I had done small parts in some films, and I had done a bit of radio. Things were going well, and there was a big breakthrough just around the corner. When Eric Sykes was invited to do the scripting for a BBC radio show called *Educating Archie*, he thought that I would be ideal as Archie's tutor. Archie was, of course, Archie Andrews, the ventriloquist's dummy of the excellent Peter Brough. Today, people would have you certified if you suggested a radio show starring a ventriloquist — it would be like Radio 2 hosting a mime festival! In those days it was totally acceptable, and proved to be a milestone in radio history, and also in the history of yours truly.

From the moment that I made my vocal entrance with: "I've arrived, and to prove it — I'm 'ere!", my character became a national hero. People embraced the catch-phrases as part of the English language. We had a listening audience of about 25 million and, as well as myself, there were other members of the gang like Beryl Reid, Julie Andrews, Hattie Jacques and Tony Hancock.

That radio show turned me into a celebrity. I was still doing my theatre work but now I also started to make records in my own right. The first was *The Cowpuncher's Cantata* and it appeared in the very first Top Ten ever compiled, and stayed there for several weeks. The funny thing was, I did very little singing in my stage act at this time but, as the records began to prove popular, I could no longer leave them out. I recorded some unbelievable titles, *When You Come To The End Of A Lollipop* and *Gilly Gilly Ossenfeffer Katzenellen Bogan By The Sea* to name but two! If you look back into the archives you will see that they were one hit after another. If you recorded them now as *Top of the Pops* material, everyone would think that you were on something but, in those days, they were a bit of fun that most people liked enough to go out and buy.

At last we were able to buy our own house, in Barnet. Maxine, our second daughter, was born there and life was really good. Just before then, I had even received my first call for the *Royal Variety Show*. I was appearing at the Nottingham Empire when I received the telegram. I was to appear before King George VI and Queen Elizabeth, now, of course, the Queen Mother. From the moment that I received that telegram I was shaking in my shoes each time that I thought about it.

In those days the show went out on radio. There was no television coverage and you had to think about that when you were preparing your material. Eric Sykes and I put a little piece of script together for my appearance, which was only to be for a few minutes. The routine went something like this:

I walk out, greet the audience, explain that I'm supposed to make them laugh, and plead with them to respond as the theatre manager finds other jobs for you to do if the audience don't like you. I tell them a gag and, as the laughter subsides, a stagehand walks out and gives me a broom. I start to sweep the stage while using more material. When I get a good laugh, I appeal to the wings that this one was worth more than a broom. From the other side of the stage a mop and bucket are thrown on ...and so it went on.

I had a maximum of seven minutes to fill. The big night came on November 3rd 1950, and 28-year-old Max Bygraves went on and did his stuff, while his mate, Eric Sykes, sat in a pub round the corner. I went two minutes over time but nobody seemed to mind and, after the show, I was the chief target for the press who were keen to talk to this 'new star'. It was just after this show that *Educating Archie* got under way.

The theatre tours, summer shows, pantos, radio and recordings were keeping me more than a little busy and I have always been thankful that I have been blessed with the ability to sleep well. It has always been a battery re-charger for me. A lot of people get over-tired and then cannot sleep and before long are so fatigued that it makes them ill. I have never had that problem. It is rare that I cannot sleep when I want to.

My appearances at the Palladium continued and I was thrilled to find myself working with some of the giants of the game, among them Judy Garland. We got on well — so well, in fact, that I later received a telephone call from her at home in the United States, asking me to support her in a season she was doing in New York. At the time I was getting £150 a week in a show at Great Yarmouth but, for this engagement, I was to receive £2,500 a week. Even after expenses, I was still in pocket by about £2,000 a week — I never knew such money existed!

America was an education. Elsewhere in the book I shall tell you of some of my exploits but, suffice it to say that, working with Judy Garland and performing *A Couple of Swells* with her, in front of a never-ending line-up of stars who were constantly coming to see her, was just amazing. I had the opportunity to meet and talk with most of them and found it quite difficult to believe that I was in the company of people like Elizabeth Taylor, Frank Sinatra, Gary Cooper, Montgomery Clift and countless others that would drive an autograph hunter crazy. I was not on the fringe either. I was totally included in their chatter and their invitations. It was an incredible experience.

I got to know James Mason while I was over there. He had been to see the show and later sent me a congratulatory letter, which I treasure to this day. At the time he was married to the beautiful Pamela Kellino. I was invited over the telephone to come to dinner, but I explained that I had all the family with me. I was told to bring them all so, sure enough, we went along to the Masons. Sounds a bit like a pub doesn't it? It was a typical Hollywood Palace with large rooms, ornately and beautifully furnished, a large garden with magnificent lawns and an immense swimming pool. We were not the only guests — Frank Sinatra and Ava Gardner were among many others, and it was noticeable that they were having words.

I was sitting with my back to the pool talking to James Mason when suddenly his face changed and his eyes went wide. I wondered what was the matter, but not for long since James dived toward the pool where my Anthony was in difficulty. But for Mason's quick action, Anthony might well have drowned. He was hauled out, wrung out and laid out. It was a terrifying moment which ended in smiles all round. I suppose that Anthony can always boast that not everyone has had their life saved by James Mason with Frank Sinatra helping.

I did other shows with, and without, Judy Garland in the States but, as always, it was nice to return home to Britain. Now that I had a few bob, I wanted to do something for my parents. My father was still working in the docks. He was an independent man and I had to be tactful about what I did. I bought them a house in Welling, Kent, and he still commuted to the docks for a while, although he was coming up for retirement and was beginning to enjoy more time spent in the garden. He took the move in his stride. My mother, though, was a little different. I made sure that they were quite well off but the trouble was, my mother liked the shops in London and was used to getting on a bus and going 'up West' or 'down the lane'. She didn't know anyone in Welling and she found the choice of shops very limiting compared to her previous territory.

She never complained, though. In fact, I can't ever remember her complaining about anything. She used to make daytime trips back to Rotherhithe and join her pals for a lunchtime session in the local pub. I'm sure that, sometimes, her return journey to Welling was successful only because of a natural homing instinct rather than her ability to read the signs very well.

When my brother Harry came to visit me he looked ill and I didn't hesitate in saying so. He had just married Miss Tate & Lyle. Her real name was Jean Lewis but she had won a beauty contest at the firm she worked for, hence the title. She was a sweet thing with lumps in all the right places. I had a chat with Harry and suggested that, for the sake of his health, he should give up his work at the docks and do something else. He resolved there and then to become a publican and eventually he became a very popular landlord at the Norbury Hotel. My mother used to go and stay with him and his family quite regularly, so everyone was happy.

I later asked my mother if she would like me to get her a flat in London, instead of the house in Welling. Immediately she said: "No fear! It would be like going back to the buildings!" As I said: everyone was happy.

There was still a lot more to come from my career but, as I took stock of my situation in the early 1950s, I could not fail to be as happy as everyone else. Thanks to Jock Jacobsen, my career had not just taken off but was really flying. Eric Sykes had become a great pal and had supplied me with some great material, and I had worked with some of the biggest names in showbusiness and at some of the top venues. I had hit records. It was hard to imagine that things would get better still.

On the family front I had a lovely wife and three smashing children. I had been well and truly blessed in every possible way. Every time I walked into a shop or an office someone would say, "I've arrived! And to prove it, I'm 'ere!"

I had, and I was!

CHAPTER SIX

You Need Hands

HERE'S only one thing better than appearing at the Palladium and that's topping the bill at the Palladium. I have done that a number of times in long seasons at that great theatre and have many happy memories, except, perhaps, for the time that 'Goldie', the wonderful horse owned and trained by Joan Rosaire of the famous circus family, stood on my foot. I have never felt pain quite like it.

There was another classic incident when I was starring in the show entitled *Wonderful Time*. Shows were produced in a different style then. Today, when you are topping the bill at a theatre, you usually do one major spot in the second half. In those days you made several appearances in various productions and sketches. One such sketch in *Wonderful Time* was a western saloon scene, in which I played the 'Dead Shot Kid'. Joy Nicholls was 'Lil', the saloon owner, and Billy Cotton was the sheriff.

I burst into the saloon and everyone runs for cover except Lil and the sheriff. I steal a kiss from Lil and am then challenged by the sheriff. Bill Cotton was never a great one for lines and on one famous night he sauntered up to me and drawled sneeringly, "So, you're the Dead Shit Kid, huh?"

The audience erupted, and Bill went redder than I had ever seen him.

"Will you repeat that line, friend?" I drawled back at him.

"No bloody fear!" said Bill.

The audience were in hysterics, but a few days later Bill got a memo from Val Parnell which said that it had come to his attention that he had used the word 'bloody' on stage, and that this was not allowed. Would he please keep to the script in future. He was absolutely right, of course, and we were thankful that he had not heard Bill's earlier slip of the tongue. I wonder what he would have made of some of today's foul-mouthed 'comics'?

After that particular Palladium season I went to Blackpool for a Tom Arnold season, in a show called *Latin Quarter*. Winifred Atwell and a new comedienne named Hylda Baker — yes she was new in the early 1950s — were also in the show. We did 16 weeks of record-breaking business. In the finale, Winnie Atwell used to precede me and every time she walked on there was a sudden roar. After some nights of this I asked my musical director, Bob Dixon, what was happening. He made some investigations and discovered that, as she walked on, her husband, Lou Levison, was making a roaring noise into a hidden microphone off stage. He made it sound just as if Brazil had scored a winning goal. Having sussed this, I began walking to the very edge of the stage and encouraging the audience to shout "More!" Lou quietly confronted me and said that it was a bit ungentlemanly to do that with another star on stage. I said he was right, and I would stop it just as soon as he stopped that roaring noise. We agreed to a truce.

It sometimes must seem that if you have a Rolls-Royce with a personalised number plate, then you are a bit of a show-off. I suppose that if we didn't like to show off a bit we wouldn't be in showbusiness, but I promise you, my first Rolls was almost an accident. I was rehearsing for *Cinderella* at the Palladium, a show which also starred Julie Andrews, Jon Pertwee, Mr Pastry (Richard Hearne) and a host of others. I arranged to have lunch with Billy Cotton, and what a lunch it was! The food was great, the wine flowed freely and our brains were well pickled.

On the way back to the Palladium we stopped at Jack Barclay's motor showroom to admire the gleaming limousines.

"That's what you need now," said Billy, pointing to a beautiful, nearly new, silver-grey, 'Silver Dawn' Rolls-Royce. We went inside and were told that it was £4,500, too rich for me!

"I'll give you £2,000 deposit and a tenner a week!" I blurted out, getting carried away by the idea. To my utter astonishment, the salesman agreed and within ten minutes I was signing all the necessary forms. Two days later it was delivered to my home carrying the number plate MB 1. Billy Cotton had gone to the trouble of tracing the number and buying it for me. I have had a number of Rolls since then, but I have always kept that MB 1 number plate.

I must tell you one other Billy Cotton story. I used to take the family to Alassio in Italy for our holiday each year and, quite often, Billy was on holiday there at the same time. On one occasion we discovered that there was a foot-ball match taking place locally, so Billy and I went along. During the game, Billy was hit by a Coca Cola bottle thrown by a visiting supporter.

"Look what he did," said Billy, as a lump began to rise on the side of his face.

"It shouldn't have done that," I remarked. "It was a soft drink!"

For years after that, whenever we were out together, I would always buy Billy at least one soft drink.

I was back at the Palladium the following year to star in *Mother Goose*. Peter Sellers was among the other stars and he also got it in the neck from Val Parnell when he started doing an unscripted Groucho Marx routine during a matinee. The band were in hysterics and it was very funny, but Peter was devastated when he received a curt note from Val Parnell threatening him with the sack. That may sound a bit harsh, but there is not one performer who wouldn't agree that we were better entertainers as a result of that sort of discipline.

In 1956 I was back at the Palladium for another long-running show entitled *We're Having A Ball*. It ran until Christmas and kept the Kaye Sisters, Joan Regan and myself, along with a number of American and Continental acts, very busy for months. During this show, once again I was invited to take part in the *Royal Variety Show*. As usual there were so many big names involved that it is difficult to remember them all. I do recall some: there was Laurence Olivier, Bud Flanagan, Harry Secombe, Dickie Henderson, Ben Lyon, Bob Monkhouse, Gracie Fields, Alfred Marks, Tommy Trinder, Jimmy Wheeler, Alma Cogan and Liberace.

We were all shocked when Val Parnell interrupted our last rehearsal, just a few hours before the performance was due to start, and told us that it was cancelled. The Suez crisis had taken a turn for the worse and Her Majesty did not think that it would be appropriate for her to be sitting in a theatre watching a show while Anthony Eden was addressing the nation to explain how close we all were to another conflict. We were all disappointed to say the least, and Liberace was in tears. He had travelled overland in the United States and then crossed the Atlantic by boat, all at his own expense, and had even brought his mother to witness his appearance before Her Majesty, The Queen.

We all stood around like an undertakers' convention. Winnie Atwell was there, and even she was downcast, even though she was not involved. Suddenly Jimmy Wheeler opened his violin case and went into his routine saying: "I've been rehearsing this for a fortnight so someone's going to see it!" We all began to laugh then, including Liberace. Winnie Atwell invited us all back to her place for a few drinks and snacks and the whole affair turned into a party. It was quite a sight to see Winnie and Liberace at four o'clock in the morning, sharing a grand piano to play *Chopsticks* together.

It was during the run of *We're Having A Ball* that I turned my hand to song writing again and came up with a number that was to stay in the Top 20 for about 16 weeks and win me the Ivor Novello Award as Songwriter of the Year. The song was called *You Need Hands*, and it has been a major part of my life ever since. Everyone still wants to hear it, so it is rare that I leave it out of my act — even now, 40 years on! It was followed by *You Gotta Have Rain* and, for that, I won the ITV Songwriter of the Year Award.

Of course, the advent of rock 'n roll in the late 1950s produced a whole new form of entertainment, and people like Frankie Vaughan, David Whitfield and other entertainers — myself included — became 'old hat'. Television turned its back on us in favour of stars like Tommy Steele, Marty Wilde, Cliff Richard and others. Fortunately, the theatres and radio still welcomed us.

I'd had a film success with *Charlie Moon* which had also spawned a hit record, *Out of Town*. My son, Anthony, was in the film, too, playing me as an eight-year-old. It was good to be working with him and we had a lot of fun filming in Hampshire, especially when we were doing the circus scenes. Another film was *A Cry From The Street*, which won the New York Critics Award for the best film of the year, and also won a number of awards at the Edinburgh Film Festival. It was also the only British film selected for the Moscow Film Gala so we were quite thrilled about it.

In 1961 I had an idea for an outdoor comedy show and suggested my favourite haunt in Alassio as a potential location. ITV liked the idea and, along with Eric Sykes and Peter Dulay, I spent three weeks in the Italian resort shooting six half-hour shows called *Roamin' Holiday*. The show proved so popular that Alassio's average of half a million tourists per year rose to two million, and the town made me honorary mayor.

Television turned full circle and was good to me for years. You may remember the show entitled simply *Max*, in which I was joined by the Geoff Love Orchestra. It was very popular and ran for some years. We had a decent blend of songs, gags and guests and it worked. It also helped with my record sales. *Tulips From Amsterdam* had been a big hit and I followed it up with an album of favourites. During one of the TV shows, Geoff Love announced that he had been asked to present me with a Gold Disc by Astor Records in Australia. I was speechless. It was completely unrehearsed and I had no idea about it. When I said: "I don't know what to say", Geoff Love said: "Don't say anything …sing something!" Bob Dixon went into a four-bar intro and I followed with a little medley. The audience loved it and the next morning Pye Records started getting calls from all over Britain from record stores asking for *Singalong with Max*. Pye pressed copies for all they were worth and within four weeks I had another Gold Disc.

In the next couple of years I made another nine discs which Cyril Stapleton called *Singalongamax*. They all went either Gold or Silver — and they are still selling all over the world today.

Although television turned on its head again and, for the most part, shunned performers like myself, I have never been short of work. Many of the lovely old theatres have gone, but Civic Centres have replaced them. The plush carpets and chandeliers have been replaced by parquet flooring and computerised lighting systems, but the stage is still there and so are the seats. My own experience shows that people are still prepared to forsake the fireside and the television in favour of a night of live entertainment.

I have been back to the USA to perform a number of times and I have also been in fairly constant demand in other parts of the world, which is why I fly off to Hong Kong, Singapore, Australia and New Zealand so often. There is also a great hunger for artistes like myself on the various cruises that are constantly circumnavigating the globe.

On the family front, we did have a terrible upset when Christine's husband, Michael, was tragically killed in a car crash. She has since remarried as you will read. We have remained a close family, and I consider myself to be a very lucky guy to have been blessed so much.

I sometimes think back to my childhood, the tearaway days of Rotherhithe. I am a millionaire now, with an OBE, numerous awards and countless experiences. I have many wonderful friends and a lovely family. Is it any wonder that I am so happy?

It would be nice to invite each and every one of you round for tea and a chat, but that would take me several lifetimes so, instead, I thought perhaps that we would bring you into today's world of Max Bygraves in a slightly different way. You see, I could go on writing about the adventures and experiences of yesterday until we had a book that would give *War and Peace* a run for its money but, from the many letters which I receive daily, it seems that many of you are interested in how I spend my time nowadays. I even get asked for political opinions, my views on the latest films, advice on marriage guidance or how to bring up the children.

So, come on in and I'll try to give you some insight into the everyday life of Bygraves folk.

We begin as the summer cools into autumn 1996. I have finished a long summer season in Bournemouth and, apart from some radio shows and a few more theatre dates, most of my attention is on Australia. Why Australia? Let me explain.

Mention Australia and many of us probably start thinking about *Neighbours*, *Home and Away*, or one of the other countless television soaps which have not only invaded the British small screen, but also the pantomime side of showbusiness as well.

There is another side to Australia that you need to see to appreciate it fully. It is a lovely country and the people are genuinely very nice. We often get the impression, here in Britain, that they are all a bunch of Pommie-bashing sheep-shearers and beach bums, and that the country is little more than a desert, both culturally and literally, with nothing to offer other than deadly spiders, crocodiles and an overdose of sun and cricket. Nothing could be further from the truth.

Australia is not in any sense a desert. It has desert regions, of course, but it also has beautiful beaches, forests, plains, hills, waterfalls, rivers, and some of the most exotic wildlife ever created. Australians are often presented as being slobs who never do any work. What nonsense! They are a hard-working people with all sorts of international backgrounds. If they are seen to play hard, it is because they have earned the right to do so and nobody is able to deny anyone that right.

I was impressed from the very start of the very first tour that I ever did in Australia. Little did I know then, that one day I would become a property owner in that great country and spend half of my time there. I am and I do, but in a sense it was an accident.

As the 1990s began, I was on one of my trips to Australia. For this journey we decided on using a different route. We thought that we would try dropping off at places that we hadn't seen much of in the past. Blossom traced a route from London to Miami, then a stop-over of one week in the Bahamas. From there it was Mexico City, Acapulco, Tahiti, and finally Sydney.

When we arrived in Nassau, a phone call informed us that some friends were trying to contact us from Australia. Having just purchased my very first fax machine, I used it for the first time to get in touch with those friends. They were John and Sheila Taylor who lived in a place called Attunga Park, in northern New South Wales. We had stayed with them previously on a couple of occasions and thought that it was the most beautiful spot that we had ever seen.

"If you ever think of selling this place," I remember saying once. "Let me have the first refusal!"

This was exactly what their call was all about. John and Sheila had run into financial difficulties, the bank had foreclosed on them and wanted to sell off the property. Remembering my words, John got in touch as quickly as possible to inform me that the home, land and four or five outbuildings were going up for sale by auction on that very day. He assured me that the bank would consider any offer made. I was aware that the figure originally quoted when a possible sale was discussed was in the region of three million dollars, but nevertheless John told me that the bank would be sure to listen to an offer of one million.

One thing that I didn't want was a property of 84 acres in a spot named Murwillumbah. I showed John's return fax to Blossom, who was in ecstasy at the thought of owning Attunga Park.

"Buy it Max! Please buy it," she begged.

I did try to calm her down. I reasoned that Australia was on the other side of the world. It wasn't as if the property was in Bournemouth. Who was going to look after it? After all, I am still a working entertainer ...and so on. Nothing seemed to work, however, all she could see were the rolling hills, the seclusion, the scenery. She argued that we could get Christine and Barry to move in and be caretakers. She made everything seem so simple. I faxed an offer that I knew they would be bound to refuse.

Four hours later, a fax arrived from the house agents and auctioneers: "Congratulations on being the new owners of Attunga Park ...!" They had accepted my offer and suddenly I was numb with worry. We cancelled Mexico City, Acapulco and the rest and made plans to get to New South Wales as quickly as possible, which was within 48 hours. As we flew toward the scene of this folly, I was trying to think of a way of saying to the bank, "Hey, I was only kidding!"

We arrived in Brisbane early one morning to be greeted by a radiant, smiling Christine. On the two-hour journey to Murwillumbah, which I was still unable to pronounce, she told us that both of the 8,000-gallon water tanks were empty and that we'd need to get the local water suppliers to send in a bowser to fill them. The swimming pool would also need 1,000 or so gallons. Some cattle belonging to a neighbour had broken through the fences in several places and they would have to be fixed and, to cap it all, an eight-foot long carpet snake, which is a protected species, had been visiting the gardens and taken up residence on the front lawn!

That was the greeting we received at Attunga Park; we were a couple of English townies in real Crocodile Dundee country. Innocents abroad, both in our late 60s with not the slightest clue on how to manage an estate, neither of us knowing the difference between a bull and a cow or how to ride one of the horses we had inherited.

My first thought was to cut our losses and put it up for an immediate resale. Then I looked about me. There was something about the place that seemed so welcoming, so tranquil and yet still challenging. I made up my mind to wait for just a little while. Our nearest neighbour was half a mile away, the nearest doctor almost three miles, shopping in town was about the same distance.

As we woke up each morning we were welcomed by the dawn chorus of the birds greeting the sunrise. Birds which I had only ever seen in captive aviaries were abundant in our trees. Beautiful parrots, kookaburras, finches and many that I could not even put a name to. It was a daily wonderland that they seemed to be creating just for our enjoyment.

Sheila and John Taylor had moved to Queensland, so there was nobody who could tell us where the fuses or other domestic necessities were. However, we had a couple of good Samaritans in Barry and Christine and gradually we began to get the property under some sort of control.

Just after the delivery of the water, it rained solidly for three days and nights. The front gate was flooded and none of us could enter or leave. Luckily we had stocked up well with food and drink — we had inherited two large Frigidaires plus a cold room — so survival was not a problem. Then the telephone was cut off, closely followed by the electricity. Fortunately, the Taylors had left a good supply of candles and matches. Did they know something that we didn't? Just as we began to wonder what to do about all the food in the fridge, all the power came back on again.

In the meantime I had two concerts at the Concert Auditorium in Melbourne, 600 miles away. There was no way of getting out of that gate, the

The year is 1941 and 1212094 Aircraftsman Bygraves endeavours to save Britain.

On our wedding day, 12 September 1942. It's why the war took so long.

With Roger Welch, the brother of Vera Lynn, playing two bomber pilots – Wizard Prang!

It's 1951 and I'm in *Tom Brown's Schooldays* with John Howard Davies. He was almost run over by the coach – stage struck, I suppose!

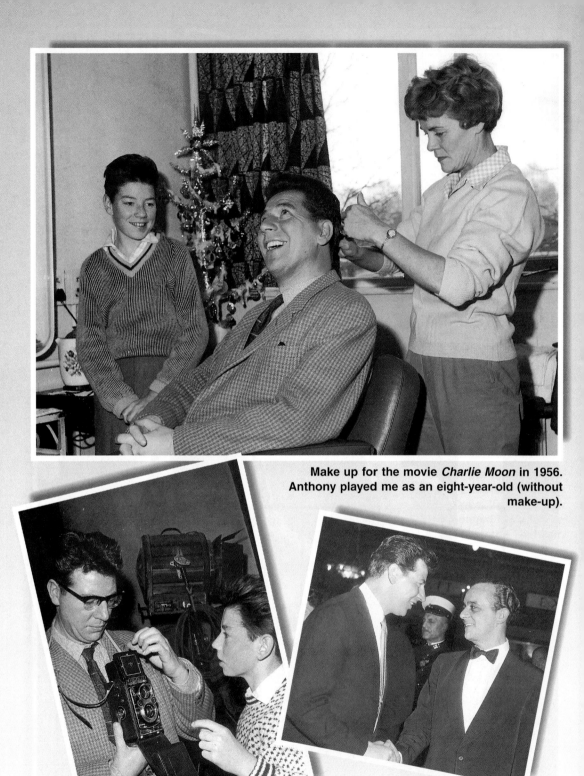

Make up for the movie *Charlie Moon* in 1956.
Anthony played me as an eight-year-old (without
make-up).

"Dad, d'yer think this is a
bit too close for a close-up?"

We all looked
young in 1958. Now Larry
Adler is an octenergarian –
but I'm catching him up.

car would have been submerged. What to do? I looked up the number of a helicopter service at Coolangatta International Airport and they gave me the number of a pilot who just might come out. I spoke to him and he told me that he knew the area well and he would be about half an hour. He instructed us to listen for the noise of the helicopter, then lay a large white sheet on the ground well away from the trees and any overhead cables. Barry and I did as he requested and, almost to the minute, we could hear the whirl of the helicopter's blades overhead. The pilot (Bob) phoned us and told us he could see the white sheet and to keep clear as he was coming in to land, but we must be ready for take-off immediately. With my stage suit and orchestra parts packed in a suitcase, I ducked low under the revolving blades and blew a farewell kiss to Blossom, whose face, with her hands up to her mouth, looked petrified.

Away we went, over all those flooded fields and swollen rivers. Bob got me safely to the airport and, with no customs or baggage to worry about, we were in good time to make the connection to Melbourne. Once at Melbourne, I was met by the promoter at the entrance to the airport, then whipped away by the longest stretch limousine that you could imagine. Just 40 minutes later I was on stage rehearsing with the band.

That's the way it seems to be in Australia. Travelling by air is a normal way of life, obstacles are easily surmounted, it's all in a day's work. I finished that concert to a standing ovation from the 2,000 audience, and was rewarded with a magnum of Moet Chandon for breaking the attendance record for the two performances with 4,000 people. The manager, a very nice lady, made me promise that I would come back again. I assured her that I would, providing that it wasn't raining.

When I arrived back at Attunga Park the following lunchtime, the place looked bone dry, the birds were singing their heads off once more, and the plants and flowers were full of colour. The only clue to the previous day's deluge was the sheet we had spread for the helicopter landing. Because of the ensuing mildew, Blossom, the ever-thrifty housewife, had cut it up into small pieces for dusters. We had 'arrived' in Australia — home is where the dusters are!

There are many hazards to be wary of in the Australian climate. One is the powerful sun that can make the unsuspecting Brit really sorry if he or she doesn't take the proper precautions. Another is swimming off the famous Bondi Beach, where the pollution can be absolutely horrendous, with many stories in circulation of swimmers swallowing something quite unsavoury!

There are, of course, the well-known hazards of crocodiles and sharks, but one for which we were totally unprepared happened to my son-in-law, Barry the Artist. We call him that because both of my daughters are married to Barrys!

Apart from his work as a painter, which earns him a comfortable living, he gives a hand on the property at Attunga Park. He is Australian by birth and therefore is aware of most of the pitfalls of country life, having been brought up on a farm in Victoria. However, even he was unprepared for what happened to him

He mentioned one day that he was suffering some discomfort around his groin. Upon investigation, a tick was discovered in his pubic hair, probably from cutting the grass around the house in his shorts. Like me, Barry dislikes the very idea of a doctor's surgery and so I motored some 16 kilometres to town, purchased a pair of tweezers, and set about removing the tick. It wasn't easy to find and it was even harder to pull out. It is very important to get all of it, otherwise they keep growing.

You can imagine the ribald comments and laughter that greeted this operation, especially from the womenfolk who found it hilariously funny. Barry didn't ... he found it extremely hard even to smile and finally asked for a shot of brandy, which was a real surprise as his only tipple was an occasional glass of wine.

As I bent over to make the extraction there were several comments, such as: "I hope the Consorting Squad doesn't walk in!" When I asked Barry to keep rock-still, a voice chimed in: "Don't you mean cock-still?" Another — from my comedy routine — "Who needs tickets?"

As I found the tick and pulled it free, Barry exploded with several four-letter words which I wouldn't have used on my wedding night. Then after much blasphemy and another request for a double brandy, I triumphantly showed him the insect at the end of the tweezers. Looking it straight in the eye and, as only an Australian can, Barry shouted: "You little bastard! In future, feed off the British — and I hope you get mad cow disease!" Such is life in Australia.

I spend most of the British winter months there now but, believe me, I do not stagnate. As well as concert engagements, TV and radio appearances, there is never a dull moment. Let me take you through a typical stay in the land of Oz. In 1996 I travelled out at the beginning of December — and this is how it went ...

CHAPTER SEVEN

Waltzing Max-tilda

December 2nd 1996

"We drew the short straw," said our Australian pilot ("My name is Greg!"). What he was actually saying was that five aeroplanes had all left for Australia at about the same time. Therefore we were each allotted different heights at which to fly and, as we were bottom of the stack and in cloud most of the time, we could expect to encounter a great deal of turbulence and buffeting. We had it all the way to Oz — only the QE2 has been worse!

Just as I was about to enter the toilet, after a couple of hours of flying, the most attractive stewardess asked: "D'ye mind if I go first — a baby has just had a sickie over my hands?" I told her to go ahead, of course, and stood cross-legged for the next ten minutes, trying not to appear incontinent to the queue that had gathered behind me.

An Australian lady, clutching a sick bag, told me that she was about to burst and could she go next. I told her that if she did then Qantas were going to have a flood on their hands, but I would try to be quick. Hating myself for being so ungentlemanly, I stood and did the longest pee ever. She almost knocked me over when I opened the folding doors. I knew exactly how she felt and did a sidestep that any Spanish bullfighter would have been proud to shout "Ole!" for, as she flew past me.

It was a relief to reach Brisbane and one of those Australian days of blue skies, red soil and Avis all ready with the ordered car. The trouble now, was that neither Blossom nor myself like red cars, it is something I have nursed since being involved in minor accidents when other cars have hit my Rolls — they were always red ones! Blossom, on the other hand, is a redhead, and she dislikes the colour clash! I also prefer an automatic because of the long journeys in Australia, and this car was not. A young chap ("My name is Darren!") did a quick swap for us and came up with a white Nissan. He then helped us out to the bay with our 'lotsa' luggage. We were on our way, home to Attunga Park.

December 4th 1996

My daughter Christine had told me, that before she left for England, she had interviewed a young lady to help Blossom with our large house. The young lady's name is Emma, she is about 18 and seems very willing. We know her parents and feel sure that she will turn out okay.

The reason that I mention this is because staff help is such a lottery. In the past we have had couples and sometimes it is the man who is all right, and sometimes the lady. We have never been so lucky as to get two satisfactory workers at the same time. It's a bit like backing horses. The people who I see at the racetrack, which I sometimes enjoy, back trebles, or trifeclas as they are known here. To back one winner is an achievement, yet now they are betting the bookmaker that they can name one, two, even three in the same frame. No wonder the bookmaker smiles when he takes a bet from a punter!

The only time that I ever came out on top in betting was last year at a club in New South Wales. The rain was torrential, too bad to get to the car without being soaked, and so Blossom and I went back into the club and settled down with a sandwich and coffee. I took the few coins change I received and popped them into the restaurant's slot machine. As I pulled the lever for the second coin, I wondered what had happened when bells started to ring loudly. Two men in suits hurried in, cut the sound of the bells and informed me that I had just won the jackpot of A$4,986 — did I want cash or cheque?

I settled for cash, bought champagne for everyone in the restaurant, gave Blossom half and tried to buy an umbrella from a lady. She told me to take it as a present — my luck was certainly in that night! When we got to the car with dollar bills in every pocket, the warning from Bloss was: "Drive carefully! If we have an accident with all this cash sticking out of our pockets, the police will think that we've held up a petrol station!"

Well, she had seen *Bonnie and Clyde* at least six times!

December 5th 1996

It must have been quite a storm during the night. Apart from the overflowing pool, the roof-tiles on the gazebo are all uplifted and the plant life looks blown to pieces. The food that we usually leave out for the foxes remained untouched, which means that they had decided to stay at home and give it a miss.

Christine tells us that a mother and her three cubs come regularly to the side door for their rations. They are incredibly tame and, because of the look of one of the cubs, she has been adding a vitamin powder to their meals. She has asked me to note the smaller one's progress as it has been quite puny. She fostered this 'Friend of the Foxes' campaign because she believes it keeps others away — she means those squawking crows, fieldmice and snakes. I don't know if she is right or not but she tells me that she once read in a book that there is a certain smell from foxes which makes other animals keep clear. Humans cannot detect it, she says, but other pests can, and, after all, books don't lie do they? Oh, sweet trusting Christine, who has never known a Pat Quinn.

Emma is upset today. Yesterday she put out two lines of washing and, with beautiful, clear blue skies, decided to leave them until this morning. She was crestfallen when she arrived to see them still sopping wet. I told her to put them through the wringer. "What on earth is a wringer?" She asked. The young have a way of making one feel very old!

On days like this, so overcast and threatening, I like to get out the foolscap and pens and settle down to write. At this moment I am writing six half-hour shows for BBC Radio Two, to be read on air in the spring. It is good to go back and test the memory. I have so much to recall of childhood, puberty and teenage days. It is a joy to keep putting it down and certain words have a way of bringing whole sequences to mind — 'wringer' is one such word!

Our wringer was a tall cast-iron contraption with two large wooden rollers. As you turned the handle at the side of the machine, the gears would engage and, as the rollers turned, wet laundry was fed through by hand and the excess water was squeezed out and caught by a galvanised tin bath placed beneath the rollers. In those days you had to be fairly comfortably off to own a wringer. The only reason that we had one was because my father had won it as second prize in a raffle. The first prize was a complete set of gardening tools — spade, fork, trowel etc — which would have been pretty useless in a two-room council flat with just one window-box.

Because we were owners of the wringer, neighbours would come to borrow it. It did have wheels, but it was still a major job trying to get it from A to B. Every Monday, my brother and I would struggle to get it to a neighbour's house, leave it for a couple of hours, and then move on to the next. For this labour of love, Harry and myself would be tipped tuppence from Mrs Dempsey or Mrs Lyons.

Harry, always in a rush to get the job done, would go much too fast for the small wheels. One day it toppled and looked to be going right over. We both rushed to support its mighty weight, and succeeded, but at a cost! Even today I still have a damaged thumb with a half-grown finger-nail because of that accident. When I arrived back home after my visit to St Olave's Hospital with my damaged hand supported by a sling, the only sympathy I got from my father was a grin and: "Hello there Lefty!"

December 6th 1996

Mobile phones can be a pain. On the other hand, in a continent the size of Australia, with long journeys sometimes taking six or eight hours, they are an absolute must. On two occasions in the past I have known what it is like to be stranded in the outback. Aussie drivers aren't full of courtesy. If they see you standing helpless beside a breakdown hut in the middle of the night, not too many of them want to stop and help — and there aren't too many that you feel like accepting a lift from either.

This week I purchased a mobile. On the very first day that I bought it, I lost it. It is not a part of my everyday thinking like wallet, credit cards, watch and all the other paraphernalia we're accustomed to carry around. I found myself leaving it on shop counters or in wash-rooms. I don't know what to do about it other than 'get used to it', especially as I've already had to drive back over 20 miles to retrieve it from a cafe where we'd had lunch. "You're not the first one mate!" said the waiter, showing me a box with at least half a dozen mobiles in search of their owners.

Yesterday I was startled to hear it ring. A dear friend, Russell Roylance, who is managing-director of a club that I work each time I come to Australia, was calling with an invitation to see the current show which he had booked. The show was the *Riverdancers* with headliner John MacAnnally, an Irish troubadour. I am a great fan of *Riverdance* and, even without Michael Flately, I assumed that it would be decent entertainment.

It was! It was just six-handed, but those young ladies and energetic young men, with hands stiffly at their sides, kicking in unison to pre-recorded tapes making an exciting beat, had the 1,100 people in the audience calling for more. Very well deserved! John MacAnnally was a pleasant surprise. He is a mature and experienced performer and knows how to play his audience. The show, a two-hour all Irish effort, provided really first-class fare.

The most surprising part of the show to me was when John asked if there were any Irish people in the audience. About two dozen hands were raised. He then asked how many of the audience had actually been to Ireland and a show of hands almost doubled the first question. Finally, how many in the audience had Irish ancestors. The whole auditorium raised their hands, me included!

John was, of course, sounding them out for his next batch of songs starting with *When Irish Eyes are Smiling* — and did they sing! All around us some of the sweetest sounds that I have ever encountered were giving voice to song after song.

I couldn't help thinking: "Are these really people from the same land where some kill and maim with their terrible bombs and are responsible for the deaths of so many innocents — people who are so bloody-minded that they can't come to any agreement or discussion that might end this unnecessary bloodshed?"

John MacAnnally closed the show with the most moving rendition of *Danny Boy* I have yet heard. Ladies unashamedly wiped their eyes as John, in a clear falsetto, sang the closing "Oh Danny Boy I love you so", to rapturous applause. I have often said that I have yet to meet an Irishman that I don't like — including Pat Quinn — and John MacAnnally was no exception.

After the show, John, Russell, Blossom and I, went to 'Oskar's — a restaurant on the beach, where the Atlantic salmon was a treat. John, whose home is in Nashville, knew many of the showbiz people that I knew, so we had a lot to talk about.

We had almost decided on yet another bottle of that superior Australian Chardonnay, when Russell's mobile phone bleeped. He had to leave and so, happily, we all went our separate ways.

Next day, I called in at Oskar's very early to say how very much we'd enjoyed the service, the salmon and the wine. Oh yes …and to pick up my new Nokia mobile which somehow I'd managed to leave behind!

December 8th 1996. Byron Bay, NSW.

This place has altered, and not for the better. Not only does almost every cafe have 'thump' music, — that's music where only the bass is heard — but nearly half of them have bearded glassy-eyed hippies half out of their minds on 'Persian rugs'. Everywhere, and I honestly mean everywhere, are teenagers in shorts and baseball caps worn back to front, devouring fast food at a frantic pace.

This must be a cafe-owner's goldmine. If they are not eating fish and chips from newspaper, they are swilling cans of Coke or Seven-up. The one thing that can be said in their favour is that they appear to use the waste bins for their rubbish, which is a lot more than they do near my apartment in Victoria, London.

Pizzas and tubs of potato chips are consumed with an unsmiling manic look — it reminded me for all the world of my idea of a leper colony. I told Blossom to have a good look around because although it is only 30 miles from our property, today is my farewell appearance at Byron Bay. We don't get on well at all.

Four of my grandchildren are teenagers. I spoke to Lily, the eldest, and gave her my opinion of this town. She listened intently from her home in Truro, Cornwall, and, when I had finished telling her about all the slobs and slobesses that we had just encountered, she drooled — "Ooh, how wonderful!"

I keep forgetting what it is to be young!

December 9th 1996. Surfer's Paradise.

Today is the end of our first week in Australia. For me, life here takes on a different pattern to the one in the UK. For instance, I am awake most mornings at around 5.30am, have a cup of tea, check the weather and decide on my activities for the day. If it looks overcast, I head for my small office to do some writing, answer mail and sign cheques — don't they seem to gather? If Blossom has a good peaceful night then I leave her in.

Invariably there are faxes to be answered, so I write to Jennifer who wants to know if I will attend some function or appear for some charity. She is aware that I am selective about where I am booked nowadays, so I give her a 'yes' or a 'no' and fax it off to her in London.

If it looks like the good weather is going to last we get in the car and decide where to go. Today it is Surfers' Paradise. Our girl Emma is turning out to be most reliable and cheerful, nothing at all seems to worry her. She doesn't know it, but we've christened her 'No worries Emma'. We can leave the house in her care which always seems to be okay. Of course, we might return one day to find that she's sold it, but, as I said earlier, staff is a lottery!

My first glimpse of Surfers' Paradise was back in 1971. Then, it was just a few scattered buildings with some fast-food sheds that satisfied the young blond surfers who had discovered their own waves that were comparable to Hawaii, or any other part of the world for that matter. Now, it is a staggering town of high-rise blocks, casinos and some of the finest hotels and restaurants imaginable. I think that it puts places like Miami or Nassau to shame, and today as I wandered around I saw workmen working on yet another high-rise on no more than a couple of acres. I could not help thinking — as no doubt many others of my age think — "If only I'd bought something in 1971 ... Oi!"

As I strolled around, a second-hand car salesman, with a large selection of 'almost-new' cars, smiled as only second-hand car salesmen can, and said: "Looking for a car mate?" I stopped, which was fatal — and the SHCS was in like Flynn.

"I have just the car to suit a gentleman like yourself sir ..." He guided me to a smart-looking Mercedes. "One owner, a dear gentleman who treated it like his own child ...this car will see you through the rest of your life sir". I noticed that he'd stopped calling me "mate", and that it was now "sir".

"Where y'from sir?"

"I come from England."

"Oh, what part?"

I just couldn't resist it. "Why all of me of course!"

A big raucous laugh. "I see my lord has a sense of humour. Would this car appeal to my lord?"

I explained that I would only be able to use it for about three months and therefore the price of 62,000 dollars would be a waste of money from my point of view. He hung on doggedly.

"What are you paying for the rental car?" he asked.

"Seventy-four dollars a day!"

He did some quick mental arithmetic. "Christ! That's ten grand over 12 weeks!"

He then proceeded to give me a lesson on leasing. Ushering me toward a Mitsubishi that was immaculate, he went on to give me more lessons on 'smart money'.

"But I don't really need a car," I protested weakly.

"Look your highness, buy this one for 12,999 dollars and, when you're finished with it, I'll buy it back for 2,000 less. That way you have a superior car, air con, power steering, warranty for 12 months, CD player, electric windows ...and all it has cost you is about 160 dollars a week. You couldn't do better than that your majesty!"

I signed the forms and 'Darren' will deliver the car — 'clean and in perfect condition' — tomorrow. I don't know if he will honour the agreement to buy it back, but it was a most entertaining half-hour spent with him. It's always good to see a professional who knows his trade and, just as I hope audiences appreciate a little bit of experience and know-how from ourselves, I had to hand it to a fellow who persuaded me to buy a car that I didn't even know I wanted.

16th December 1996

I read a piece in a newspaper where a woman has written to an 'agony aunt' saying: "My husband forgot to pack his pyjamas ...I suggested that he should sleep in a spare set of silk undies that I had bought. He did, and since then, three years ago, he has never slept in anything else. He thinks that they are more comfortable than pyjamas, more sexy, his appetite is aroused more quickly — and so is mine ... Name and address supplied.'

You cannot help but smile at the thought of some butch rugby player climbing into bed in silk undies with lavender needlework around the hem, getting into a scrum with his wife. If she gets too demonstrative, would he say: "Careful dear — you'll tear my undies!"

I read about this last week, and in today's follow-up edition there are no fewer than eight confessions from men — husbands and boyfriends — all admitting to the fact that they hit the sack in ladies' underwear.

I think that there must be a tidy sum waiting for the reporter who, having never before done so, decides to go to bed in his wife's undies. Start from the time that he comes in from the pub, yawns and says to his spouse: "Fancy going to bye-byes?" When she agrees, he takes the undies and, trying to look nonchalant, he changes into them. Sitting casually on the edge of the bed, he carefully notes down in shorthand his wife's reactions — then he puts out the light! I have given him the plot, now he must finish the piece himself. It could end in three different ways: divorce; joining the Gay Libs; or wedding bells at the new lesbian church in East London!

In the same newspaper there was a full page on Frank Sinatra, who is estimated to have wealth exceeding seven million dollars. The US government will be looking for at least two-thirds of that sum when Ol' Blue Eyes faces the final curtain.

Sinatra says that he hasn't worked all his life to leave such a sum to the US Internal Revenue Service. He has taken immediate steps to reduce the sum that Uncle Sam is poised to snatch — and who can blame him? He has paid tax all his working life, and he has also generated work for the scores of people involved in selling and pressing his records, distributing his films and taking part in his many business ventures.

Quite apart from the immense pleasure he has given with his singing and acting, Sinatra has never been one to kow-tow. "All I owe is to give the public a good performance," he once said: and, while he has been able, that is exactly what he has done.

I once had the pleasure of Sinatra's company at James Mason's house in Hollywood. It was in 1951 and, at that time, he was in bad shape. He had had a disastrous affair with Ava Gardner and, if he managed a few bookings, they were only half full. He was 'all washed up' as so many reporters delighted in telling everyone. The film, *From Here to Eternity*, was to change all that. It unearthed an actor of real quality, and a name that became respected throughout the world.

My thoughts as I met him and chatted for a while, were that here was a fellow who really loved what he was doing, who was well aware that his latent talent was about to erupt and, when it did — you'd better watch out!

Once again the odds are against him as I write, and so he is trying to salvage some of those dollars for his family, Nancy, Frank Junior, Tina and the grandchildren. OK, perhaps they don't need it, but neither does Uncle Sam. The reports are that he is ailing and in a poor way and so, as a devoted admirer, I hope that he surmounts the problems that he is facing and, whatever the outcome, may I say "Thanks, for doing it your way."

Christmas Day 1996

Yesterday Bloss and I arrived at Sanctuary Cove, a luxury resort in Queensland. Usually at Christmas time I get one of my daughters to wrap presents, but this year we were on our own. I could not very well ask Bloss to wrap her own presents so I nipped down to the local Post Office for wrapping paper, ribbon and sticky tape, and what a mess I made of it!

Both presents were round, and I did not know how to make the paper, with teddy-bears all over it, round, and so I used half a roll of sellotape trying to fix it into the required shape. The other present was oval — a jewel-case with ear-rings — and that was even worse to wrap. Still, she seemed to like both — the pot-pourri with sea-shells, and the ear-rings in a jewel-case — and I got a big kiss for my efforts, which, on a scale of 1-10, I would think deserved at least one for my wrapping expertise.

Blossom had hinted that a pair of ear-rings would be welcome and that saved me from racking my brains to find something pleasing. She always puts me to shame by going out and finding something really unusual, and this year bought me a book on masks.

Almost at the same time last year, I received a box containing a plain white ceramic mask from England. It was accompanied by a letter from HRH the Prince of Wales asking for my ideas of what I could make of it with some paints that were included for my artistry — something at which I am quite new.

For my contribution I concocted the face of a woman that looked amazingly like Madonna. I had read somewhere that she had been chosen to play the lead in the movie *Evita*, to be directed by Alan Parker. There was the usual blurb about it being an artistic challenge — and very little about the fee and the millions of dollars that it hoped to make upon completion.

Quite cynically, I designed a hat made of 100-dollar bills, and with a tear falling from the eye, titled it, 'Don't Cry for me, Andrew Lloyd Webber'. Now almost a year has gone by and the film has been acclaimed, Madonna got pregnant and made all the front pages, Alan Parker confessed that it was the most worrying time of his career but still managed to get an award-winning performance from his star, and Andrew L-W is going to help the Exchequer to balance its books and, hopefully, stop a Labour landslide in the forthcoming General Election.

The Prince's Trust looks as though it will bring several millions of pounds to help young people set up in business — this from the auction of the masks, the entrance fees and the limited edition of the book that Bloss went to such lengths to get for my Christmas present, which arrived at the foot of my bed this morning.

One of the most interesting and novel presents that I have ever received, the leather-bound book is in colour, and contains pictures of the masks made by celebrities as well as articles written by pundits to persuade us that, if studied, the masks will give insight into the personality of the one that did the art-work.

There must be something in it! Thumbing through the pages, the one by Richard Branson tells us that here is work done by the country's greatest self-publicist. Open any newspaper and it is almost an each way bet that there will be a picture of those half-closed eyes and protruding teeth somewhere, and an account of some stunt or other that Branson has dreamed up. Clint Eastwood is quite a surprise, and so too is Michael Crawford. Barry Manilow seems to be working on self-exploitation and my favourite comedy actress, Patricia Routledge — or Mrs Bucket — really does seem to have got her knickers in a twist. The Prime Minister goes for a tranquil country setting, whilst Opposition leader, Tony Blair, plugs the red roses of the Labour Party. Paddy Ashdown's, meanwhile, is absolutely beautiful, but totally bewildering!

On page 136 is my effort. I wish the caption, 'Don't Cry for me Andrew Lloyd-Webber', had been included, because the whole idea hinged on the title, but, so what, the project was a mammoth job of organisation, made a lot of people happy and brought some originality to the hum-drum appeals that most charity organisations keep pushing through our letter-boxes.

Boxing Day 1996

There could have been no greater enthusiast than myself about the adorable *Riverdance* video that took everyone by storm after the Eurovision Song Contest from Dublin. The innocence, the enthusiasm and the sincerity with which it was performed made it a world-beater. The originality and novelty turned *Riverdance* into a No.1 hit — and deservedly so.

I told relatives and friends — in fact, anyone who was prepared to listen — that Michael Flatley and Co were the best things to come out of Ireland since Guinness. "Go out and get a copy!" I demanded of everyone.

My family must have remembered my ravings, especially since I sat next to Michael Flatley at this year's Television Awards at the Royal Albert Hall. A few days prior to Christmas, a packet arrived from England — another version of the Riverdancers entitled *Lord of the Dance*, with choreography by Michael Flatley and filmed before a live audience.

What a disappointment!

The talent was still there. So were the musicians and the music but, if ever a goldmine could be ruined, then this was it. Why? It was totally over-produced! Filmed like a rock-concert, never dwelling on a 'take' for more than three seconds without cutting, never dwelling on a close-up to show the sheer enjoyment of the dancers, digital lighting that assaulted the eyes, and never getting anywhere near the souls of the performers, the video is a lesson to every up and coming TV director of how not to direct a show! All the fun, all that innocence and enthusiasm that I mentioned before was simply not there. How could such a great idea go so badly wrong?

One thing learned is that, 99 times out of a 100, theatre does not transfer well to the small TV screen. It should have been done again and the audience shots only put in when really needed. Half a dozen friends began to fidget and talk, completely losing interest in the video. Before starting, I had told them that it would blow their minds. Instead, they left their armchairs to go to the loo or have a smoke, and it was completely understandable. I notice on the credits that the producer was a man named John Reid. If he has to answer for this production of Irish talent being wasted, I can only think that he must have a grudge against the British and wants to make us suffer.

New Year's Eve 1996

Today we say farewell to 1996 — tomorrow a brand new year. I am going for my last swim of '96 as soon as I have made this entry in my large new desk diary, one of the nicest I have ever had. It reminds me of that large five-year diary that my father gave me on the day I joined the RAF back in 1940. It is on moments like these that his words come back to me: "Anything worth remembering, jot down! You'll never regret it."

When he eventually died, almost 20 years ago, we continually discovered old Woodbine packets and small bits of paper with the day's events, neatly dated and written down in his own particular brand of shorthand: "Feb 19 — Tram strike, w Bellamys. ND hand plast — mend pumps". Deciphered, this read: "There was a tram strike and so I walked to Bellamy's Wharf. There was no work (ND — nothing doing). His hand was in plaster but he managed to do a repair job on his boots (mend pumps)".

I have two regrets and may possibly do something about them in 1997. One is that I should have learned shorthand, and the other is to type as competently as Jennifer, my assistant. To her it comes as easy as ABC. I write in long-hand, pass it to her and, shortly afterward, she hands me a pristine copy. I never cease to marvel at lyrics that I have dashed off in a way that sometimes even I can't read — and yet Jennifer nonchalantly hands them back to me complete and neat — and I am so impressed! I look at my scribble, which is now beautifully typed, and think what a genius I am, thank you Jennifer …and your word-processor!

The old year is going with a flourish. The plants and bushes have never looked more radiant. In full bloom, the tippichina trees and poincianas make the grounds here at Attunga Park into a wonderland. It is hard to stand at the entrance and not feel the poem that has been carved in stone in so many gardens all around the world. I read the words by the bird bath that Bloss put in place more than five years ago …

> The kiss of the sun for pardon,
> The song of the birds for mirth,
> You are nearer God's heart in a garden,
> Than anywhere else on earth.

I once asked a gardener who had written those words, but it seems that it was by that writer named Anonymous. It's a shame to think of all the pleasure his or her words have given and yet have to miss out on the copyright!

It is hot — 85 degrees — not a bird in sight it is much cooler to stay in the trees. Now and again a crow squawks. The news is that Europe is experiencing the worst winter in a decade with quite a few old people dying. The protest marches in Belgrade have dwindled because the rebels can't face the cold — and I feel so very lucky and humble that I am in a profession that allows me to travel away from all those tribulations. Mind you, we still have to watch out for sunburn, skin cancer, mosquito bites, snakes and so on, but there are few places that I would rather be.

When you are used to Christmas and the New Year being all that winter wonderland stuff that the traditional Christmas cards portray, it comes as a bit of a culture shock to spend that time in Australia. Gone are the robins, the log fires and the gentle snowflakes — instead there are parrots, barbecues and the sort of sunshine that enables you to fry eggs on the rocks. There are, of course, exceptions to even Australia's beautiful weather.

New Year's Day 1997 — 7am

I woke up to the loudest clap of thunder that I have ever heard. In seconds the heavens opened up and the noise of the rain on the roof sounded like a rock band whose amplifier needed adjustment. Thankfully it did not last too long and we are always grateful for a downpour to fill the water tanks. If we go more than ten days without rain — suddenly there is a crisis. For this reason we have learned to conserve — to turn off the shower when soaping — to use just a glassful of water when teeth-cleaning. In fact, to take extreme care that we don't lose water through running the taps unnecessarily.

One of the main reasons for this conservation is that if the tanks do get low, then we have to phone the water supplier who turns up with what looks like a large petrol bowser. It is the dickens of a job to get near the tanks, and that bowser churns the drive up badly — not to mention that each delivery costs 95 dollars. For these reasons, saving water becomes a habit — even back in England I remain conscious of this and, even though water is plentiful in the UK, I still wash and shave in a bowl of water with the plug in. Maybe I should try putting the shaver plug into the electric socket!

10am

Opened the *Sydney Morning Herald* to read some scathing readers' letters replying to Conrad Black's departure from the Australian scene. He had obviously said something derogatory about the politicians who had stopped him expanding his newspaper chain. The Canadian tycoon decided to write his impressions of some of the government party that, according to one letter, 'only allowed him to make half a billion dollars profit in five years'.

I met Conrad Black at a small apartment in Toronto almost a decade ago. He had been to see my show at the Roy Thompson Auditorium. When we met he told me a fascinating story, fascinating to me because, even then, he was one of the richest men in Canada — and he hadn't even got around to buying up the *Daily Telegraph* in London.

The story was that when he was a student at Oxford University, it was the practice to get a job during the summer break. Conrad's job was to take tourists sightseeing around London. One of the treats that he stored up for them was a trip on the river boats from Westminster Pier to Greenwich. On the way, as they passed Rotherhithe, he would point out St Mary's Church and inform the party: "That spire was a place of worship for mariners — and the building at the side of it is where one of Britain's entertainers, Max Bygraves, was born!"

He could have mentioned that, like him, I was also once in the business of selling newspapers. I sold the *Star*, *News* and *Standard* at one penny each to customers passing my stand. The price of the *Sydney Morning Herald* that I am holding at this moment is 80 cents (40p). I suppose it's the same as when I had some air put in my tyres not long ago — the attendant held out his hand for two pounds.

"Two pounds?" I said. "Just for a bit of air in my tyres?"

The attendant nodded sagely. "Well, yes sir, I'm afraid so. You see it's inflation!"

11-30am

Like most newspapers, there is a review of the past year, and a story that caught my eye is about a group of men who put money into a kitty and make a competition between themselves called 'Run for the Lillies!'. They then each guess the names of ten people that they think will die during the coming year. At the year's end, the one with the biggest collection of corpses takes the pot.

It's quite amazing what Australians will bet on. I know three betting men, one of them happens to be English — Des O'Connor. Each time that these three walked toward the elevators at a certain hotel in Perth, they would bet on which one would arrive first — left, right or centre. On a three day stay one of them lost 400 dollars! On another occasion, during a tour of Victoria, where it's possible to drive for several miles without seeing another car — the bet would be ..."the next car we meet will have either an odd or an even number at the end of its number-plate". You wouldn't believe that one of the trio could end up, on an evens bet like that, owing almost 1,000 dollars! It's true!.. just ask Des!

12 Noon

It's sad to read about some of those who have passed on during the last 12 months.

Juliet Prowse, aged 60. I will never forget Juliet as principal dancer in *Cinderella* at the London Palladium in the early '50s. She could only go on to greater things, which is what she did when Hollywood called. What I will never forget is that pixie-like dancer from South Africa seeing snow for the first time. Her disbelief at snowflakes melting in her hand was a picture to cherish.

Beryl Reid aged 76. We were together in the radio show *Educating Archie* for a number of years. The last time that I saw her she was in a wheelchair. We were behind schedule for a television production from the Palladium at the time. In the dressing-room for this nostalgia show were Eric Sykes, myself and Harry Secombe, with Beryl, in the wheelchair, in the centre of the room. Coyly, she said: "If they don't get a move on with this show, I'm going to break a golden rule and have a drink!" Gin and tonics were promptly ordered ...then some more. It was a good thing that the show was recorded. Paul

Merton asked Beryl a question, which she fluffed. "Shall we try it again?" asked the patient director.

"If you like," said Beryl. "I'm game for anything when I'm pissed!"

Apart from George Burns and Michael Bentine, of whom I've spoken elsewhere, there was also Tiny Tim who left us at the age of 71. He was mad on betting, especially on horse racing. We had the same manager in Australia — Lionel Abrahams — and one morning Lionel received a call from 'TT', asking if he would place a bet for that afternoon at Randwick. Lionel said that he would oblige and so TT relayed his fancies over the phone.

"I'll have 25 on the first race, 75 on the second choice and …" His list went on for the next eight races. Lionel totted up the requests then told TT. it came to 240 dollars. In a panic, TT shouted down the phone: "No, no, I bet in cents!" Lionel, who is no mean better himself — told TT that there was no way he could get a bookmaker to take a £2.40 bet with so much work involved. It was then that Tiny Tim, a world star attraction, confessed that he was allowed only ten dollars a week pocket money. He didn't even get a raise when he got married. Tiny Tim made a good living out of one of the strangest acts that I have ever seen. He sang terribly, but his audiences loved him. He must have been some sort of a genius!

January 2nd 1997

One thing that is noticeable about my diaries of the past is that they all start off with good intentions — the months of January and February are always quite full with entries, but then I either get lazy, or else nothing noteworthy seems to happen. When the summer arrives I only ever seem to jot down such entries as 'golf', 'laid in garden' or 'planted some tomatoes', etc, etc.

In the summer of my 1996 diary I am surprised to see how many blank pages there are, and not because there was nothing happening — in fact I had a most busy time. Contracted for a ten-week season at Bournemouth's Pavilion Theatre, every show a different audience, relatives coming to stay, fly-fishing on the River Test a couple of days each week, golf with good friends like Gordon Dean, directors from the BBC in London to talk over proposed shows, phone-ins, charity appearances etc. (The strangest charity show was to cut the ribbon at a pedestrian crossing on the Poole Road, to allow old folk from a retirement home to cross without having to walk a quarter of a mile down the road to another crossing). Looking back, there are quite a few entries that I could have made interesting, so I can only plead laziness!

After cutting that tape on the Poole Road, I was invited back to the home for tea and cakes. Because I am in the business of entertainment I am usually button-holed by the senior citizens to do something about the appalling quality of programmes on television. They must think that I am some form of Mary Whitehouse. One lady, while making a point, made the company laugh when she said: "Why don't they do something about all that swearing on TV? It's bloody disgusting!"

I just have to stand there helpless. All I can do is nod and agree, but they think that I can just pick up the phone and say to the Director-General: "Now look here, folk don't like four-letter words that they hear on TV. With very little being done to chastise the guilty actors and directors you should do something about it — after all, you're the boss!"

That's what they think that I can do. And I have to pass it all off with a shrug by saying: "It's not bloody right is it!" A sneaky way to get out of an argument with a little of what they call comic relief.

Another entry is for May 16th. I promised to appear for Jack (known as John) Profumo at Toynbee Hall in the East End of London. John does such wonderful work at the 'Hall' for the poor and deprived — not just now, but for many years past. One stupid mistake forever labelled him as the man who brought down the Tory government because of the Christine Keeler affair. The country lost a very good bloke.

I knew him slightly before the Keeler affair, when he was Minister for War. It was during those days that we went to different parts of the world entertaining our troops. John was such a gentleman, and a real pleasure to talk with — he didn't become charming after the affair. His wife, former actress Valerie Hobson, is a sweetie too. They both work hard at Toynbee Hall. You know what I'd like to do? I'd like to walk down Park Lane holding the biggest banner that I could carry, emblazoned with the words: 'John Profumo and Co ...public benefactor ...let's hear it for John!'

Another entry is for Monday, April 22nd 1996. All I noted down was "'QE2 to New York.' This turned out to be one of the best trips ever on this lovely ship. I am not quite sure if it was my eighth or ninth voyage, but it was really enjoyable. My son Anthony came with me to help out with the lighting, look after the props, take the bandcall and be general dogsbody. He is good company and we get along well.

The other joyful part was that my good friend Gordon Dean and his attractive wife also came aboard to celebrate their tenth wedding anniversary

— a cruise to New York, then fly back to Heathrow on Concorde. We shared a table with two other good friends from Bournemouth — Jim and Jane, so the six of us had some splendid meals in the Queen's grill. Colin, the mâitre d', excelled — every dish was a banquet.

I did two concerts in the main lounge, which had been refurbished since our last trip. I thought that the good old QE2 had suffered badly with the publicity surrounding the fact that she had not being ready in time on a previous trip. Many of the passengers had complained and Cunard had been forced to pay out some pretty hefty sums in compensation. On this trip, however, all faults had been rectified and we were there to enjoy it. The audience appeared to enjoy my stint and I finished by doing several encores and everyone was most complimentary.

I had written a parody to *A Life on the Ocean Wave*. It's usually a good idea to poke a little fun at any crisis, such as the one that Cunard had just suffered. I sang what I had just written to a senior officer to make sure that it was in order and wouldn't upset anyone. He laughed his head off and then pleaded — "Please don't do it! We've got enough problems as it is!"

This is the parody:

A LIFE ON THE QE2

Oh, a life on the QE2
Is something you shouldn't do,
If you wanna be sick
Well you've gotta be quick
Aboard the QE2.

I went down to Southampton,
To sail into the blue,
I shook hands with the Captain
And also met the crew.
They showed me to my cabin,
But when I got inside
The bed and all the furniture
Had gone out with the tide.

Chorus: (Oh, a life on the QE2, etc.)

The Captain he was wonderful,
He made us all feel fine,
But then the ship hit something
It could have been a mine.
The Purser tried to calm us down,
He said we'd struck a rock,
"Women and children first," he cried,
In a Laura Ashley frock!

Chorus: (Oh, a life on the QE2, etc.)

I'll save it in case I ever appear for a rival shipping company.

Anthony, my son, is an asset on these trips. I suspected that he would want to see as much of New York as possible in the 24 hours that we had before returning to London and a show I had to do in Skegness. There's a great follow-on for you — New York to Skegness. It was a beautiful day as we steamed slowly up the Hudson. A red sky, that did a wonderful lighting job on Miss Liberty, made you realise what a great lyric writer Sammy Cahn was, when he composed *It's Very Nice To Go Travelling* for Frank Sinatra.

We were booked into the Helmsley Hotel — that's the one now owned by the widow of the former owner, who went to prison for income-tax fiddling. Poor old Jim, our friend from the QE2, had cause to regret his stay. While taking a bath he pulled himself up by the side-rail. Unfortunately, the rail pulled straight out of the wall and he fell — finally ending up in a neck brace.

He went to the doctor, who refused to come out to him at the hotel — and had to pay the receptionist 100 dollars before she would even take his name. When he eventually got to the doctor he was in so much pain that he asked if he could have a couple of codeine. The doctor went mad with fury: "This isn't a junkie visit is it?" he demanded. Jim, an absolute innocent, tried to explain that codeine in Britain can be purchased without prescription at any chemist. That New York doctor wouldn't listen however, and couldn't get Jim out of his surgery quickly enough. "What are you trying to do? Get me struck off?"

All in all, that little visit set him back quite a large amount. Jim is a millionaire but is still staggered by the treatment he received — he has a case going on with them now.

Back to Anthony. After breakfast we took a cab to Times Square. He had a vague memory of coming to see me, while he was still in short pants, at the Palace Theatre where I appeared with Judy Garland. I had lived in New York for several months and knew the Broadway area like the back of my hand but, when we got out of the cab to look for this once-famous landmark, there it was — gone! An ultra-modern building was in its place with the Richard Branson logo — 'VIRGIN' — across the entrance. Every trace of the old days had vanished. All those stars from the Hollywood musicals, with the often-heard ambition: "One day I'm gonna play the Palace," were just a memory.

I watched an old film starring Dean Martin and Jerry Lewis recently. The dressing-room that they were purporting to be in at the old Palace was more like the Oliver Messel suite at the Dorchester. It made me smile to think of the reality of my dressing-room in that theatre. There was an open lavatory with a chain hanging, the whole affair was only about the size of two telephone kiosks, and there was one of those twirly fly-papers hanging down from the ceiling. Judy Garland, the star, was a little better off of course. Her lavatory had a lid so that visitors could sit down. My last memory of Dick Powell, the famous movie actor, was sitting on that loo with June Allyson on his lap!

Anthony went off to explore on his own, eventually coming back with a large packet of Cuban cigars for me. How in the world he managed that, since America doesn't trade with Cuba, seemed little short of a miracle to me. "Where on earth did you find these?" I asked. He winked at me. "Simple really, I just put a call through to Fidel Castro!"

One incident that should have been recorded from that QE2 trip was when the entertainments officer, knowing that I was the owner of a vintage car — I had King George's 1950 Daimler — asked me if I would talk to an audience of car-lovers who were aboard. I told him that although I wasn't any sort of expert, I didn't mind talking for a few minutes on how I came to get hold of the king's car. It was an interesting story and so, the following morning, I made my way to the Main Lounge and found it packed with standing room only. I expected other 'speakers' from some of the organisers who were on their way to a vintage auction in New York. There was no sign of anyone and then the cruise director informed me that I was the only speaker. It had been announced in the ship's newspaper that I was to 'lecture' from 11am until midday. I have never felt so scared! It seemed that the entire passenger list had turned up to hear my comments on owning a vintage car.

Technically I knew nothing except for a few points that I had been given during the restoration of the Daimler. I knew that the Queen Mother and our present Queen had spent some time in it, but that was all. How was I going to fill a complete hour with my knowledge of old cars?

I did a quick sketch in my mind of nine Rolls-Royces that I'd owned since my first in 1954, and I made those my milestones. I decided to go from Rolls to Rolls, trying to fill in 20 minutes on each one. I did give fair warning to the CD that I might only last for 15 minutes or so. I was duly introduced to general applause and with "Good morning car lovers …" I was on my own.

Being a 'ham' and facing up to the challenge, I began by telling the crowd the story of my friend Billy Cotton talking me into buying my first Rolls from Jack Barclay in 1954: "It cost £4,500 — I ran it for ten years, etc. etc." From the corner of my eye I saw the CD looking at his watch. I was genuinely surprised to discover that I had been 'on' for an hour and 20 minutes, getting big laughs and finishing with a standing ovation.

"I don't know how you do it dad," said Anthony. "You told them stories that I'd never heard — and I thought I'd heard them all!"

I didn't really like to disillusion him and tell him that he'd just been listening to one of the biggest 'bluffers' since Donald Trump.

January 3rd 1997

The international editions of the British newspapers arrived this morning. The New Year's Honours list is always interesting. We had read and heard through the Australian media about some of the recipients. I was elated to see that my buddie and fellow Water Rat, Frankie Vaughan, was awarded a further accolade.

Frankie is one of the nicest and most-caring individuals you could ever wish to meet. Johnnie Riscoe, another friend, once said to me that there was not a jealous bone in Frank's body, that he had never heard him say a bad word about anybody and, that if it's humanly possible to help someone in need, Frank is always there. He has been under the weather lately but is almost back to his old self.

Just a few years ago he was our King Rat, and he made such a good job of it they would have liked to have him as King for ever. Stella, his lovely wife, reminded me that there are only 24 hours in a day — and some of them are for living. Good on yer Frank! Give Stella a big kiss.

Cilla Black was awarded and well deserved it. She brings so much pleasure to so many. Starting out as a young vocalist, raising a family and keeping husband, Bobby, smiling, and then rising to become one of the highest-paid females in the land, is no mean achievement.

It seemed that it was the turn of the Liverpudlians to be honoured this time around. There was Paul McCartney and a couple of others as well as Frankie and Cilla. One moment from the past that I remember was at the Prince of Wales Theatre when admirers of Jimmy James's talent had given their services free to help JJ's family.

While standing at the back of the stalls watching the 'turns', a young man sidled up to me and introduced himself. It was Brian Epstein, the man who gave The Beatles to the world and later shocked the pop world by taking his own life. Brian asked my advice on whether a young lady he had suggested for the show and who was coming on in the second half, should sing one, or two songs. I said that as there were quite a few big stars on it might be shrewd to sing just one song then, if she went well, have the MD ready with an encore.

I couldn't stay to watch the new singer as I was on myself a few 'turns' afterward, and it was not until we were on our way home in the car that Blossom asked me if I had heard the new singer. I told her that I'd missed the act and asked if she'd sung one or two songs. "She only did two, but she could have done 52 — the audience loved her!" That 'new singer' was, of course, Cilla Black!

Blossom is proud of herself as a star forecaster. She never misses *Blind Date* or *Surprise, Surprise*, actually applauding in our own lounge as Cilla walks in at the top of the show. Good luck to you Cilla. Keep it up!

Another acquaintance of mine is Willie Carson, the jockey. Each year that passes I expect to see him being elevated to knighthood in the same way that Sir Gordon Richards was. What a career! What a great sense of humour, and what a lovely man. We received our OBEs on the same day at Buckingham Palace, back in 1983. For the ceremony you proceed in alphabetical order. As I was the last of the Bs and Willie was first of the Cs, we found ourselves standing together like a comedy double act. Even if Willie had worn his top hat, he would still have only reached my shoulder. As he looked up at me he said: "I wish you had been Charlie Drake!"

Willie got a kick from a horse last year that, up until the time of our leaving in December, had put him out of racing. It was good to see that he fully recovered and is now a top racing presenter. Well done Willie!

CHAPTER EIGHT

Arise Sir Paul

January 4th 1997

The New Year is already into its fourth day. It seems like only yesterday that it was January 3rd! We get the newspapers a day late over here which explains why I have only just seen a very nice picture of a smiling Paul McCartney who has just received a knighthood — and deservedly so. Now that the barnstorming days of the Beatles are over, it is good to see that he is a serious-thinking human-being, who cares about his family and the community.

In an interview today, he thanked the other Beatles as well as the City of Liverpool, and he came over as a very genuine person. He is articulate, concerned and I can't think of a more popular choice for the honour. You wait and see! I'll bet that Sir Paul will be a great asset to many of the people that he has given so much pleasure over the last 30 years. Paul we love you — yeah, yeah, yeah!

I sent Paul a fax of congratulation. I would have loved to have told him a 'story' which he may not have heard before. An Australian agent named Ken Brodziak, who was my agent when I first came to Sydney back in the '60s, took a night-club owner named Denis Wong — a Chinese gentleman — to see the Beatles, who were appearing at the Horden Pavilion, since demolished.

Ken was hoping to sell the Beatles to Denis as an attraction for his club. As they both sat among the screaming fans — all tearing their hair out and crying in their ecstasy — Denis became more and more impressed. At the end of the show, Ken asked Denis if he would care to book them. Denis, who was notorious for driving a hard bargain, watched as the four young men acknowledged the thunderous applause — then, quite seriously said: "I really like them ...I take two!"

January 6th 1997

Disneyland must be one of the greatest organisations in the world. Today's papers are carrying a story that a gentleman by the name of Michael Ovitz, who is 54, is to be sued by two shareholders who are questioning how a man employed by Disney for only 14 months can get severance pay of 164 million dollars. In case I had read that wrong, I wrote it down: $164,000,000 — that's it! And Disney are expected to pay it!

Ovitz, it seems, was president, and the two shareholders claim that his position was so unnecessary that Disney haven't even bothered to find a successor to fill his place. Two brothers — Richard and David Kaplan — claim that during his term of presidency, it was both 'undistinguished and unproductive'.

When you read about these claims, it makes you wonder how such a 'Mickey Mouse' company can survive. The brothers Kaplan must be wondering the same thing, because they have taken their case to the Los Angeles Superior Court. It got me thinking of a day I spent at Disneyland. I loved it — every single minute. I had two of my youngest grandchildren with me, and I think that I enjoyed it even more than they did!

On the third evening there, we packed them off to bed with a baby-sitter to watch over them, and went off to dinner in a place called 'The Last Frontier'. This was a saloon modelled on the days of the old wild west. Pretty waitresses, in gingham that matched the tablecloths, cheerfully served the steak, grits and apple pie, while, at the same time, two musicians pounded away on piano and banjo as the diners joined in the singalong.

As we ate, an attractive hostess wandered in and out of the tables with a hand-held microphone, asking patrons where they were from and what, if anything, they were celebrating. Each response brought a generous round of applause.

"A couple here from Nebraska!"

Applause.

"You are celebrating your golden wedding?. How lovely!"

More applause.

"Two young people here from New York who have been married only 24 hours!"

Thunderous applause.

"Let's hear it for them!"

Now it was our turn.

"Where are you good folk from?"

"We're from London, England!"

Applause.

"Hey, well that's a long way — are you celebrating anything?"

"Yes, we're celebrating the 15th payment on our washing machine!"

I have used that same line in many of the shows that I have done, and it usually gets a reasonable laugh …but that night the roof seemed to fall in. People actually stood up and cheered, it was almost embarrassing. Blossom, who usually takes a back seat whenever I am inclined to show off, did precisely the opposite this time. She stood up shaking both hands above her head like a prize-fighter entering the ring — and all this on one glass of champagne!

As I read the article posing the 164 million dollar question, I wondered if there is really anyone in the world pulling down that sort of loot. And if there are, what are the requirements for his job?

I folded the newspaper and turned to Bloss.

"There's a man in the paper who works for Walt Disney and he is going to get 164 million for 14 months work. What d'you think of that?"

Bloss continued staring out of the window.

"Do you want peas or brussel sprouts with your dinner tonight?"

January 8th 1997

A well-written letter in today's post from a woman in Darwin. The writer, who emigrated from Aylesbury in 1965, was missing the novelty songs that were a part of the music scene of those days.

This interested me because, once upon a time, I was recording more novelty songs than anyone else. Classics like: *You're A Pink Toothbrush — I'm A Blue Toothbrush*; *Gilly Gilly Ossenfeffer Katzenellen-bogan By The Sea*; *What Noise Annoys An Oyster?* Plus knockouts like *When You Come To The End Of Your Lollipop*. All of which, I might add, made the Top 20 best-seller list.

About the same time as I received the letter, I picked up a month-old copy of the *Financial Times* which had an article on the same subject, written by a gentleman named Anthony Thorncroft. To be honest, I can't make up my mind whether he was writing to be cynical or if he is just plainly out of touch!

He blames people like myself for resurrecting such songs as *Yes, We Have No Bananas*. And one which I recently recorded will no doubt also fit into that category: *I've Got A Lovely Bunch Of Coconuts*, the Billy Cotton novelty hit from the 1950s.

On the one hand you have Mrs Ashurst from Darwin asking what has happened to such delightful melodies as *How Much Is That Doggie In The Window?* and on the other, Mr Thorncroft of the F.T. telling us that we should be ashamed that contemporaries like Charlie Drake were ever allowed to curl our toes with songs like *My Boomerang Won't Come Back!*

The last Frank Sinatra concert that I saw had the audience calling for *My Way* — a song that was slammed by the music critics yet managed to be not one of, but *the* biggest hit of his long career. Sinatra's words were: "Ladies and gentlemen, I am reluctant to sing this song as, in many circles, it was judged to be a 'yuk'. I would just like to say if anybody — anywhere — could write me another *My Way*, I would go down on my knees and kiss their feet".

You're A Pink Toothbrush … was part-written by Dick James who was responsible for publishing most of the Beatle songs. The writers of some of the world's classics were unashamed to come up with *Oobla-dee — Oobla-da* or *Yellow Submarine*, and I'll bet that Sir Paul McCartney would like to have another inspiration like *When I'm 64*, which he penned with John Lennon. When I think back to *Why Does Everybody Call Me Big-'ead*, and novelty songs like Lonnie Donegan's *Does your Chewing-gum Lose Its Flavour?*, I feel rather proud that I refused to record *I Haven't Had A Bang Since Bonfire Night* …Mr Thorncroft would be justified in slamming that one!

Talking about unusual songs, whenever I arrive in Australia the same old topic comes up: "Do we want to be a republic?" The Monarchy comes under attack and the anthem gets a good going over. This situation goes back many years. When Gough Whitlam was Prime Minister he got the idea of creating Australia's own national anthem, and gave an open invitation for any composers to submit their ideas to the government.

The song which they chose was the one still used today: *Advance Australia Fair*. It's a good anthem but it seems that half the population can never remember it. On a recent TV quiz game, one intelligent contestant couldn't even get past the first line, while another started singing *Waltzing Matilda*. At about the time that Mr Whitlam had his idea, I wrote a song which I simply called *Australia*. The lyric went:

Australi -ay
The land of the Koala — the Kangaroo
The billabong — the boomerang — the didgeridoo.
But wait a minute — there's much more in it
They've got a whole lot of people who say,

I'm so proud now — I'm one of the crowd now
in Australi-ay!

...I wrote several choruses which still go down a treat with Australians. I include it whenever I come here, and this is my 26th visit in the last 30 years. Two years ago, I received a letter from an all-lady choir in Melbourne who were off for a world choir gathering in New Orleans. The letter was to seek my permission to include *Australia* in their repertoire in the competition. I was flattered and said that it would give me the greatest pleasure. The choir didn't win, but they came second, and were kind enough to say that it was my composition which helped to sway the judges in their favour.

I still think that it would have been more popular than the present one *Advance Australia Fair* — not because I fancy myself as another Elgar, but because a commercial song sung with sincerity is often better than one which can't be remembered.

Waltzing Matilda is as Australian as an Aussie can get for a signature tune, but I think the reason that it was passed over was because of its English origin.

The Australians, more than any other nation, like a bit of humour in their lyrics. At the moment, one of the big songs is *When Beryl Went Feral*, about a heavy 'Sheila' who has gone vegetarian and joined 'Weight-Watchers'. It is very funny and the chorus is just made for an audience to join in. Aussies seem to have the keenest sense of humour. They are not turned on by American comedy and, although there is lots of talk about being a republic, the British are still their number-one preference as a people — and as performers they earn a considerable amount of respect.

That's why I keep returning to this faraway land, which I hope will never go republic. Mainly because it is so near to many of those over-populated Far Eastern lands that seem to be continually increasing their numbers. One day — perhaps not tomorrow, but soon — they could be looking for ways to feed those hungry masses and the continent of Australia might be just the place for a takeover. My act in any other language just doesn't seem to travel that well!

January 9th 1997

Just about to doze off when the phone began to ring. I guessed that it wasn't Jennifer or one of my children because we have an understanding, if it is late at night and nobody answers after three rings, to hang up as we are either asleep or too tired to take the message.

The call was from the *Times* newspaper in London. A journalist named Brian Viner apologised for the disturbance but could I give him a few words for an obituary he was doing on a gentleman named Phil Hyams, who had just passed away aged 103. The journalist had learned that I had once made a movie for Phil Hyams, who incidentally was Brian Miner's grandfather. The movie, in which I played the lead, was *Cry From The Streets*, a dramatic story about an orphanage. I work there as an electrician, become involved in the children's lives, then fall in love with the social worker, played by that very fine actress Barbara Murray, and we finish by adopting three of them. Phil Hyams was the producer and from day one we got on like the proverbial 'house on fire'.

The movie, which comes around regularly on TV, was directed by Lewis Gilbert — *James Bond, Shirley Valentine, Educating Rita* etc. It was most successful and had quite a lot to do with Alfred Hitchcock's selection of me for his last film, *Frenzy*, in which I was unable to appear because of other commitments.

My boyhood days spent in South London enabled me to regularly visit cinemas like the Trocadero at the Elephant and Castle, the Trocette in Tower Bridge Road and the Troxy in Stepney, all within a short bus-ride of Rother-hithe and all owned by Phil Hyams.

The success of these cinemas had a lot to do with the presentation of 'live' acts. In those days, for sixpence, you got two feature films, a stage show with well-known names and an organist named Bobby Pagan who played the Wurlitzer. I can't tell you what Mr Pagan looked like, we only ever saw his back. I cannot ever remember going to one of Phil's cinemas without having to queue, and that included the State Theatre, Kilburn, which, at that time, was the biggest cinema in England.

Phil related stories about these picture palaces that are treasured memories. One took place at the Troxy in the East End and I laugh every time I think about it. Brian Viner laughed more than I did when I related his grand-father's telling of it. There were dozens of others but this one was my favourite.

Before the war, one of the biggest attractions anywhere in the UK was Gracie Fields — she was comparable to a name like Barbra Streisand today. She appeared three times a day between films and the audience would queue all round the Troxy, in any weather, to get a glimpse of this talented and well-loved young lady. Phil, an astute business man, would put an attraction like Gracie on when he had a couple of duff films to show, knowing that someone like 'Our Gracie' was the crowd puller.

In the middle of the week of the Gracie Fields booking, he got a phone call to say that his star had laryngitis and could not appear, on doctor's orders. It was Phil's job to walk on as the live show started in order to announce that the star would be unable to appear. Even as he walked on to the stage the audience sensed that something was wrong and the booing began. Orange peel and ice-cream cartons were thrown, but Phil, an East Ender himself, knew their way of thinking and began: "Ladies and gentlemen, a terrible thing has happened!"

Lots of booing.

"Let me explain, please."

Less booing

"Our Gracie, who we all know and love, is ill."

Aaah!

"The heavy schedule that she has taken on in appearing here three times a day, plus all her charity work, has made her doctor insist that she take today off to rest that wonderful voice."

Applause.

"We will send her your regards and I know that you all wish her well."

Voice from the back" "We want our money back!"

"Wait one moment please. In order that you won't be disappointed we have a young lady from the West End who is going to fill in for Our Gracie!"

More booing again.

"Hold on please, let me tell you something. Two years ago the name of Gracie Fields was unknown. She came from a small mill town in Lancashire and tried her luck in London. The audience loved her and made her a big star. Now, when this young lady comes on, who knows? You may be discovering another Gracie Fields!"

This pleased the audience, Phil gave her introduction, the audience was pacified and Phil made his exit.

"How was she?" I asked.

"F✳✳✳✳✳✳ awful!" came the response.

January 10th 1997

Today I decided to have a rest from writing. When I faxed Jennifer to tell her I would be absent from the office for a couple of days, she faxed me back with this tongue-in-cheek reply. 'Please don't stop writing and sending me your copy — it's 27 degrees below here in England and it's only the typing that stops my fingers from freezing.'

She is a lovely person, somebody I put my trust in and if I searched for another ten years, I don't think I could find anyone so diligent, so cheerful and trustworthy — she is 18 carat.

PS. She will probably delete the above paragraph as she is most humble and thrilled at having such a fine boss — not just for the present but for the past 30 years.

We will only know when the book is published.

January 12th 1997

At the moment I am sitting on the verandah at Attunga Park becoming more aware that I am the owner of some 84 acres of lush parkland that, today, is greener than Ireland. In the 30 miles that I am able to see to the distant mountains, there are only two other properties that I can make out. It is Sunday, and somewhere in the opposite direction a church bell is tolling, making me wonder where the people will come from and wonder also what the next owners will do with the place.

There are many possibilities here. If I were younger, my ambition would be to grow grapes. The many hours of sunshine, plus the rainfall that makes this land so pleasant, would be a natural for a vineyard. It is a banana-growing area, but I think grapes would be my choice. I seem to have an affiliation with this wonderful fruit.

Thirty years ago I was asked to make an appeal on BBC Television for Cancer Research. A few days after the broadcast I received a letter from a Mr Osborne in Barnstaple, Devon, who told me that I would have done a lot better with the TV time if I had talked about the 'Grape Cure'. He assured me that there are far better results from the humble grape than from the drug research on which millions are being spent, so far without appreciable result. I became so curious that I wrote back and we kept up a correspondence that continued until last year when he died peacefully at a ripe old age.

Mr and Mrs Osborne were firm believers and sent me books to back up their point. I became hooked. They pointed out that ever since the Roman Empire, the grape has been used for nourishment. Diluted, it would wash away skin complaints, when we visit people in hospital we take grapes in preference to other fruits. Then, lo and behold! In yesterday's *Sydney Morning Herald*, Melissa Sweet writes a long article about US scientists who have just made an amazing 'discovery'. They have discovered that grapes contain Resveratol which helps to fight off fungal tumours — something I wrote about in my first book, *I Wanna Tell You A Story*, 20 years ago!

I am sceptical of these articles because of knowing about some of the skullduggery in politics. It would not be beyond the scope of a government to spread the word promoting the grape, especially if the farmers had a glut on their hands. A little propaganda could sell millions of tons to a gullible nation but, in this case, I am convinced — and have been for over 30 years — that you'll never go wrong with a couple of pounds of grapes in your diet once a week.

This is Doctor Bygraves — News At Ten — Murwillumbah — New South Wales.

January 14th 1997

The television on the commercial station in this country is almost unwatchable! A movie that you want to watch is continually interrupted — about once every five minutes — by the most raucous sellers of wares who shout and rant to get their message across in the time that they have.

In the middle of a love story, which a director has spent hours in crafting, comes some yobbo telling us he has got the answer to smelly feet, or some model, thinking that TV exposure is an absolute 'must' for her career, informing us that constipation can be cured with a particular laxative.

Nothing is sacred, and so we usually go to the ABC which shows no commercials, or SBS which does, but only in the natural breaks. The alternative is to dig out some videos taped in the past and, on a yuk evening with dreary stuff forecast, watch the oldies on video.

Last night I came across *Heroes of Comedy* which was shown in the UK about three years ago, but which I don't I had seen before. It involved comedy clips by the best of our British comedians, Morecambe and Wise, Tommy Cooper, Arthur Askey, Spike Milligan and others. This very fine show by director-producer John Fisher was welded together by unending laughter. And who do you think closed the show? Yours truly, and with some good and original material that got big roars of laughter. Most people in this part of the world are unaware that I do a pretty good stand-up.

Des O'Connor was full of praise for my section of the show and told the story of a letter he sent to me asking for advice. This is the way I tell that particular story.

Many years ago, I had a letter from Des O'Connor, which I remember well for the sheer ;modesty; of the writer. Des, now a good friend, wrote: 'Can you help me get into showbusiness?' Des kept the letter which I sent him and still has it to this very day.

I read his letter which explained that he was in the RAF serving his conscription, but that when he was released he was going to try the entertainment business. He added that he sang a great deal better than I did, he told better jokes and that he was much better looking.

What does he do with all this God-given talent?

He asked me to advise him on how to start, where to find an agent, and to look out, because when he got going he would unseat me from my perch and become the new Max Bygraves!

I took my time in replying with the only advice that I knew how to give. Learn to walk before you start to run, get audience experience, gather material, work in pantomime and summer shows, and don't be afraid to experiment. I also wished him good luck.

Several years later our paths crossed and he introduced himself as the writer of that cheeky letter. He had taken my advice and got a job as a redcoat at a Butlin's holiday camp. He thanked me and each time we meet he tells the story to anyone who cares to listen.

I was guesting on his Thames Television show not too long ago and he was expounding the story to some of the technicians. I interrupted him to ask: "But Des, now that you are an established entertainer, surely you get similar letters asking how to break into showbusiness don't you?"

He confessed that he did and so I asked him how he responded to them. He got a big laugh when he told the assembled crew: "I write back to them and say, get in touch with Max Bygraves!"

Now I can tell any potential entertainer asking the same questions — get in touch with Des O'Connor!

CHAPTER NINE

Was Anthony's Fez Red!

AVE you ever noticed how a diary becomes a good friend. You can tell them your innermost secrets and they never tell a soul unless you give them permission. Also, no matter how much you go on and on, they never start yawning. I talk to my diary — I think I'm going crazy.

January 19th 1997 Sunday

A beautiful day. Yesterday our neighbour, Graham, together with his brother, came down with two tractors and cut the grass down toward the billabong — about 16 acres — and today there is the smell of new-mown grass in the air. The birds are swooping down and there is a cacophony of bird-calls and, as my brother-in-law John, just remarked: "I'd hate to be dead on a day like this!"

John is here from Greenwich in London with my sister Kath for a few weeks holiday. They are taking it easy while John, an ex-security officer, recovers from a sinus complaint that has bothered him for some time. Each morning he strides out, long before the rest of us are awake, to draw in a few lungfuls of fresh, unpolluted air. He sniffs it in so deeply that it's a wonder there's any left by the time the rest of us surface.

Kath, who I have mentioned before — she was the bedwetter when we were kids — is at peace with the world and only exasperated when I ask her if she could do with a rubber sheet. "Won't you ever forget the buildings?" she demands.

They are both fun to have around as they have the London sense of humour, which is quite different to any other part of the world. I told them about a letter I had received from our son, Anthony, who told us all about how they had spent Christmas.

On Christmas Eve, Anthony had taken his family of three children, Lily, Tallulah and Ashley, and his wife Celia, to lunch at Alveston Manor. After lunch, Ashley disappeared to the toilet, returning a few minutes later looking quite shaken. When prompted he said that he had opened the door to the toilet to disclose a man seated on the loo with his trousers round his ankles.

"Did you say anything?" asked Anthony.

Twelve-year-old Ashley, who was quite stunned, said: "All I could think of was 'Happy Christmas' — so I said 'Happy Christmas' and shut the door!"

My brother-in-law John, with that Cockney sense of humour that I mentioned, said: "He should have added — 'and a crappy New year!'"

John is a teetotaller and he worked at the Barbican, a large block of dwellings in the City. During Christmas-time, the residents, who are unaware of the fact that he doesn't drink, ply him with gifts of whisky, gin, brandy and other spirits. He claims that, at Yuletide, his house 'looks like an off-licence!'

Last summer I visited their beautiful home in Greenwich. We left late at night and John insisted that I take some bottles of the hard stuff with me. I don't drink spirits, a glass of wine is my limit, but we have plenty of visitors who can make it disappear quicker than Paul Daniels, magician par excellence. I tried to refuse but John insisted and laid several bottles on the back seat of the car. Driving up the Old Kent Road I was pulled over by blue flashing lights for a random breathalyser test. I was clean as I never have a drink when I am driving and when people do get done for this offence I can never raise any sympathy for them. If ever I was guilty of driving under the influence, anything that they threw at me would be deserved.

Next day John told me about a mate of his who was also asked to blow into the bag. As he did so, a large horn came out of the side of his head. "Do that again!" said the policeman. The man blew into the bag again and another horn appeared on the other side of his head. "What on earth have you been drinking?" gasped the copper.

The man shrugged and said: "Bovril!"

"Did the police say anything about the bottles on the back seat?" asked John.

"Yes, they did," I lied. "I told him they were all empties and belonged to my brother-in-law. When the policeman asked me where my brother-in-law was, I told him that you were asleep in the boot sobering up!"

John, who is quite a tough individual, was sitting at breakfast with Kath and Blossom the other morning. I walked in to show them the most beautiful little creature that I had ever seen — a lovely emerald-green tree frog about the size of my thumb. As I opened my hand to show them, the frog jumped — and so did my three-strong audience. It was quite the quickest exit of three terrified human beings that I have ever witnessed. I was helpless with laughter, mostly at John's frightened expression. What a tough security guard! It makes you think doesn't it?

January 20th 1997

Last night we watched a video hired from the local Flick shop. It was quite the worst movie that I have seen in many years, far worse than *Lord of the Dance*.

On the cover was an interesting story about a young fellow trying to find his original parents. I was impressed by the names of the star players which included Alan Alda, who is most likeable and has been a favourite since the first *M.A.S.H.* series. It also included Mary Tyler Moore, who knows her way around a movie camera, and Lily Tomlin, an accomplished comedienne who played the telephone operator in the *Laugh-in* series.

The movie was badly cut, inarticulate, with half a dozen actors treading on each other's lines and a story so hard to follow that I fell asleep, to wake up 15 minutes from the end. Alda and Tomlin had not made an appearance — they had top billing on the video cover so it really was a con as far as the paying public were concerned. They eventually appeared for about ten minutes.

When John returned the video and told the salesperson that it was quite the worst film that he'd ever seen and, what's more, contained more pornography than he had witnessed in years, the only comment was — "Have you tried *Noddy in Toyland*?"

Tonight we rented *Godfather 2*. You either like this movie or you don't. We were sorry when it finished — very little swearing and only one 'F' word from the senator. The craftsmanship in the joining of the scenes, plus the acting — not only from the stars but from the supporting cast too — make this a classic. Even the violence was acceptable. Tommy-guns, that made the '30s gangster films so memorable, were used for slayings and a character being strangled was shown by his feet twitching through a broken windscreen. It was all understated but gave more melodrama than a graphic display of the slaying.

Of course, Francis Ford Coppola had a few more millions to spend on *Godfather 2*, probably more than its forerunner because of that one's enormous success in the cinema. Maybe the director of the previous movie, which we had voted as being the worst film seen in a decade, was only experimenting, trying to bring us a newer style in movie-making. If he was, then it was a no-no as far as we were concerned.

Having made half a dozen movies myself, that hardly put me into the Marlon Brando mould, I am fully aware that it may sound like 'sour grapes' to knock the work of a producer or director. I would never blame the actors because it is the producer-director that has the last word and, if what is finally up on the screen cannot be defined as entertainment, then they must stand or fall by the result. Rarely does the producer-director have to take the stick that actors are forced to take.

"Have you seen Alan Alda in that yuk effort? . . . Lily Tomlin was hopeless . . . Mary Tyler Moore should give up!" That's how a bad movie circulates down to someone who hasn't yet seen it.

In short, if the director of THAT movie makes another. Let's put it this way . . .

January 21st 1997

There is a scenic route to Brisbane that leads out to the Pacific Highway. Halfway up the mountain that goes over the state-line which separates Queensland from New South Wales, is a 'tick-gate' shed, where an officer checks the coming and going of cattle between states. I make this journey quite often and all I have ever seen of the officer on duty is a newspaper held on high and a hand that appears to tell me that it is OK to cross.

About a mile or so from the Queensland border is a small bungalow that sells Devon teas, scones freshly ovened with cream and strawberry jam. "All very slimming," we tell ourselves as we enter the establishment. The enterprise, which also sells home-made pickles, jams, salad dressings and so on, is run by a charming lady named Angela, a grey-haired, middle-aged, happy-go-lucky sort whose greeting is always "G'day Max, — G'day Bloss!"

If we are early, Angela will call out from the kitchen: "Hang on while I put me face on!" She enters with a pot of English Breakfast tea on a tray accompanied by some of the seven deadly sins …scones, jam and thick, thick cream. She is in a freshly laundered pinny, hair combed and lightly lip-sticked and, between feeding the colourful wild rosellas a few crumbs, she tells us how Norm — her husband — is progressing. Norman has Parkinson's Disease and spends 12 hours a day 'doing something or other'. At the moment he is on the tractor making such a noise that we end up shouting at each other. She goes out and waves a red serviette at him and the noise shuts off.

Norm comes in and obeys Angela's good-natured 'wipe your feet' by using an oily rag on them and gets a laugh. We get another "G'day," and then we get into the gossip.

Angela tells us that the place is thriving, coaches delivering 40 or more tourists during the day, but she finds it a bit too much, she has only one lady helper who is not always there and the tourists are so demanding. She likes the Singaporians, who are always clean, well-mannered and cheerful. She isn't too sweet on the Japanese because they give tokens, supplied to them when they leave Japan to use instead of money. It is all a bit of a nuisance. She doesn't care for the Chinese, finds them arrogant, dirty and unappreciative. But she LOVES the English.

She came originally from Adelaide, which has a large British area. I have appeared there several times at theatres and made a few TV shows from there, too. On the edge of town is a large museum of old vehicles and I remember making a documentary on vintage cars.

I told Angela of the time we pulled into Adelaide aboard the QE2. It was the first time that this massive ship had tried to dock in the port. There was a big turnout of people and I think the whole city was on the quayside. The bands played, the crowds cheered, it was a cloudless sky, the big liner steamed in at about two knots and tied up. As I descended the gangplank in blazer, flannels and deck shoes, escorting Blossom on one arm — she looked like a front cover for Vogue — a middle-aged Cockney purser in uniform said from the corner of his mouth: "Ere Max, don't it remind you of Rotherhithe!"

January 22nd 1997

There are several British newspapers that have come out weekly. They are a combination of the dailies in the UK with parts of the Sundays included. The editors are wide-boys. If a writer has a go at some dignitary, then turn a few pages and find another writer singing the praises of the one that suffered. That way there are less complaints from readers.

In the *International Daily Mail* this week are Lynda Lee Potter, who never misses 'having a go' because she is a good journalist, and John Junor who is clever and starts almost every bit of controversy with: 'Am I right in assuming …?' It's a great journalistic ploy from the editor, whose job it is to see that not too many complaining readers end up by saying: "I will never buy your paper again!"

Lynda Lee Potter is on about Sir David Frost who has flown to Barbados for a holiday. Sir David and Lady Frost travelled Business Class, but bunged their young family in Economy. Lynda Lee Potter wouldn't do that. Unless the whole family travels together it's a no-no. She wonders if Sir David's father would approve — he was a reverend and so she cleverly quotes the *Holy Bible*: 'Do unto others my boy …'

Makes good copy, of course, and also gives John Junor a chance to 'have a go'. He starts with the same subject: 'I don't entirely go along with the criticism …'

But Sir David Frost is a wide-boy too. I have been on several shows with him and most of his talent comes from the very fact that he is a wide-boy, and an old saying is 'Never try to con a con-man'. So we'll wait and see what transpires. Or am I right in assuming that they are both wrong? Answers on a post-card please.

As a parent, one who had to make similar decisions on children's travel, I can tell you that my son Anthony, who had a fear of flying and was coming to Sydney as part of my act, wanted to travel on the Oriana, a three-and-a-half week trip. As caring parents we booked him a first-class return. It was the worst thing that we could have done to a red-blooded 16-year-old travelling by himself.

At meal-times he sat at a table alone — the First-Class passengers were mostly retired people — and for the first few days at sea he felt completely lost. Then, one evening, a ship's waitress who noticed that he always seemed to be alone, invited him to a party below decks. From that moment on he spent most of his time below decks and had the time of his life, so much so that he changed his ticket to economy for the return journey. The only time that he did go above was to accept an invitation to a fancy-dress evening and cocktails hosted by the captain.

Anthony decided to attend the party as an arab: fez, painted moustache and beard, his pyjama jacket and in bare feet. I have seen the photographs and the make-up was really good. Full of confidence, he bounded up the stairs to the captain's quarters and breezed through the door — straight into a crowd of exquisitely gowned women, men in tuxedos with champagne in their hands. Wrong night! The fancy-dress party was on the following evening.

Anthony beat an eager exit, a bit like Peter Sellers, hoping that no-one had recognised him.

January 23rd 1997

What does the song say? 'Just direct your feet to the sunny side of the street.' Not here you don't! Not in Murwillumbah.

We recently had to go to town for Blossom to have a blood test. After we had seen the pathologist and he had taken a few drops of blood — 'nearly an armful' as Hancock once said: we decided on a slow stroll round the shops.

It was here that I became aware that Australians don't want to know about the sunny side of the street, they choose the shade. Every town is built very much the same, large canopies or awnings are all part of a building's structure. Most shoppers are eager to stay under them — they have been warned.

Australia has the highest rate of skin cancer in the world, with the State of Queensland having the unenviable distinction of having the very worst cases. If you are thinking of coming here for the Olympics in the year 2000, think about getting yourself a wide-brimmed hat, not a baseball cap. I wore one of those over last week-end to play golf and now the tops of my ears are peeling and my neck is the colour of a Smithfield turkey.

Thank goodness that a collar and tie is such a rarity. If a fellow is seen in one, it is assumed that he must be an undertaker. The last time that I wore a tie — apart from when I go onstage in a suit, was almost three years ago when I was asked to speak at a Rotary luncheon. I turned up in a blazer, white shirt and RAF tie. They just stared at me — I should have worn trousers! It's a joke, it's a joke!

The local businessmen that made up the audience were in awe. One man told me that he had never even owned a tie, or a top-coat. He was a friendly sort of fellow in his mid-50s and told me that he was going to London in a few weeks. I warned him that it would be cold but that he could, if he liked, call at my office near Victoria and borrow an overcoat that I always leave there. He was about my size and I assured him that the large woollen topcoat would keep him warm and save him carrying one half across the world.

He did call at the office when he arrived during London's bleak winter weather, took the coat and returned it just before he left. When I saw him about a year later, I asked him if the coat had done the trick. He confessed that it was, by far, the heaviest garment that he had ever worn. He was a farmer, and wearing it, he said was like 'having a couple of Angus bulls on my shoulders!'

After my speech, which most seemed to enjoy, it was time for a drink and, as the drink flowed, so the tongues and the reserve got looser. By this time I had ridded myself of jacket and tie and I had, to them, become a lot 'more approachable'. Everybody had a joke to tell me. Most I had heard before but one local comic had some good original stuff that really made me laugh. He had a lugubrious face and that, together with his doleful delivery made his jokes even better.

"I got in this taxi at Heathrow and said to the driver, 'Take me to the smallest and cheapest brothel in London!' 'You're in it!' he said."

With the same sorrowful expression he told about the coloured girl who asked him if he'd like to come home. "What! All the way to Africa?" he responded.

When he was propositioned in Soho, he said: "Nothin' doing sweetheart, it's too cold!" She said: "It's OK, I've got a blow-lamp!"

I never did get his name but he was a really funny man. When I was asked by a few of his friends if he would have any chance in doing it professionally, I said: "Sure, he ought to have a go!"

He would need to clean up his material a bit, find a venue like Comedy Store as a showcase, and he could make it for exposure. Then it would be a matter of finding something to do between bookings, finding enough original material, and hoping that a mixed audience would enjoy him as much as his mates at the Rotary.

I didn't mention that all this takes a long time and therefore he should hang on to his day job. If I had sounded a bit negative I would have been thought a 'bludger' by his cronies. So I said again: "Sure, he ought to have a go!"

I'll probably hear some day that he is topping the bill somewhere and heading for international stardom. I hope so. Then I could say: "Didn't I tell you to have a go?"

January 24th 1997

This morning, my sister Kath dashed in, wide-eyed, to tell us that she had just seen the biggest frog she had ever set eyes on swimming around the pool. She was wrong! It wasn't a frog at all, but a cane toad, a big coconut-like creature that is the curse of many Australian farmers.

Way back in 1922, a few of these toads were brought in from Hawaii and released into the cane fields. Sugar from cane is one of Australia's most lucrative exports. Below us we can see acres and acres of canefields which are harvested all the year round.

The original idea was to rid the canefields of the field-mice and other vermin that damage the crop. From those first few dozen that were brought in there are now literally millions of cane toads. The population is steadily moving south from where they were originally released at quite an alarming rate.

At night they can be seen on the roads in canefield areas and motorists do their best to run over as many as possible. Next day their squelched-out bodies can be seen everywhere. They have no natural predator in Australia, they are ugly yet, unbelievably, many schoolchildren keep them as pets. A song entitled *Cane Toads Are Coming* is played quite often on radio.

There is no answer to the plague at present — they are coming slowly southward like an advancing army, secure in the thought that they cannot be stopped. I have seen only three in all the five years we have been here. A neighbour tells me that a good way to exterminate them is to use a fully swung golf driver!

I have an inborn revulsion of killing any of God's creatures — even ultra-ugly cane toads — so I have always just shooed them off, hoping that they won't go off and tell their mates that "It's good up at Max's place!"

I heard that there was an Irish scientist who had been approached to begin experiments on ridding the land of these awful looking creatures. When they checked up on him, however, they decided against him. Among his prior inventions were:

Waterproof tea-bags.

Wheelchairs with pedals.

L-shaped mobile homes.

Beer glasses with square bases; they never leave 'rings' on tables!

Apparently his last suggestion was a brewery from cane toads — you could make beer from the hops!

January 25th 1997

One of today's dominant stories in Australia is the account of two yachtsmen, from different boats, lost at sea at the bottom of the world. They have been spotted by RAAF aircraft clinging to the hulls of their boats and an Australian warship is racing toward them in the hope of picking them up before the cruel sea — and the Southern Ocean can be cruel — claims their lives.

Each news bulletin keeps us all aware of how the rescue is progressing. A few days ago, a Frenchman, Raphael Dinelli, was rescued by a British yachtsman named Peter Goss. It was moving to see the distraught men embracing each other after the rescue. Many people become irked by the astronomical costs of these rescue operations — which, of course, comes from their taxes — and the fact that the rescued mariners sell their stories for colossal amounts of money to the newspapers. The Frenchman sold his for a reported 10,000 dollars.

At first light a helicopter will be trying to pluck another Frenchman from his upturned yacht and then go on to locate a Britisher. If they find him they will drop a diver who will listen for sounds of life from the hull, which at present seem most unlikely. The British yachtsman has been in the freezing water for three days and nights, so the outcome of this operation is real *Boy's Own* stuff.

According to the experts, heading south cuts the journey for the round-the-world race by many hours, but conditions are far more hazardous. It is to be expected that several governments are asking that a set route be adhered to; a route that can be better monitored and the dangers lessened. Of course, that would also lessen the thrill — and there does have to be a challenge.

Yesterday, Richard Branson took off in a giant balloon in an attempt to circumnavigate the globe in a blaze of publicity that only he knows how to generate. He made very little progress and was forced to abort after a very short distance. It is said to be the last aviation record left and Richard dearly wanted to achieve it. He had all the money, the equipment and the know-how and yet the elements defeated him. Remember the saying: 'Time and tide wait for no man!'

I became aware of this on trips that I've made on the QE2. This ship is equipped to contend with the roughest of seas, but one trip that I made across the Tasman Sea, with waves reaching up to the top deck — is something that I never want to experience again.

There was another occasion in the Pacific, on our way from Hawaii to Fiji, when 80 per cent of all aboard, crew included, were confined to cabins. On this particular trip we had to cross the International Date Line, where a day is lost. My fellow entertainer was the supreme Victor Borge. I had done my shows but Victor still had his to do.

I suggested to him that he could get a laugh from the previous, awful 24 hours of storm by asking the audience if it were true that we lost 24 hours when we crossed the Date Line. Following their response he should say: "Why the hell couldn't we have lost yesterday?" It got one of the biggest laughs of his act and when we met afterwards he said: "Max, have you got any more lines like that?"

On another occasion, Neil Armstrong was talking about what it was like to be the first man on the Moon. The entire passenger list crammed in to hear what he had to say, some even securing their seats an hour before the lecture began. Then a swell started and we began to sway. About 400 people began to get more and more restless and one by one began to leave their seats. By the time the much-admired and respected astronaut made his appearance, the audience had dwindled to a quarter of what it had been.

The next day, when I was introduced to this wonderful man, I apologised for leaving the lecture halfway through because I was so sea-sick. Knowing a little of the rigours that astronauts have to go through, I was quite surprised by his response. "You were sea-sick? I was sea-sick! I've only just got up!"

If you have never travelled across some of the world's great oceans, it's very hard to appreciate that sometimes for days on end you will never see another ship, land or even a bird, nothing but water, water, everywhere. One old lady, travelling across the South Atlantic for the first time, enquired of the purser; "Does the crew sleep on board?" It's one of the QE2's stock jokes.

It is 7pm and Richard Moorcroft, the very professional newsreader for ABC Television, has just announced the successful rescue of the two yachts-men. Australia has earned the gratitude of the whole world for one of the most spectacular and dangerous rescue missions ever attempted.

To pacify all those tax-payers who were up in arms about the cost of the operation, why not give the captain of the HMAS Adelaide permission to sell his story to the tabloids. Get the money and then pay the ship's expenses from it — then secure the TV and film rights and really cash in. No! On second thoughts the Southern Ocean would be like Hollywood Boulevard, with Max Clifford directing the ship!

CHAPTER TEN

A Mysterious Stranger

THE Australians take their public holidays very seriously. Any excuse for a party will do. That's why my diary continues with a very serious announcement.

January 26th 1997

Today is Australia Day. That same old Captain Cook joke has been cracked twice already — the one about Captain Cook landing at Botany Bay, pointing to an animal and asking what it was named. An Aborigine told the captain: "Kan-ga-roo!" It wasn't until 150 years later that it was discovered that 'kangaroo' in the Aboriginal language means "I don't know!"

There are celebrations that can only be achieved in a climate like Australia's — but unfortunately it rained! If you can imagine Manchester with fireworks that's how it is.

In Melbourne it was overcast but OK for the Australian Open Tennis Championship, won by Pete Sampras, who demolished new-boy-on-the-block Carlos Maya, 6-2, 6-2, 6-3. It was a no-contest and embarrassing for the 20-year-old Spaniard who had fought his way to the Final by disposing of top seeds Boris Becker, Michael Chang and British hope, Tim Henman.

There were few words that the presenter of the trophy could find to say except, "Better luck next time," and the sponsor, Ford Motors, had to be content with the commercial channel filling in with an old Pat Cash tournament from years ago, a match with Mats Willander which had far more thrills than the present demolition, over so quickly that the programme was running an hour short.

Six hunded kilometres away, at Hope Island, was the Johnnie Walker Golf Classic, won today by Ernie Els, a young South African player who is so good that it makes me wonder why I ever bother. In a field of top players, which included Faldo, Langer, Couples and some formidable Australian talent, Els sailed home with a two-stroke lead. South Africa must be really proud of this young fellow, especially since they were kept off the world sporting stage in the days before before apartheid was ended. Not since Gary Player has a champion of Els quality arrived from that land. Before Player, of course, was the great Bobby Locke

I once had the pleasure of partnering Locke in a foursome which included British professionals Brian Barnes and Hedley Muscroft, on a course just outside Johannesburg. We were playing for £10 a hole and we were one up at the 16th. As I approached my tee shot, which made the centre of the fairway, Bobby said: "Steady master," — he called everybody master — "Take your five-wood and hit it straight at the green." I told him that I didn't have a five-wood in my bag, so he let me borrow his. To my utter amazement, the ball finished three inches from the pin and the money was ours.

In the club-house, Bobby was as pleased as Punch with my great shot, and so was I because you get few of those in a lifetime at my handicap. He asked me: "Why haven't you got a five-wood master? You used it so well." I assured him that I would purchase one upon my return to the UK.

"Don't do that master! I will write to Lillywhite's in Piccadilly Circus, and when you are next in London, pop in and there will be a five-wood waiting for you."

Bobby was notoriously forgetful, the result of an accident when his car stalled on a railway-crossing, so I didn't really give it much more thought.

Some weeks later I happened to be passing Lillywhite's in London and Bobby's words came back to me. The salesman nodded and said that they had indeed heard from the great man and that the wood was there waiting to be wrapped. Having taped it up in brown paper, the assistant handed it to me and said: "That will be eight pounds and ten shillings please Mr Bygraves!"

That's not the end of the story of that wood. That same day, as I returned from London to Leatherhead, I had to board the train during the rush hour. As I shoved my way into the crowded train, clutching the wrapped club under my arm, a porter shouted: "Mind the doors!" and slammed the carriage door right on the end of the protruding club. The result was a decapitated wood with the head of the club dangling from the twine.

I still haven't got a five-wood in my golf set, but I have wonderful memories of Bobby Locke, who sadly passed away in March 1987.

January 27th 1997

Anthony phoned me from Cornwall last night. He lives in Truro and tried to make a living there. His timing could not have been worse when he purchased some land, together with his partner, which they developed to build some award-winning houses.

It was the late '80s, the housing slump came, the banks called in the loans and, after putting in all that enthusiasm and time into the project — over two years — he finished up bankrupt.

On the 50th anniversary of D-Day he planned a celebration at Bovington, with tanks, World War Two aircraft, side-shows etc, culminating in a big open-air celebrity concert with the Glenn Miller Band, the Beverley Sisters, myself and supporting acts. The outdoor stage, sound equipment, lighting and seats were aimed at an audience of 2,000 to 3,000. I expect you remember the torrential rain on that day? Anthony finished up owing £15,000. There were a handful of people in the audience, all equipped with snorkels and waders, and three months of preparation were wasted.

Anthony's wife, Celia, supports him in his losing battle for survival. Luckily his three children are bright. At the private school in Truro they each won scholarships which will cut the school fees down a bit. His phone call was to tell me that he had finally, after ten years, decided to leave Truro and move up to Bournemouth, where there will be more scope for his talent. He really does have a lot of talent — his handicap is me!

Although he is a capable performer, a very good lyricist, script-writer and PR man, the only work he could get in Truro was as a shop assistant. As a youth he often came on TV with me, we did live shows at the Palladium, Prince of Wales Theatre, tours, Scotland's Alhambra Theatre, summer shows at Brighton etc. When his teenage years were coming to an end he finished up in Hollywood as a writer, then he played drums at a night-club in Hong Kong.

We both went to Tokyo and laughed our way around the world, playing the Tivolis in Sydney and Melbourne. We even did a *Royal Variety Show*.

Anthony has never 'sponged', never asked for a hand-out. He laughs his way through life but, as he said on the phone: "Dad, I have a young family. I have to do something!" I don't know what it will be. I would like him to run my music company which I don't pay enough attention to ...we'll see!

My favourite story concerning Anthony was this one. I call it 'Anthony and the Wallet'.

Most families have gatherings at weddings, funerals, Christmas etc, where their favourite family story is trotted out time and time again. My family is no exception and one of the yarns that we enjoy most is the tale of 'Anthony and the Wallet'. It happened many moons ago when I took Blosssom and the children for a two-week holiday at a luxury hotel in Jersey. Anthony was about seven or eight at the time.

I would crack gags about him training to be a miser. I would tell of a tramp who knocked at our street door. Anthony answered the knock and the tramp said: "Any old clothes?" to which Anthony replied: "Yes please!"

We arrived at the hotel on the Saturday and I gave the children £5 each, telling them that it was their holiday spending money. The two girls spent half of theirs over that first weekend, but Anthony invested sixpence in a plastic wallet. The pound notes, the ten shilling note and the silver were compartmented in the wallet, which he kept with him at all times. He is now one of the most generous people that you could wish to meet, but in those days he was tighter than a duck's bum — and that's watertight.

As we were going to bed one night we heard a shrill cry from the childrens' bedroom. Rushing in, we found Anthony sobbing and our baby-sitter, Phyllis, laughing hysterically. It took some time to get the story out of her.

This is what happened. Anthony, in order to make his wallet more difficult to find if burglars should happen to break in, hid it under the mattress of his bed. After about five minutes he decided that it would probably be the first place that they would look, so he got out of bed and found another hiding place, this time placing it under the carpet.

Another five minutes went by and he decided that the new hiding place was not good enough, either, so up he got again. This time his hiding-place was in the cupboard next to his bed — inside a china chamber-pot. Again he returned to bed, only to get up again after a short while to try to find an even safer place. As he removed the wallet from the chamber-pot, he discovered that it had not been emptied from the previous night. No wonder Phyllis was in hysterics every time she thought of the situation. She laughed even more when I gallantly retrieved the wallet, took it to the bathroom to remove the muck and placed the notes on a radiator to dry.

The last time that I told that story was to friends and relations at Attunga Park last Christmas. I had flown out the entire family — 12 in all — for an Oz Christmas and, once again, Anthony had to listen to the tale of the wallet.

Anthony, who never misses a chance to make a pun, muttered, for my ears only: "I remember it well — I was really pissed off!"

January 30th 1997

Anthony is really proud of his own son, Ashley. Today he faxed me a copy of the choirmaster's report from Truro Cathedral on Ashley's progress as a chorister.

' ...It took a little while for Ashley to adapt to the necessary standards of concentration and behaviour ...His rich, warm tone gives an excellent lead to the younger boys ...Adopts a perfectionist's approach to all our work, especially our recent live BBC broadcast, CD recordings and numerous concerts in England and Germany ...I value his work in the choir very highly indeed. 20/1/97.'

I hope you will forgive a grandfather getting a warm glow from the above, but it gives Blossom and myself a real thrill to listen to his singing and we feel that there is much more to it than a boy singing with a top-class choir.

He is the youngest of the three and, being the only boy, was sometimes left out of things by his sisters who had similar interests. Because of this, he teased, sulked and did what most boys do when they are annoyed at being left out of things. At one time it was quite worrying for the family trying to live a peaceful existence and Anthony was at a loss to find the answer.

It came one day when he heard Ashley singing to himself. He was pitching some notes that grabbed Anthony's attention and they were in a range that was unusual from a boy of ten. Being very aware of the fame of the choir in Truro, Anthony first asked Ashley if he would be interested in auditioning for a position in it. A little non-committal at first, Ashley gradually warmed to the idea. He was keen because it was something to which his sisters were unable to attain, a chorister in the famed Truro Cathedral Choir, although they were both pleased for him.

As a chorister he sang, not only for High Mass and special events, but he was also paid for weddings and funerals — not much, but enough to give him pride. His personality improved from the time when all he could think of was different ways to pull his sisters' hair.

Most of all, it built his character and a nice person began to emerge. I don't know what will happen when his voice breaks, which will be fairly soon, but I have a gut feeling that he will be a credit to the young Bygraves household.

I have some affinity with Ashley, because at his age I also sang solo at both Westminster and Canterbury Cathedrals. The only difference between us was that, after all my effort and practice, the only compliment I got from my father was: "You sounded just like a tart!"

January 31st 1997

There is a greengrocer's shop in town run by three personable ladies who love a joke or two. I don't think they know what I do for a living as they always refer to me as 'the gentleman from England'. They know that I have three horses on the land; two are mine and the other belongs to Graham. The horses mix with Graham's cattle and, periodically, the ladies give me carrots that are past their sell-by date to give to Pepper, Sandwich and Fred.

When I drive down to the field and toot the horn, the horses come galloping toward me and try to outpace the car alongside the fence as I accelerate down to the gate. They almost make it! That time together with the horses, watching them crunch their carrots and swish their tails, is one of the best ways I know of being at peace.

They are not rideable as their mouths are too soft for the bit and they have roamed in comparative freedom in the five years that we have known them, but they are chummy and full of fun.

Something strange happened today. As I was stroking the blaze on Pepper's head, a stranger appeared round a bend in the road. It is rare to see another car along this road — rarer still to see someone on foot. This, however, was no ordinary pedestrian. I gaped and thought that I must be dreaming, but I swear that this is true!

The stranger was in full eastern garb, with a turban, kaftan, sandals and a grey beard. He walked with the aid of a long staff and looked anything between 60 and 80 years of age. It was not really the sort of image you would normally expect to see on an Australian country road at 11 o'clock in the morning!

I bid him "G'day," and he replied in a language that I had never heard before …and don't forget that I once lived near Southall. All three of the horses began to whinny and puff loudly, but when the stranger murmured something to them, they immediately settled down. I had recently been reading a book entitled *The Horse Whisperer*, and this stranger was doing exactly what the hero of the book did — he was talking to the horses!

I asked the stranger his name but he just made signs to explain that his English was not very good and that he must be on his way. I was becoming convinced that I had been visited by some celestial being.

Excitedly I returned to the house and began to gabble out my story to Blossom.

"Was he wearing a turban and a kaftan?" she asked, and went on to describe my strange visitor exactly.

"Yes, yes — that's it!" I cried excitedly.

Blossom smiled, a little condescendingly I thought, and said: "That was Gary Singh's grandfather!"

Gary Singh is our local garage mechanic!

CHAPTER ELEVEN

Lew, Roy, Paul and Greg

ONE MONTH of 1997 has already gone. The months seem to go quicker as you get older, but the library of memories just gets bigger and bigger.

February 1st 1997

I received a very warm and affectionate letter from Lord Grade today. 'Lew', which is the only way that I can think of him, celebrated his 90th birthday last week and I had, of course, sent my congratulations to him. I have known him for over 50 years and have the greatest admiration for the man who will always be 'Lew' to me. I think that he, too, prefers the warmth generated by the use of his — I was going to say Christian name, but, of course, Lew is Jewish — and one of the nicest gentlemen that it is possible to meet. He has so many friends and admirers. It would be difficult to say how many different honours he has received. Kathy is Lew's wife and a perfect support for the solar-powered dynamo that she married all those years ago. She still has a proud smile for his achievements which seem to go on and on without end.

Lew, together with his two brothers, Leslie and Bernard, dominated show-business for over 30 years, and were responsible for giving the public some of the best entertainment ever, which will be remembered for many years to come.

It must be a trait of the Grade family, something which I hadn't realised until I re-read Lew's letter, but the three of them were always generous with sound advice. In today's letter he writes: "I am glad that you're working consistently and the secret is — never retire!"

He goes on to say that he is still in the office by 7am, working on a movie, *Something To Believe In*, and already planning out his next project when that one is wrapped up. All of this at the age of 90!

Bernard Delfont, Lew's brother, also a lord, was also always full of good advice. We were rehearsing a show called *Swinging Down The Lane*, early on in my career at a time when I was just starting to make good wages. During a break, Bernie, who was quite a bit older than me, sat alongside me in the stalls and gave me a bit of that advice.

He pointed out that I was now top of the bill, and that meant that my wages were bound to increase even more. He also pointed out that, as top of the bill, the only way to go was down if I was not careful.

"Always make sure that you have a few quid in your pocket. If you are broke, and people sense that you are looking for a hand-out, you will be shunned. When you are solvent, you will always be welcomed at any banquet, premiere, first night or what have you."

To seal this advice he popped a six-inch Havana cigar into my mouth and said: "Muzeltov!"

For a long time after that I thought that Muzeltov was a kind of cigar. I became quite fond of cigars and every time I walked into the tobacconist in Charing Cross Road, I would say: "Muzeltov!" And the tobacconist would hand me my cigar and say "Shalom!"

It wasn't until I met Moishe Dyan in Tel Aviv some time later and was greeted with "Shalom!" that I realised it was a greeting. Up until then I thought it was a brand name the same as Monte Cristo!

Leslie, the father of Michael Grade, was quieter than Lew and Bernie, but no less dynamic. I remember Leslie being very flattering to an old performer who didn't have a very good reputation and was reputed to be a bit of a ****. Afterwards I remarked on how nice he had been and Leslie put his arm around my shoulders and whispered: "Always be nice to performers at the bottom of the heap because they have a strange way of coming back to the top of the bill!"

I was made aware of this several years later with a comedienne named Hylda Baker, who, it seemed, had had the best of her days. Agents weren't able to give her away and she was going through a terribly lean time. Suddenly she landed a role in a comedy TV show in which she starred with Jimmy Jewell. Both of them became national TV stars and Leslie's words came back to me with a vengeance.

Lady Grade — Kathy — and myself appeared in a film together, which I think we'd both prefer to forget. Honestly, I can't remember the name of it! It was in the late 1940s and we had to travel out to Stanmore by tube, then wait for a bus which took us to Bushey Park Studios. They were small studios and I sometimes wonder if Kathy, knowing that Lew was once the boss of the famous Elstree Studios and became eventually Lord Grade of Elstree, still remembers those days. If she does, she will understand my admiration for her husband, Lew.

Muzeltov Lew — a big Churchill size!

February 2nd 1997

Just before I left for Australia I received a line from Roy Hudd, asking for the words of a song that I recorded many moons ago entitled, *That Old Straw Hat*. It was a very good composition, sent by a songwriter named Murphy from Liverpool. I liked the song and worked on it and recorded it, hoping to get it into the best-sellers list.

It did OK but didn't exactly set the world on fire. Now, 30 years on, Roy wants the words and music for a friend in the States who has heard the song but is unable to trace the origin.

Roy Hudd is a collector of showbusiness memorabilia and immediately got on to me to help his friend, a well-known international performer by the name of 'Topper' Martyn. Mr Martyn was a juggler whose trade mark was a top hat, hence the 'Topper' as a nickname.

After quite a search I finally came across *Straw Hat* on an LP that I'd recorded years ago. While recording the song on to cassette for 'Topper' I began to realise that here was a very good piece of stage material. It could well be that modern audiences would go for it more than they had for the original recording of 1959. I made a cassette for myself and, only last week, got a local pianist and arranger to put down a routine for me on manuscript. Just two nights ago I put the routine into my act at a concert in Sydney. It proved to be a sensation. The lyrics suit a soft-shoe dance routine, which I did — and you haven't lived until you have seen a 74-year-old doing soft-shoe:

> That old straw hat
> My Poppa wore
> I'm gonna take it down
> And wear it just once more.
>
> I'm putting on his blue-striped coat
> And his spotless clean white pants
> I'm rolling back the rug
> To do his fav'rite song and dance
>
> I'm gonna swing his walking cane
> And serenade the ladies once again
> I hope perhaps a tear might fall
> Like Momma's did before
> When I wore that old straw hat
> My Poppa wore.

An audience can always sense when an entertainer is enjoying what he does and they certainly let me know it the other night. Of course, it will get stronger and be more presentable, but I can always tell that if a new routine is about 80 per cent right, then the polishing and know-how will be sure to follow. It may take as many as half a dozen shows to get it absolutely right, but I just know it will be a 'must' once I have worked on that *Old Straw Hat* routine.

Friends in the business are usually very helpful when you are in need of something. For instance, I didn't want a full-size walking cane among my props because of the difficulty in packing it. Then I remembered the way stage magicians produce a walking cane 'as if by magic' from thin air. I sent a fax to Paul Daniels asking where I might get one. Two days later, a small box arrived by air-mail containing the stick. I warned my wife to be careful as she opened the box: "You never know, Paul Daniels might be inside!"

The straw hat was harder to come by. I had no luck at the various theatrical costumiers and other likely places in Sydney. One turned up at one place but they would not sell, only rent. Then my luck changed. I was driving home, through a place called Rose Bay, when I saw two schoolboys at a bus-stop wearing the ideal hat, 'straws', similar to those worn by students at Harrow.

"Where did you get those hats?" I asked them.

"From school," said the one, jerking his thumb in the direction of a large building behind him.

Without more ado I drove down the drive to the main school building and searched out the principal. I introduced myself and explained what I was looking for. With a smile he threw open a cupboard and a whole pile of straw hats cascaded out.

"Try one for size," he said.

The second one fitted perfectly — from the label inside it had once been owned by a pupil named seven and one eighth.

"How can I purchase this?"

Again the principal smiled. "Just let me have two tickets for your next show!"

The pleasure was all mine.

As I left the school grounds, several other boys had joined the two at the bus-stop. As I passed I raised my hat to them and could almost hear them debating which class this strange looking fellow in T-shirt, shorts and sandals, and the regulation school head-gear, was in.

I couldn't resist it: "Bygraves Senior — needlework and domestic science!"

February 3rd 1997

Greg Norman, the golfer, made the front pages today. He was at a dinner in Queensland and made the confession that he regretted becoming so cynical over the past few years.

I remember my first meeting with Greg, long before he was labelled 'The Shark' and writers had not sensed that killer instinct by which he is known today. It was at the airport in Hong Kong and he was trying to get a single seat to London but there weren't any. Greg was quite concerned as it was the last flight to London that night. I happened to know the fellow at the desk so, when Greg had told me his problem, I informed the clerk that the young golfer had a tournament next day in the UK and, if he could help, it would be wonderful. To cut a long story short, British Airways found him a seat. When we finally landed at Heathrow, Greg told me that he had slept all night, 'like a log!'

I suppose that when you get to be the world's No.1, sleeping like a log doesn't come too easily. When millions of dollars are rolling in, the pressures must be immense, not only from the manufacturers who are eager to use your name to make their own fortunes, but family and friends can become distant.

When Greg was just beginning to make a name for himself and getting his face in all the Queensland newspapers, I was playing a round of golf with some friends at his home course, Southport, near Surfer's Paradise. As we were having a drink at the bar after the game, I was introduced to Greg's mother. I asked how Greg was.

"I'll give him bloody Greg," she replied. "Two weeks and not even a postcard!"

The great golf battle that went on when he squandered a six-stroke lead to finish up five shots behind Nick Faldo, hurt him a lot more than he could admit at the time. Ten months have gone by and Greg seemed to want to get it off his chest. He told his fellow diners: "If I did all this again, I wouldn't become so cynical." He put it so well when he said: "Everyone wants to know how you feel when you screw up. You try to explain, but you can't get it out because you are the only one who knows".

I once played a foursome with him at Moor Park, just outside London. Watching him play a shot, he stood poised watching the flight of his ball and looked like some hero from a western movie. This was long before he wore the Akubra-styled hat that has become his trade-mark. His blond hair and his near-perfect physique made him stand out. His bright eyes, half-smile and encouragement to a lesser player — me — makes me proud to have known him for more than 20 years.

The moment I remember most was at the second hole. I drove my ball into a bunker. I closed my eyes, hit the sand — and wished. When I looked up, the ball was two inches from the flag, and this from a really difficult hazard. Since that day, Greg always says the same thing: "Will you teach me that bunker shot you did at the second at Moor Park?"

No, there was no sign of cynicism in those days. I think it comes with the territory.

There is very little that anyone can add to the comments that he made, except to say that in almost every profession there comes a time to move over and make way for the next fellow. It's been a great innings, try to enjoy the fruits. That's very hard to do when you have been the supremo but, like Frank Sinatra, you did it your way and there's still a lot of golf in those broad shoulders, still a lot for you to pass on.

If we ever play another game, and Greg is still interested in that bunker shot, here's how it is done:

1. Select your sand-blaster.
2. Make a firm hold with your feet in the sand.
3. Play the ball off the right foot.
4. Come slowly back.
5. Close your eyes — swing — all the time saying softly:
6. Our Father, Who art in Heaven ...

February 5th 1997

There is no way that you can sleep in at Attunga Park. The birds begin their singing at 6.30 every morning. It can be a very pretty sound or a 'go-to-hell' sound, depending on the day ahead. If I wake up on one of those 'thank God I'm alive' mornings, I can be shaved, showered and cornflaked in 15 minutes, dressed — that's a laugh — in a pair of shorts and sandals, and then it's down to the den to pick up the paper and open the writing pad to pen a few lines for the book which you are reading at the moment.

Some mornings are a doddle. The memory is sharp, the ideas seem entertaining and there are no worries. Today, by way of a change, it is slow. The only glow that I get today is from a famous lady journalist who has been caught out 'thieving' her copy from the Internet and passing it off as her own.

With my hand on my heart, I can honestly say that, good or bad, brilliant or trash, I have written every word in longhand, enjoyed it all immensely, and fulfilled a desire to come up to the publisher's deadline.

If I do get a 'block', my mind turns to the writers of comedy that I have used in the past. When I was on TV every week, I used the services of Londoners, Eric Davidson and Spike Mullins, both with a quick wit and often coming out with lines so funny that I refer to them as 'gems'.

Talking on one show about my dog meeting his end:

"...then one day he was running after a ball and couldn't stop — our French poodle became a bulldog ..."

Enter Nicky.

"Then we got Nicky. He's a wonderful house dog, we always know when burglars are near the house — he faints!"

Camera close-up of dog.

"A great house dog, we've had him six months and never lost a house. Carpets, valuables, yes — but never a house ..."

"He's so keen. I sent him for a paper the other day — he came back with the newsagent!"

"He wouldn't eat yesterday so I sent for the vet — he ate every bit."

"We got him as a pup. He looked like two dirty mops tied together — sometimes I wonder if I've been talking to the right end. I get some very unusual answers ..."

I did this routine with our dog, live on the end of a lead. At each funny line, the camera went to a full-head shot of Nicky, who did the 'Ooh blimey!' look at every 'boom-boom'.

Spike and Eric *had* to come up funny lines every week. That's what Thames Television was paying them good money for, and for many years it worked.

Eileen, who was Eric's wife, used to deliver the new script and I always said a little prayer that there would be a few 'gems' within its pages. If there were, I would say another prayer that I could give them their value when I used them on the show.

Spike, like Eric, was a chain-smoker and a non-driver. His wife, Mary, transcribed his awful scrawl into legible type-script, as well as keeping him cheerful when the ideas didn't flow. Both of them became big names in the world of script-writing. They wrote regularly for *The Two Ronnies*, *The Des O'Connor Show*, and several light-entertainment shows.

Sadly, they both recently passed away, having 'coughed' their way to that great script-writers' meeting in the sky but, every time that I look at a blank sheet of paper, I admire those two fellows and their prolific pens. Week in and week out those two script-writing experts helped to make me an accepted humorist to the great TV audience. Thanks a lot both of you!

February 6th 1997

My friend, Lionel, called earlier today to remind me that it was Chinese New Year and would I like to have lunch? Yes I would! Where should we go?

"At my golf club — really good Chinese food."

As you're no doubt aware, Chinese restaurants vary a lot more than English ones. One of my favourite memories of great Chinese eating places was back in the 1950s.

The food at the House of Chan in New York's 7th Avenue has never been surpassed. I was the guest of Danny Kaye and he was amused at the way I delightedly cleared my plate at each course.

"You don't get Chinese food like that in England, huh?"

I told him that you don't even get Chinese food like that in China!

I was a bit doubtful about Lionel's invitation to eat Chinese at his golf club. A ham or bacon sandwich maybe, but I'd never heard of a Chinese restaurant on an 18-hole course! He assured me that it would be OK, so I went along for the ride, which he had arranged — in a rickshaw!

Our driver, dressed in denims and a large coolie's hat, seated us and then pulled us through the main thoroughfare of Surfers' Paradise at a cracking pace. He even remembered to leave two large fans on the seat. At the end of town, the 'coolie' stopped and bowed us into an air-conditioned stretch limousine, together with nine others, and off we went to the golf club.

Lionel is a very wealthy man — he should be, he's my Australian agent! When we arrived at the golf club, we were met by the owner who greeted us with: "Kong Lei Fat Choi", which, I was assured, meant "Health, Wealth and Happiness", and so on. We were ushered into a cheerful-looking restaurant, hung with lanterns and bunting, and seated at our tables.

Soup to start, then spare ribs, followed by the tastiest dim sims, rice, fish and a suckling pig. Wow! The greatest Chinese meal that I have ever — ever — had. I must send a menu to the House of Chan in New York — if it is still there!

After the meal came the liqueurs, followed by the 'stories' for the next hour or so. The one that got the biggest laugh was told by Tom Spencer, another Australian showbiz agent. Tom is married to a Chinese girl named Mona, who comes from Hong Kong. She is not into the ways of the western world, or, at least, wasn't at the time. Tom related the story of when he was driving me to Melbourne after appearing at a concert in a place called Wollongong. We got pulled by the police doing 80kms an hour in a 60kms area. He got a ticket, of course, but, since he never heard any more from the State of Victoria police, he assumed that it had gone no further.

Two years later, Mona phoned Tom at his office to tell him that there were two policemen at his door with a summons. They wanted 100 dollars from Tom, or else 14 days in the nick. Tom, who makes more than that every ten minutes, asked his wife if she had paid the 100 dollars.

"Of course not!" she answered innocently. "I didn't know what you wanted to do!"

February 10th 1997

A very good friend of many years is very ill. I phone and write regularly but he is now gasping when I call. He quite openly tells me that 'it won't be long!'

He has had a good innings and is now 89. Even at that great age, though, he is unmuddled and has the clear thinking of a man half that age.

His name is Archie Collins, originally from Scotland but now living in Australia with Olga, a native of New South Wales. They have had a good marriage for — I don't really like to ask, but it must be well over 50 years. We first met when Olga Varona, as his wife was then known, was on a first-class variety bill at the London Palladium. In those days, Archie managed Olga who did a most unusual act. The orchestra played an opening fanfare and then Olga, a ballerina, walked on her points to a rope that hung from the flies at centre stage.

Olga, who had the reddest of hair, which hung to her ankles, now ascended the rope in a series of graceful moves. The orchestra played some classical pieces which perfectly matched the gymnastic movements being carried out by Olga. Suddenly the music would change and, face-first, Olga would begin to descend the rope. Archie, at the bottom of the rope, would begin to twirl it until it described great loops until Olga reached the bottom. The music would cut out and Olga tripped forward to take the applause. It was a class act that worked all over the world.

Whenever we talk nowadays, he loves to go over the events of times past. His recollections of almost every act that graced the variety theatres, before they were turned into bingo halls, is truly amazing. His knowledge of the czars of showbusiness, small-time agents such as Lord Lew Grade and his likeable brother Lord Delfont, is hard to believe. I got to know the Grades personally later, but Archie can remember the time when they would hound him for their ten per cent, which came to about 30 shillings in those days. It makes for great nostalgia.

Archie talks candidly about the demise of variety. He puts his finger on the closures and, as you listen, you know that he is talking sense. Variety was a part of our history and, if it is to be put aside, then it should be done truthfully and without favour.

He believes that the closure of the theatres in the UK was accelerated by the agents, to whom ten per cent became mere chicken-feed. The laziness of people who ran the Moss and Stoll Empires was another contributing factor.

At one time, every week, almost 60 theatres in the UK needed a show containing eight or nine acts. It was quite a nightmare trying to provide the public with artistes that had not been seen before, or finding new talent that would attract, and so if an agent represented an act that was 'top of the bill' and guaranteed attendances, it became the practice to fill the rest of the bill with 'washers' — the term 'washers' was used to mean 'cheap' acts! The agents would then submit a complete bill, made up mostly of artistes that he or she represented, and go on a 70-30 per cent split of the box-office receipts for the week.

Not only did they collect from each individual act, they also took a percentage from the theatre. It didn't always come off, but 90 times out of a 100 there was no gamble. Every artiste knew that with all this went a few 'sweeteners' to the bosses, so all concerned were making their crust.

To give you some idea of how it all worked, let me explain about a time that Louis Benjamin, the boss of the London Palladium, had a week to fill. He was going on holiday and didn't want to be bothered with the assembly of a supporting bill, advertising plus orchestra payments and so on. He asked if I would like to take over the package. At that time I would earn a flat rate of £5,000 per week.

I agreed to his suggestion, fixed a supporting bill and played the week at the Palladium on a 70-30 per centage deal. To cut a long story: instead of £5,000 salary, I came out with more than £27,000, the most that I had ever earned in my career — and, what's more, it gave me some idea of what theatres were able to take.

From then on I asked my agent, Jock Jacobsen, to make sure of theatre capacity, prices and expected attendances before making arrangements for me. It resulted in a few years of lucrative bookings, simply through understanding the ways of theatre production. Mind you, Louis Benjamin never let me forget that he had lost well over £20,000 for not being more of a business tycoon. He put it about that I had an astute business brain, which I haven't. He was the cute one! Louis was also managing director of Pye Records and tied me up with contracts that are still binding as I write these words.

The closure of the music halls and variety theatres was inevitable. The cheap way of watching entertainment in the future would be television and, as Archie explained, all this hurried the last days of my sort of entertainment along. It was time to look at fresh pastures.

I don't know if Archie will be around when this book is published, so Arch, it has been wonderful knowing and learning from you. So long old pal, see y' the noo!

February 15th 1997

I keep meaning to tidy my desk. The faxes come and go and my filing system is a lot to be ashamed of! I decided to do just that today. I was about to start when a truck driven by two ladies arrived. They had come in response to a call from Blossom, who had seen a request for wood to be used as fuel for a pottery kiln.

We have loads of wood as our handyman, Graham, has just replaced most of the fencing. There must be a couple of tons that they can help themselves to. Trouble is, of course, I'll have to leave the desk-tidying to go and open the gates ...any excuse!

I drove down with them to the paddock on the back of the old boneshaker of a truck. Upon seeing the wood the lady said: "Would five dollars be all right?"

I said it would and fished in my pocket for a note — I thought she meant it would cost that much to take the wood away. Instead it was she who gave *me* five dollars. Five bucks tax-free — at least I think it is!

I still have to pay tax here as well as in the UK, so I'd better have a word with my accountant. It's these paltry little amounts that the Inland Revenue want to know about and I have a fear of forgetting them in case there's a knock at the door, like one Boxing Day as I was preparing to leave for a holiday.

I opened the door to a well-dressed West Indian gentleman, who informed me that he was from HM Income Tax office, I was asked why some forms had not been filled in and returned. Knowing that all my tax affairs had been dealt with, I called my accountant, Mr McKey, at home.

Mr McKey could not believe that anyone from the tax office would be calling on Boxing Day and asked to speak to the man. After satisfying himself that the man was genuine, McKey, who has a great memory, gave him dates, cheque numbers and so on, and convinced him that the necessary papers had been returned. The official apologised, hung up the phone and, turning to me said: "Can I have a couple of autographs for my children?"

This is a true story and I often wonder what brought a man from the tax office out on Boxing Day for two autographs. Anyone got any ideas?

I helped load the wood on to that old truck with the temperature standing at 85 degrees. I would gladly have paid anyone my five dollars to do the job for me. I had no gloves, as the ladies sensibly had, and finished with splinters which I'm still trying to get out of my hands. My last words to Bloss were:

"Next time you decide to get rid of any wood, make sure I'm not here!"

The desk-tidying has been abandoned for the day. To be honest, I don't think that I'll get round to it this week. Next week will be difficult, too, because I'm busy.

Come to think of it I might as well leave it because we'll be going home to dear old Blighty very soon. As we prepare for that, my desk is going to slip down the queue of things to be done. I have just realised that gaps are beginning to appear in my diary again. Tomorrow's priorities are beginning to take over yesterday's events. Maybe I'll fill in the missing bits when I get back to England. Maybe …maybe it's because I'm a Londoner that I'm starting to get excited about seeing her again!

CHAPTER TWELVE

Max The English Patient

W HEN I looked at the calendar on the wall, I realised that my return to Blighty was further away than I had been thinking. I would have to tidy that desk after all. But not today! Life in Australia is too good to be worrying about desk-tidying. Not tomorrow either. It is Sunday and as good an excuse to do nothing as I could possibly find.

February 9th 1997
I usually like to have a lie-in on the Sabbath — so I did! I listened to ABC National on the headphones. National is similar to Radio 4. By that I mean there are some nice surprises along the way. Just after seven I got a programme called *Macker* — I don't know if that's the correct spelling — and when I told Bloss about it, she asked if it was a religious programme. I said some parts of it were 'God-speak' and she punned: "Next week I'd better turn to the east and face Macker!"

Macker goes all over Australia to different parts of the outback and interviews interesting people, very much like *Down Your Way*, except that he also takes phone-ins and reads letters from listeners.

This morning he interviewed a very articulate gentleman with an amazing sense of humour, who had just turned 102! He had been married three times, the last time being at the age of ninety-three. One of the quest-ions that Macker put to the centenarian was: "At what age does the sex urge go?"

The old fellow replied: "I dunno! You'd better ask someone a bit older than me."

Another story that brought a smile was this. In a very small country town, miles away from city life, anyone who wants a driving licence is usually tested by the local constable. In this particular town — I missed the name, but Australia has so many — the constable would take the applicant halfway up a very steep hill and ask them to drive to the top, changing into the right gear on the way. On this particular test the interviewer's mother-in-law didn't quite make it. The car rolled back down the hill and both she and the constable finished up at the bottom. The constable turned to the lady and said: "OK Mary, I'll give you a licence, but don't come into town when it's busy!"

February 11th 1997

Another beautiful morning. It is a constant source of surprise to me that a bird that is so small it can fit into the palm of your hand, is able to make a call that is so loud and piercing. It can be heard all over the park — just when I need to concentrate! I shoo them away and go down to my den to write. At the moment it is 35 degrees Celsius, which is over 90 degrees in old money — and to be blunt …it's bloody hot!

All I have had to eat today is a slice of water melon because it's much too hard to work up an appetite on a day like this. Talking about birds, there is a baby butcher-bird that cries all day to be fed. At first we all went "Aaah!" when we put out food for the hen to pick up and pop into the baby's mouth. As a result, the chick has done nothing about learning to stand on its own two feet. We don't say "Aaah!" any more, we've changed it to "The lazy so-and-so!"

Bloss just brought me a double-decker salmon sandwich, topped with salad, and that baby bird, which we've named 'Gercha!', has sensed that it is feeding time and has commenced screeching like somebody's car alarm gone wrong. Throwing a bit to him does no good — he just swallows it and begins screeching even louder than before. Fortunately, along comes mum who takes over the popping in baby's mouth bit, and peace is restored. It is so tranquil that I quite forgot what it was I was going to write. Oh well, I'll finish my sandwich!

Later that day, as they used to put on the screen of the silent movies, it is still extremely hot but I have remembered what it was I was going to write about. It was a letter from Eric Sykes. He is due to open in a play at the Piccadilly Theatre after already being on the road with it for several months.

"The audience loved it," he told me. "Especially the interval!"

Sykes has a wonderful 'like it or leave it' approach. I really wish I had. If I get a bad notice it can keep me awake for a full five minutes.

He goes on: "We'll be here at the Piccadilly until May 3rd and, barring accident, acts of God, or bad crits, I'll expect you and Bloss to pay a visit."

Eric stresses that it is not a hard part. " ...Plenty of opportunities for me to put my feet up, but that's what Nuryev said!"

So many times I have asked Eric and his wife, Edith, to come out here and stay for a few weeks, but I think that the long journey is a bit of a turn-off. In a previous letter he had asked: "What is there to do?" When I write back I can tell him. "We'll feed the birds!"

February 12th 1997

This evening I leave on the Quantas 7 o'clock flight to Melbourne for two concerts at the Melbourne Concert Hall. It is going to be a bit of a slog as I have to change planes in Sydney, have a 40-minute wait and then on to Melbourne, a distance of some 1,000 miles. Had it been a direct flight, I could be there in three hours. As it is, I will be lucky to check into my hotel before midnight.

I decide against having a meal and have a glass of champagne instead. I've been trying to read Alan Bennet's book *Writing Home* but, having made up my mind to put some new material into the act, I am mentally rehearsing instead. I have written what I think is a very funny piece on the Australian entrepreneurs who have taken many shareholders for millions of dollars. The song includes references to Alan Bond, Christopher Skase and Ned Kelly, and trying to fit the patter and syllables into the song forces me to concentrate on tomorrow night's concerts. I get many strange looks from the opposite seats when they realise that I am not chewing gum, but obviously talking to myself!

Tom Spencer, the agent, is waiting at the deserted Melbourne arrivals gate and takes my case, for which I am grateful. The case is heavy with props, straw hat, band parts, suits, shoes and so on. At times like these I wish I was a rock singer — one of those who walks off the street on to the stage and starts the stint without even a glance or a 'Good evening,' to the audience, one whose only baggage is a pouch full of cannabis and cigarette papers. I usually have Bert Mortimer to sort out all my things but he isn't on this trip and I really miss him after a day like this one.

Blossom is always saying: "I don't know why you do it! All this travel — hotels — in all sorts of weather. Why? You certainly don't need the money!"

It's very hard to explain that I need the stimulation. It's hard to explain that, when 2,000 people stand up to applaud, with cries of "Bravo!" and "More!", there is nothing else quite like it in the whole wide world. Yes I know! You can say that it is just ego, but I call it achievement. Each audience must include some sceptics as to your ability. You have to prove them wrong and win them over, you have to be fit, you have to present the right stuff. You have to give them their money's worth and make them appreciate why they have left the comfort of their homes, travelled some distance, taken the trouble to book ahead and then sat through your performance. If, by the end of the evening, they are applauding you, then you know that you have succeeded.

Try explaining all of that without sounding like a big 'ead!

I'm going to bed!

February 13th 1997

Still in Melbourne I called room service for a morning pot of tea. I waited. Then I waited some more. After 20 minutes and still no tea, I found kettle and tea-bags in a cupboard and decided to make my own. As I finished preparing the tea, a knock at the door informed me that my order had at last arrived. A Vietnamese waiter wished me, "G'day". My own tea was definitely superior to the waiter-delivered luke-warm variety.

After a quick shower, I got my band parts in order and met Tom, complete with taxi, in front of the hotel. Our rehearsal was for 8.30am so Tom told the driver — a young Hungarian — to take us to the Melbourne Concert Hall, stage door entrance.

Eventually we drew up outside a building.

"What's this?" demanded Tom.

"This is the Melbourne Arts Centre, stage door!"

When Tom came down off the roof, the cabbie explained that the Melbourne Concert Hall was only another 100 yards away, we could walk it in no time. Tom, who was born and bred in Melbourne, would have none of it. He told the driver that as we had some heavy baggage, and that the Arts Centre was not the destination that he had asked for, he demanded that we be driven to the Concert Hall.

The Hungarian explained that he would have to go all round the one-way system and that it would cost us another ten dollars. The argument almost came to blows. I couldn't believe my ears. We had something like $100,000 in the box-office and here was Tom getting into a punch-up over a mere ten dollars.

A well-built stagehand-type came out of the Arts Centre stage door for a smoke. I went over to him and asked: "Would you like to earn a quick ten dollars?" He nodded. "Then take those two bags up to the stage door of the Concert Hall!" He almost snatched my hand off taking the ten bucks.

Tom, who had no idea what I had done, shouted to the young chap: "Hey there! Where are you going with those?"

The youth, totally bewildered by all this, looked at both of us.

"It's all right Tom, he's helping us out with the bags!"

The young fellow must have thought Christmas had come early. As we entered the correct stage door, Tom bunged him another ten dollars. I decided to stay schtum!

After an hour or so with the band, in the charge of Ross Lombardo, a very talented pianist-arranger, we had completed our rehearsals for both the matinee and evening performances. I still had not eaten since early evening the day before and I was desperately in need of sustenance. Tom sent out for sandwiches which were not quite to my liking and so I had two Mars Bars instead and felt as if I'd had quite a meal.

The shows were an enormous success. On the second performance I did almost 20 minutes of encores, then it was a rush for the plane to Sydney for the same journey as yesterday, this time in reverse.

I had eaten nothing except the two Mars Bars and some cheese and biscuits in the Quantas lounge in nearly 24 hours. Once airborne, however, the stewardess presented a tender fillet steak with baked potato etc, followed by some fine Australian claret — I wanted to kiss her. Incidentally, I still have to find a better airline than Quantas. I once mentioned this to a British Airways employee who remarked: "That's because they're all British trained!" If that is true, it's the pupils who should be complimented.

I eventually arrived back at Gold Coast to find that the heat-wave was still on, but assisted now by torrential rain coming down like stair rods. It was so fierce that umbrellas were given us as we made our way to the luggage collection point. Totally dejected, I lugged my bags into the arrivals lounge and the sun came out — wearing her biggest smile was Bloss. I couldn't say anything, we just hugged! We got home just before midnight and a cup of tea, together with Bloss's banana buns, was just right.

While she was in the bathroom, I retrieved a big red heart-shaped box of chocolates from my case and placed it on her pillow. The card read: 'Happy Valentine's Day!'

February 14th 1997

I must have been really exhausted last night because I didn't wake until a quarter past ten, after ten hours of almost solid sleep. I think I could probably have managed another ten hours but it was Bloss who made me wake up.

"You still haven't done anything about your back — look at it!"

How on earth she thinks I can turn and look at my back I don't know — I'd have to be a contortionist!

However, I did know what she was talking about. There are a couple of spots on my back which just will not go away. Bloss is always telling me that I ought to see a doctor since they have been there for more than a year now. I must have got them in Bournemouth because I never sunbathe under the Australian sun. She is right, of course, so I phoned Dr Snedden at his practice in Murwillumbah and he arranged to see me at 4.30pm.

After examining me, Dr Snedden, who is a very good doctor, said: "I think it might be a good idea if we cut them out!" Always wary of any remark like that, I asked: "How?" He explained that it was necessary to cut across the inflamed part and then dig out anything that should not be there and get it analysed. Seeing the fright in my eyes he told me that there was no need to worry because it was something that he did a dozen times a week and, with a local anaesthetic, there was absolutely no pain. In a trice we had made an appointment for 9.15am next Tuesday, February 18th.

I have always been very proud of my good health and to have something wrong which is beyond my control makes me really despondent. Bloss is absolutely victorious. "I told you! What did I say? Didn't I say it was skin cancer?" When she spells it out like that, I feel that I must be heading for the knacker's yard. Those spots on my back, I can't even feel them. They don't itch or cause any sort of discomfort. I swim and play golf and enjoy lots of fresh air and, at 74, I feel in good health.

Now, with a couple of sun spots on my back, a certain doubt has crept in, especially when the Doc says that he is going to send samples off to see if there is any malignancy.

February 16th 1997

Jacqueline, better known as Jackie, keeps the property looking ship-shape and is the partner of Dave. They come up at weekends to the property at Attunga Park.

Jackie is slight and slim, very slim. I told her a few days ago that if somebody punched a few holes in her, she'd make a very good flute. They do a good job between them and Attunga Park is their pride and joy. I mentioned that we would like a good job done on the gardens as we had some potential buyers coming with the estate agent next week, and Dave's face dropped a mile.

When I asked him why, he told me that he was so in love with the place, he spends an extra five dollars on lottery tickets each week, hoping for the big win so that he can buy the place.

I wish that there was a way that he could as there are no two nicer people than them that I would like to have it. The trouble is that there is about 30 years of hard work behind the place. Otherwise, in all seriousness, I would give it to them as a present!

February 17th 1997

I watched part of the Australian Masters Golf Open on television yesterday. There was a cliff-hanger finish by two new faces, at least, new to me. Peter O'Malley and Peter Lonard fought out 72 holes, finished even and had a play-off. It ended with Lonard winning the Golden Jacket, plus a large cheque.

Afterwards, Lonard was interviewed. He is new to the challenge of the interview and managed to get in about 400 "y'knows" into the two-minute interview. I think that it's very unfair to shove microphones under the noses of sports winnners, winners in whom the adrenalin is still flowing. To answer the questions that need preparation, they should be given time. It is done to tennis players, boxers, out-of-breath sprinters and all sorts of others who are unprepared. All to get the facts from the horse's mouth, so to speak!

Today, after some quiet thought-gathering, Peter Lonard answered much more readily and clearly. He had a dilemma, the same sort of dilemma that had confronted me when I left the RAF after the war. Then, I had to face the question of what I had to do to become a full-time entertainer, entailing living out of a suitcase, travelling hundreds of miles, sometimes winning, some-times losing. If you won, you were looking at the world through rose-coloured glasses; but if you lost: it didn't bear thinking about!

Lonard, a homely and honest looking fellow, says that he loves his family and cannot make up his mind about joining the International Circuit. He is a capable golfer and has proven himself in a field that included the latest US whizz-kid, Tiger Woods, who the gallery expected to set the game alight. In fact, Woods finished eight strokes behind Lonard in the Australian Masters, even though he has since taken the golfing world by storm after his amazing performance in the US Masters.

In Australia, Woods was graceful in defeat and Lonard was being honest when he told the interviewer that he doesn't like the idea of spending hours alone in a strange hotel rooms thousands of miles away from his loved ones. It isn't just a question of what the sporting heart dictates and I hope that he chooses right. Yesterday the crowd was cheering him on and wishing for an Australian winner. It may not be quite the same on foreign soil.

I remember when Tony Jacklin won the Grand Slam, he told me that he was happiest on home ground. That's the dilemma. Tony did something that no Britisher had ever done, and nobody can ever take that away from him. The one thing that no-one will ever know is: was he happier with all those trophies than if he had stayed at Potters Bar and never become the only Englishman to win all of golf's greatest trophies?

February 18th 1997

As the day closes I look at my back with the aid of a small mirror to see what Dr Snedden did to my 'skin cancer' — how I hate that word! I was amazed when he showed me what he had cut out to be sent away for analysis. Apart from a couple of injections I had felt no pain. It was all over in seven or eight minutes.

"Try not to get the dressing wet. Come in Friday and I'll remove the stitches," were his final instructions.

That was all there was to it. No big deal, just a payment of 60 dollars. I couldn't help thinking how much better the Australians have things as opposed to the British. Not only in medical care but in every other aspect of life. Houses are cheaper, so is food. Clothes cost much less and, in this part of the world, fewer are needed. Most people go around for half the year in shorts, shirt and soft shoes — and that applies to the ladies too.

Cinemas come much cheaper for the latest releases, so do CDs and cassettes. I can buy my own recordings at almost half the prices charged in the UK. Vegetables can be bought at the roadside and Blossom is in ecstasy at the freshness and prices. For instance, two kilos of freshly-picked tomatoes can be bought for less than a pound. Large corn-on-the-cob with fresh green leaves are usually about two dollars for six. Bloss pays double that in the UK and they don't come fresh from the field to the table.

Petrol is half the price and income tax is much lower: I pay about ten per cent. There is no VAT and the government doesn't get the luxury of the millions that have suddenly come the way of our leaders through the Camelot-run National Lottery. What a windfall that has proved to be for the boys and girls at Westminster. To see the millions of people eagerly waiting to give handfuls of money to the government each week — if it had been put on their income tax bill, you'd have seen those millions marching up to Parliament each week in protest!

I recall when I went to Portsmouth as a guest artiste for the Camelot organisers. It was a part of my job to congratulate the winners of the previous week's lottery. Some 18 million people watched as I showed the cheque to a syndicate of workers who had shared in the prize. Dressed in tuxedo, I asked one young lad, a factory worker from the Midlands, what he was going to do with his share. He said: "Get a suit made like you are wearing!" I really wish we had been in vision when he answered as I would have removed my suit and the dress shirt and presented them to him. What a headline that would have made: 'Personality gives the shirt off his back!'

We all have problems and life is never easy. For example, how do I take a shower twice a day without getting the dressing on my back wet?

Bloss is no help. "Take an umbrella," she told me.

ABC Television is like our Beeb — no commercials — and on Tuesdays they show past recordings of *Yes Minister*. I try not to miss it. The show has not dated as so many others do, and the performance by the three leading actors, plus the direction of Sydney Lotterby, is among the greatest work ever done by the BBC. What a loss Paul Eddington was to the world. Derek Fowldes and Nigel Hawthorne are so convincing, if it ever comes out on video I shall purchase every one because I don't think that we'll ever again see a show for television that is so well written and welded together.

What a stupid remark: "Take an umbrella!"

I'm off to watch *Yes Minister*.

February 19th 1997

One of the most revolting words that we hear, and one that seems to be spoken with a hush by the general public is 'paedophile'. These days it seems to be on most television bulletins, most front pages, discussed freely in the media and yet the public at large seem to shrink back from any discussion of it. When a person is interviewed, it is either in silhouette or a scrambled picture. I am amazed how deep-rooted paedophilia is — and why we aren't more vociferous about it.

In the last couple of months we have heard of a judge — yes, a judge — here in Sydney, named Judge Yeldman, who took his own life rather than face up to the shame of his abuse of children. Three days ago, the headmaster of a girls' school also committed suicide after he had been found out. It is very good of these people to save the state the costly procedure of prosecution, by either gassing or hanging themselves, but it isn't the solution.

One young lady thinks she has the answer by bringing out a book with the names of known paedophiles who have been convicted, but I'm not so sure that it would solve the problem. In the long list which she has compiled there is already a snag. What if innocent people have the same name and live in the same area? Men and women are included in the book, so it might be dangerous.

The 'do-gooders' are already shouting the odds, referring to paedophiles as 'sick people'. My own personal view is that they are not 'sick', they are crafty, vile, cunning and cajoling. There is a certain person — a millionaire, currently residing in South Africa — who the Australian authorities are keen to talk to. He has abused dozens and dozens of defenceless kids to satisfy his lusts. Don't tell me that he is 'sick', because he has used every legal trick in the book to remain where he is, safe and secure, and there's very little that the South African or Australian authorities can do about it.

No sane person can call these people 'sick'. They never pick on equals. Instead they woo these young minds with gifts, or they use fear to dominate, leaving some young person traumatised for the rest of his or her life. How many times do we hear of people, now adults, being subjected to terrible ordeals at the hands of these paedophiles while they were at school, or in places that should have been looking after them properly? It stands to reason that these perverted people would want the sort of jobs that placed them near to the 'market'.

Social workers are, in the main, good and honest people doing a great job, but just go back over the past few months. When you hear of the depravity of some of those perverts who have slipped through the net, the priests, judges, schoolmasters and others that we have always expected to trust and respect, we must put aside this claim that they are 'sick'.

Why am I up in arms about this?

Having brought up three children of my own, having six grandchildren who I love and adore, I never want anything like the things I've read about to happen to them.

Do I have an answer? Yes, I do.

My answer is to find a few people like Mrs Bobbit, the woman who cut off her husband's private part when he was asleep, then, on Tower Hill, once or twice a month, do a public castrating job.

I don't think that there would be too many objections.

CHAPTER THIRTEEN

Max The Heckler

HECKLERS can be a nightmare, especially for a young comic just finding his feet in the business. You have to learn to cope with it or you will not survive. Having said that, I know of one very experienced and well-known comedian who 'lost' it one night. He was working a club and was having his gags ruined by one loud-mouth sitting at a table near to the stage. He tried all the usual anti-heckler one-liners but to no avail. Eventually he stepped down from the stage, smiled, and strolled toward the table, politely asked the chap to stand up — and when he did, he shot out a clenched fist and knocked him out. He returned to the stage, apologised to the audience and got the biggest round of applause of his life!

I would never heckle! Would I? . . . Would I?

February 20th 1997
Boys Town is a charitable trust run for boys who have done something wrong and are sent away, hopefully, to become better citizens. It is costly to run and one of the money-making schemes they have is to raffle off a luxury home. It is a very popular idea.

Apart from the home, which is usually worth a million dollars or more, there is also a car, a speedboat, and furniture throughout. They also include running costs for the house for the first year. The raffle is run annually, and it is far too tempting not to buy a ticket.

A project like this has to be 'sold' properly. They have an enormous mailing list, with sales people at the home to be raffled. Potential buyers of tickets are bussed in to look around and dream. Then the salesmen then get on with the job of selling tickets.

A friend of mine, Ronnie Dines, a native of Romford in Essex, is one of these salesmen. Ronnie used to live next door to my wife when they were children, Then, when the war came, Bloss joined the WAAFs and Ronnie went into the Navy. Almost 30 years later they met again when we first came to Australia in the early 1960s. At this time Ronnie had a chain of hairdressers which he ran together with his gorgeous wife, Anne.

Ronnie decided to retire and gave up the hairdressing business, but then got restless and, for something to do, he became a salesman, selling tickets for Boys Town. Each day he goes to the prize home, wanders through the house explaining to the 'dreamers' that, should their number come up, they can move in without even buying a teaspoon, and sells his tickets. He has to 'spiel' to the busloads that arrive, explain how to fill the tickets in and so on. Sometimes he can convince a busload of Japanese, Chinese, Vietnamese, Germans, Brits etc, to buy bookfuls that can amount to more than 100 dollars a time, but he does it and does it very well. He peppers his sales talk with jokes — the jokes he gets from my act. He comes to my shows with a shorthand notebook and writes down everything that brings a smile.

Just before Christmas, Bloss and I went to Sanctuary Cove, the location for the house that was being raffled. We joined the queue of people and, as Ron did a joke, I sank down lower in the crowd and finished it. He had no idea that we were in the audience — or even in Australia — so he was mystified. When he started: "My wife can be an angel …" and a voice from the crowd said " …and the sooner the better!" he wondered how they knew his routine. He tried again. "My wife is a lousy cook! I mean, who can spoil cornflakes …?" Me from the crowd: "She can …she boils 'em …in the boxes!"

Ronnie stared all around quite perplexed. "Is there a ventriloquist here today?"

His face was a study as I came to my full height.

"You wicked sod!" he shouted at the top of his voice, and then left his pitch to embrace us both. The Japanese smiled benignly and thought it all part of the presentation.

That same evening, over a meal in a restaurant, we had a 'memory lane' session, paid off by Ron saying: "Would you mind coming down every day to do the same thing, we sold more tickets than we've ever done!"

February 21st 1997

Getting 'dressed-up' is a rare occasion here in Murwillumbah so, last night, when we were invited to attend the Twin Towns Theatre to see Charley Pride, a great country singer, we decided to put on some finery. Dinner at seven, followed by the show at 9pm. The theatre is about a half-hour drive, so Bloss began getting ready at five. I took my time in getting ready. After all, it's only the second time I have worn a suit since arriving here in early December.

Looking sharp and feeling a bit special, I called to Bloss that we ought to be getting on our way. She made an entrance in a dress that I hadn't seen since we attended the Garden Party at Buckingham Palace the previous July. It was a knockout! Long skirt covered in sunflowers, a white top adorned with smaller flowers, hair carefully teased into careless style.

"How do I look?"

I refrained from my usual remark: "Like a well-kept grave!" and told her the truth: "Like a million dollars!"

Off we went, all sparkling and clean, into the car with 45 minutes to make the half-hour journey. "Away we go!" I said, and turned the ignition key. Nothing happened! I tried again. Still nothing. The battery was as flat as the proverbial pancake. What could we do? Our nearest neighbours are miles away, but luckily I had my mobile and tried several numbers, none of them answered. My last hope was Graham, who cuts our grass and drives a large Ford tractor. "Hang on," was his response. "I'll be there in 15 minutes!" In 20 he was with us but, after ten more minutes with the jump leads, he told us that it would need an all-night charge. He pointed to the battered yellow four-wheel drive utility truck. "Why not use that?" He suggested.

I'm afraid that Bloss nor I received that suggestion with too much approval. We felt that we couldn't start an evening, with Bloss in her West End creation and me in my Saville Row suit, by turning up in that grease-covered, battered-up FWD. It was hard to explain this to Graham, a 36-year-old farmer, who had left the district only once to go on holiday — and returned in 48 hours because he was so homesick.

"OK, let me have one last go." said Graham.

This time the engine turned over. As quick as we could we were in the car and off we went. We duly arrived at the restaurant about half an hour late, but were forgiven by our party who thought we should have settled for the FWD! Why was that battery flat? Yours truly again. Last time I'd used the car to go down to the horse I'd left the keys in the 'on' position with the air-conditioning going at full blast.

The theatre was full. The audience knew Charley's Pride's repertoire backwards. The sound system was lousy and hardly a word of the lyrics could be made out, or any of his chat between the songs. He made the mistake of working to the first three rows of the audience so that the rest of the audit-orium felt ignored. Charley's performance reminded me to never forget the advice once given by Nosmo King. He told me: "Fix your eyes on the farthest object that you can see — like an exit sign, or a light at the back of the circle — look at it and mentally hold a conversation with it, that way you get across to everybody."

Charley Pride is a handsome, personable and talented performer, but he needs to be taken in hand by an 'act doctor'. If he did, he would hold the aud-ience and they would not be getting up to leave before he had finished his stint.

Later, on the deserted Pacific Highway, we came up to a car with the bonnet up, a young fellow frantically waving for help at the side of it. "My bat-tery is flat!" he said: when we stopped.

Knowing what he must be feeling, I took him to an all-night garage a couple of miles further on and he called the NRMA, (an organisation like the AA). They'd be there soon, they told him. We arrived home just before mid-night. I switched on the radio to get the World News. A record was just coming to an end. It was Charley pride singing *For the Good Times*.

February 22nd 1997

Today is Anthony's birthday. He is a little dejected at reaching the half-hundred. I had to remind him of a lyric I wrote some time ago:

> Don't be blue — don't be sad
> Be happy — be glad
> It means you've survived and you've won
> There are millions don't make it
> So raise up your glass
> You lucky old son of a gun.

He cheered up a little at that wisdom but I guess he feels like many of us do when the milestones of life begin to slip by. As they say: "Now it's all downhill!"

The day that he arrived is indelible in my memory. We had very little money, rationing was strict, we lived in rented rooms in Woolwich in South

London. I was on the road and that week I was appearing at the Theatre Royal, York. The snow was really thick on the ground. The stage manager had made me wait until the final curtain came down before he would give me my £15 wages, less ten per cent commission to bandleader Jack Payne. With my £13 10s in an inside pocket, my band parts and my few props, I made my way through the snow to York railway station to catch the midnight train to London.

I was with a pal named Art Christmas, who was billed as a 'multi-instrumentalist'. We made a last desperate charge to get there, buy a single ticket, then get aboard the milk train to King's Cross but when we arrived at the station we were just in time to see the red tail light disappearing down the track. We'd missed it. Now we had a three hour wait.

Blossom had begun her labour pains the day before and, because in those days we could not afford a telephone, she sent Kath, then aged 13, to a kiosk to phone for an ambulance. It was 1947 and the coldest winter ever recorded. Within 20 minutes Bloss was on her way to give birth to Anthony.

In the meanwhile, I was in a freezing waiting-room with Art Christmas, a Canadian, who had been wise enough to pack a hip flask filled with whisky. I can remember that flask so clearly: it had the figure of a St Bernard dog embossed on it. He talked me into taking a swig and I almost choked. I had never tasted whisky up to that point, and I have never tasted it since. Just the smell of it is enough to make me go hot under the collar.

Many years later, I was invited by the distillers of Johnnie Walker to visit their factory. I toured the works, feeling terrible, and couldn't help wondering how it was that Johnnie Walker was 'still going strong'.

My brother Harry, who looks a lot like me, visited Bloss in hospital with flowers and chocolates. They told him that the next visiting time would be the following night. I didn't know this. They assumed that he was the father!

About 9am I arrived with my battered suitcase and without a 'wash and brush-up' because I couldn't afford the tuppence that it cost in those days. A stone-faced almoner told me that I had been advised of the visiting hours and could not see my wife until that night. After much explaining that I had journeyed down from York overnight, that I'd had nothing to eat, and felt exhausted — and could I please, please see my wife and new-born son of yesterday — they finally relented, albeit bewildered.

I was thrilled when a nurse showed him to me. The staff had christened him 'Winston' because he resembled Churchill so much, gurgling and kicking his legs. I was now a 24-year-old father of two, a boy and a girl (Christine). The woman from whom we were renting our rooms told us that there was no way we could stay with the two children. Blossom, who was as strong as a lion and as determined, said: "Don't worry, something will turn up!"

I wish that I'd had her faith.

Incidentally, my sister Kath and her husband John, who are staying with us at this very moment, had to sit through the story of the ambulance and telephone kiosk again last night.

"By the way," I asked. "When the ambulance had gone and you were on your own, what did you do?"

She told us that she had walked back in blizzard conditions, over five miles, to my mother's place. That made us all compare the changes in the world from then to today. We all agreed that there was no longer any way that an attractive 13-year-old could walk through the streets of London at night and not meet with trouble — even below zero!

When I phoned Anthony with birthday greetings he responded in a 'little-boy' voice. "Daddy, if you really loved me, why did you build me a swing facing the wall?"

Thanks Ant, thanks for many years of laughs and understanding. Happy birthday and many more.

PS Your mother said can she stop breast feeding you now — she's beginning to enjoy it!

February 24th 1997

A man came in today to fix the video. The TV programmes get progressively worse on the commercial channels and it is almost impossible to watch. The ads come at you every six or seven minutes, and with absolutely no finesse. Just at the moment of tenderness in a love story, bang! A low-brow Ocker hits the screen with: "Have I gotta bargain for you! Git dahn and be a first! I'll knock $1,000 off the first customer — etc, etc." When it happened for the umpteenth time the other night, I just gave up.

It was during one of my favourite films *The Untouchables*. Kevin Costner was just telling his wife and child that they had to leave Chicago ...then on comes this oaf and kills the moment stone dead. Everything that the director, the actors and the writers had worked for and led up to had been shot to pieces by this loudmouth telling us to rush down to the showrooms and grab this bargain of a lifetime.

That's why I bought this video. Mind you, so far all the videos that we have had don't miss out either. The first 12 minutes we have to sit through trailers advertising what's at the video store, mostly in three-second bursts.

Modern films, apart from a few classics from the past, are all bang, bang, bang, so to see an old film with the story gently unwinding is both unusual and rewarding. For two dollars I hired *Citizen Kane* and heard every word the actors spoke and was delighted with a young Orson Welles making his name as the whiz kid showing Hollywood something new. I'm not suggesting that all this should come back, but surely being able to make out what the actors are saying would only add to the pleasure of the film. My hearing, I admit, is below par, but Bloss's is well above average, when I ask: "What was that?" she often replies: "I missed it!" I don't miss the dialogue in pre-1960s films, so what's happened to voice projection?

I began hiring videos a few weeks after arriving in Australia and, so far, my Top Ten favourites are:

1. *The Sting*
2. *Of Mice and Men*
3. *West Side Story*
4. *The Untouchables*
5. *The Scent of a Woman*
6. *Cutthroat Island*
7. *Serial Mom*
8. *Thelma and Louise*
9. *Unforgiven*
10. *War of the Roses*

I rent about three videos each week, most are forgettable, but if you search the shelves and ignore the blurbs on the box, you can have surprises like numbers two, five and six in the above list. I had not seen any of these at the cinema and was pleasantly surprised.

Usually there is a movie being shown on a large screen in the video store. Recently there was a screening of an adult movie: two naked bodies, heavy breathing, writhing and grunting to heavy metal accompaniment. Bloss gave it a glance and said: "Ooh look, Delia Smith on how to truss a chicken!"

February 25th 1997

I usually write these diaries between nine and noon, that is when I feel the sharpest. Some days I sit down and try to fill in yesterday's happenings. Some days, like today, I could fill a dozen pages with all that is happening, yet I hardly ventured out of the house. It was over 90 degrees outside but I couldn't swim as the doctor had asked me not to get the dressings on my sun spots wet. (Notice that I've stopped referring to skin cancer) It's a real set-back because the pool looks so inviting, but, the stitches are still there and I wouldn't want to upset the very fine job that Dr Snedden did, especially as he takes them out tomorrow.

A piece in the *Telegraph* is entitled 'Love Songs'. Apparently, a sex-shop has come up with a speciality: musical condoms. A micro-chip in the tip of the condom activates the sound and, according to the sex-shop, Bob Dylan's *Lay Lady Lay* is the current best-seller, with Frank Sinatra's *All The Way* a close second.

I do hope that Jennifer doesn't read this before she types it — she is prone to hot flushes!

It got me to thinking what songs I could contribute from the 780 that I have recorded and, looking down the lists, there are a few that could warrant inclusion. How about these:

1. *Fings Ain't Wot They Used T'Be*
2. *When You Come To The End Of A Lollipop*
3. *Ain't That A Grand And Glorious Feeling*
4. *Coming Round The Mountain When She Comes*
5. *Please Do It Again*
6. *I Can't Give You Anything But Love*
7. *Happy Days Are Here Again*
8. *Give Me Five Minutes More*
9. *A Couple Of Swells*
10. *Any Dream Will Do*

There are a few more that would fit a musical condom, but I really have to spare Jennifer's blushes.

In the same newspaper was a piece that is quite startling: 'According to research reported in London, as many as ten per cent of rams bred for breeding turn out to be homosexuals.'

Well, I have to admit, I'd already heard of Puff Adders but assumed them to be queer accountants. This puts a whole new meaning to the words 'Ram Raid'!

February 26th 1997

Today I kept the appointment to have the stitches removed from my back. It HURT! "I'm just having a bit of trouble with one that won't come out," said Dr Snedden. He wasn't too pleased about the redness around the wound and decided to put me on antibiotics.

As I drove away from the surgery with all those pregnant women, screaming infants and the lustiest coughing that I'd ever heard in one room, I reflected on the thought that just a week ago I had been in A1 condition. Now, a week later, after Bloss had remarked on those red spots, I'd had mini-surgery, been put on antibiotics, and had pain in my back just by touching the car's upholstery. All this and a few words from people who have never endured it saying: "It's nothing, just a little nick. You won't even feel it!"

The doctor said that because of the extreme heat, the perspiration enters the wound and causes inflammation. It was nothing to worry about but better to be on the safe side, hence the antibiotics. He didn't tell me last week, that he was going in half an inch with a knife to dig out the trouble. All he said was: "Let's have that out!"

As a perfectly healthy human being, I hadn't expected to be going through all that I've mentioned, plus a dressing that stops me swimming and to run up a medical bill. Also, if I had to have it done, I would have picked a better time, not the 95 degree heat-wave we were experiencing at the moment.

I guess I've been in a bad mood all day. A fax this morning brought bad news. I found myself thinking of an old friend, Keith McAndrews, more and more. Keith is a successful agent who resides in Preston and has a very attractive wife, Barbara. He takes bookings mostly for myself and Ken Dodd. Keith wasn't always an agent. In his early days he was an act with a partner. He was the youngest dancing champion in Northern England and then he teamed up with a girl partner and made a very good living as McAndrews and Mile s, 'From Ballet to Tap'.

We see quite a lot of each other and the story that he loves to relate is when, as a younger man, he had a very bad stammer. He conquered it later but at that time he could hardly string two words together. It was in 1950 and we were working at the Theatre Royal, Bath. I had a small Anglia in those days which I drove through the night to get home to Bloss and the family. On this particular night Keith asked me for a lift into London. Conversation was quite difficult but we managed to communicate as we drove along. Halfway home I noticed that the fuel gauge was on 'empty'. Garages did not stay open all night in those days, although some did have a bell which you could ring to bring the proprietor out to serve you.

It was bitterly cold, there was not a soul about and I began to get worried about making it to Romford. As we neared Beaconsfield I saw a huddled figure struggling along head-down against the wind. I pulled up near him and, forgetting Keith's stutter, I said: "Ask that chap if he knows where there is a garage."

Keith leaned out. "D-do do y-you kn-know where we-we m-m-might f-f-find a g-g-garage?"

The man straightened up and pointed. "J-j-just g-g-go on up th-the r-r-road …"

The only other human being that we had seen for miles and he turned out to be a stammerer too. Keith smiles about it now but, he says, he was afraid at the time that the chap was going to give him one for taking the mickey!

We have had so many laughs and his partner of those days, Barbara, his wife, enjoys all the nostalgia as much as Keith and myself.

Today a fax arrived from Jennifer: 'Sorry for the bad news. Keith passed away at 1.10pm today.'

February 27th 1997

A mighty scream: "Max, quick!"

I rushed up to the verandah to find Bloss pointing a horrified finger at something that looked for all the world like a stringy wet mop. "What is it?" I went to move it off the chair cushion.

"It's a hornet's nest — and I almost sat on it!" she wailed.

Gingerly I lifted the cushion from the chair and suddenly it seemed to come alive with the buzz of hornets. Not wishing the horrible things to make a bee-line (what a rotten pun) for me, I threw the entire cushion out on to the grass below. Then we rushed inside the room to watch from a window.

The air was humming with the sound of the angry insects. They came from all directions to see who had destroyed their beautiful nest while we stood on guard with a tin of Aurogard Spray at the ready. Bloss suggested putting a flame to the aerosol to turn it into a flame-thrower. I couldn't believe my ears. This woman of compassion was suggesting that I 'torch' the nest and fry the hornets as they lay there. I couldn't believe it. Was this the same woman who, just a few days ago, was making excuses for Dr Crippen? So I lit the aerosol, the same way that Roger Moore did as 007, and watched as flame shot out of the nozzle (don't let the kids read this), then advanced, military-style, to the nest, which still looked very much like a concrete mop-head. I gave a full blast, the flame cooked the nest, and I performed an exit that would have made Lynford Christie envious.

It was amazing how the hornets had managed to build a nest as big as that in a matter of two days. Two days earlier we had been sitting on that same cushion drinking our coffee. It is equally surprising because we employ a firm of pest eliminators to come in and spray a solution, harmless to humans and pets, which keeps flies, mosquitoes and other insects away from the house interior. Several people have thanked me for introducing them to Natra-Spray. It is quite cheap and needs to be done every six months. Apparently, according to the fellow who does the spraying, it is made from dead caterpillars and has to be sent from England.

It is amazing what we export from the UK. That's what makes me angry with our tax system. Someone gets a brilliant idea to start a business like spraying and eliminating pests. He gambles on a van and all the essentials, puts in many hours getting the idea across to prospective customers, borrows from the bank to get started and hopefully eventually starts to show a profit. He doesn't live on hand-outs from the government, but they sit back in their comfortable offices and take 40 per cent of the man's profit. If he goes bust — too bad!

The nicest part about writing a book is that you are a free spirit. You can think and say what you like, whether anyone listens doesn't really matter, it's just good to get it off your chest. Like today: more IRA activity in Northern Ireland. An informer has decided to blow the whistle and he is rather proud to tell reporters that he is now reformed and that when he was murdering men, women and children, he was young and easily led. He explains that his chances of living a full life are remote. What a ball for the media — those close-ups that go into the eyes as he sucks on a cigarette and tells the interviewer that he felt no remorse when he carried out those killings.

I think that most people in the UK are fed-up with the Northern Ireland situation. I know I am. It is more than 20 years since the troops were put in and it is a fact that £500 million spent each year in policing the province. As a tax-payer I want to shout "STOP!" You are no nearer to a solution than you were 30 years ago. Bombs don't make any difference — shock maybe for 24 hours or so — then back to despair.

Yet the real solution seems easy. The British Government pulls out the troops, closes the gates and tells the people to sort it out among themselves. Return in a couple of years when they have worked it all out, when the chaff has been separated from the wheat, and give them a hand then. There is a lot in the saying: 'A country gets the government it deserves.'

Most of the Irish people that I know are wonderful people, but just like those hornets under our cushion, they probably need stirring once in a while.

Here endeth the epistle of Max. Goodness me! It's nearly March!

CHAPTER FOURTEEN

Alice Faye — Alice Faye

ARCH is a funny sort of month isn't it? Winter's long, icy fingers trying desperately to cling on to every tree, every bush — doing its best to lay its white cloak over the ground every night. Spring, however, is breathing its warmer air, claiming its own time, and being cheered on by the daffodils and early tulips. In Australia, it's flamin' 'ot mate!

March 1st 1997

I'm sitting at my desk again, staring at the wall. A sheet from the calendar tells me that February is finished, another month screwed up for the waste paper basket. My desk pad with all its varied jottings stares up at me to remind me that telephone numbers should be entered into the proper book for future reference.

BSkyB shares were £6.35 on February 8th. Today they are just £6. Why? A pundit in America named Greenspan announced that stocks in the USA were over-priced, and suddenly every stock-exchange world-wide takes a tumble. They should listen to Bygraves. I bought quite a lot of BSkyB shares when they were £3.50 or something. You don't have to be a genius to double your money: all you needed to do was look around at the increase in those dishes outside windows of even the smallest of council flats, and you knew that Mr Murdoch was on his way toward another billion or two!

Personally I think that Sky is great value for what it charges in rental, just for the sports channel alone. Providing it doesn't overprice itself it should tempt anyone who likes a bit of a gamble.

That last bit reads like I'm some sort of expert on stocks and shares. I'm not, but I reckon that I'm as good as those so-called experts who take up so much space in the Sundays and on the financial pages during the week. If they were so clever and accurate, do you think that they'd be pushing a pen in some newspaper office, giving out information on stocks that would bring riches to others? If they were all that psychic, they wouldn't be telling the likes of you and me everything, they would be in some tax haven like the Seychelles or the Bahamas where their only worry would be whether the air-conditioning was working properly!

I have stock circulars in front of me with various 'great buys' for 1996. Today — this very day, March 1st — every suggested share, except one, of the promoted 14 is showing a loss. So much for one of the top stockbrokers in Australia! The High Street bank would have yielded at least a five per cent rise — and with no sleepless nights. I bought the BSkyB shares for my grandchildren so now, for the first time in their lives, they turn to the financial pages of the dailies. When their stock has a bad day, I invariably get a call from one or the other, asking: "Gramps, what's happening to the shares?"

I can imagine how stockbrokers have to pacify punters who have taken a tumble: "Don't worry, they'll come back!" or "The market is worried about a change of government." Of course, when a boom day comes, watch those same punters cover themselves with glory.

With all this gamble, the government still has the cheek to demand a 30 per cent Capital Gains Tax. If you happen to cash in on a winning share, then be prepared to part with 30 per cent of it. If that unfair tax were abolished, you would find many more people investing to help the British economy. The only way to achieve that abolition is to <u>stop buying shares!</u> I suppose you'll still find some guru in Westminster telling us why it must stay, and don't ask Denis Healey. He would only raise those eyebrows and say: "We did it to soak the rich ...Silly Billy!"

March 2nd 1997

Kath and John came for lunch and also to return the car. They left at 5.40pm for Sydney and I ran them to Coolongatta Airport. On the way the subject of mobile phones came up again. Between them they came up with some amusing stories that I had never heard before.

One was about a young lady who wanted to rehearse her graduation speech in the centre of the city. She didn't want to appear as if she were talking to herself so she got her spectacle case out of her handbag and held it up to her ear. Among the crowds of people doing the same thing with their mobile phones, nobody gave her a second glance.

Another concerned a young fellow in a posh restaurant who was getting increasingly fed up with the lack of service at his table. Using his mobile, he phoned the number on the menu and, when the maitre d' answered it, he said: "What about some bloody service on table 17!" He got it too.

When I was at Wimbledon, watching the tennis between torrential showers last summer, the mobiles around the Centre Court were going like tubular bells, so much so that the umpire had to appeal for some constraint. I really appreciated the story that Kath told about tennis star, Pat Cash. I don't know if the story has been embroidered at all but, if you know Wimbledon and some of the prima donnas there, you can believe all of it.

Pat Cash was about to serve, a hush came over the crowd and the only sound that can be heard is the breathing of the tennis star. Suddenly the muffled sound of a mobile broke the silence. Cash appealed to the umpire who, in turn, appealed to the crowd. Again Cash tried to serve and again came the 'beep beep' of the mobile. Cash scowled but this time got on with the game. After the match Cash reaches for a towel from his bag and a small black object fell out — the noise had been coming from his own phone! Needless to say, Cash slipped the phone back into the bag until there was a more appropriate time for him to own up.

Apparently the newspapers often quote instances of mobile phone users walking into plate glass windows, but one unfortunate user actually died when he walked into a tree! *To Think That I Will Never See — A Poem Lovely As A Tree*, was not played at the funeral service.

March 3rd 1997

One of the comedy sketches that I feature now and then is where I compare myself to singer Tom Jones.

"…the women rush down to the stage just to reach out and touch him …they throw their stockings, bras and — *(furtive look toward the wings)* —

knickers up on to the stage! Of course, I attract a different sort of audience. I was singing at a concert last night and I got three pension books and a hearing aid …."

It all goes down well.

The truth is that many people in the audience use me as their yardstick. If I look healthy, energetic and 'with it' then they gauge themselves on <u>their</u> age. They know that I've been around for 500 years or so. Not many of them seem to work out that when I, or anyone else, walks out on stage, we are helped by the make-up of Max Factor, the spotlights and an expensive tailor. If what they see and hear is pleasant then you are halfway home even before the orchestra has played your entrance music.

Quite a few of the audience are genuine fans. They travel long distances, especially in Australia. They also write long letters telling about when they first saw you, who they were with, how much they paid for their seat and asking if you will sign a photograph or dedicate a song to them and so on.

Let me tell you about Peggy. She has been writing as a fan for several years. She lives in Adelaide, South Australia. Her letters are always cheerful and articulate and say that she has either seen me in an old movie, or spotted something in one of the English papers about me. On a number of occasions she has written to Desmond Zwar, one of the columnists of the overseas *Daily Mail*, to ask if he knows when I am coming to Australia again, or if he can trace a song that I have recorded in the past. She is younger than me by a few years but swoons like a Tom Jones devotee.

Until today, the last time that I heard from Peggy was when she told me that her son had treated her to a trip to see me at the Melbourne Concert Hall, a distance of some 500 miles for her. Both performances were sold out but he had managed to get the last two tickets. Her glowing letter described how much she had enjoyed the performance and how sad she was that she would not see me again until I possibly played Adelaide. She also lamented that she would love to see the green grass of England once again before her number was called but, alas, the finances just would not allow it.

Today she sent me a fax: 'The phone went and it was my husband who said: "Are you sitting down? Have I got some news for you!" …' The fax went on to say that Peggy Boakes of Adelaide had won the lottery — not only the cash, but a luxury house, plus an extra prize of a choice of nine cars!

I have never spoken to Peggy personally but I dialled her number anyway. Putting on my Ockers Australian 'common-as-muck' voice, I said: "G'day Peg, congratulations!" She had no idea who was speaking. I went on: "…listen Peg, I'm your long-lost relative and nah you've got a nice big house I was thinkin' of comin' to live with yer!" She was totally bewildered by this awful yobbo at the other end of the phone and I couldn't keep it up. I told her that it was Max Bygraves calling. There was a gasp followed by an eternity of silence, and I wondered if I had gone too far. When she came back down to earth we chatted and she then told me that she was booking to see me at my next venue, which is at the Gold Coast, over 1,000 miles from Adelaide. To hell with the expense!

You hear many sad stories of lottery winners coming to grief but it seems to have made Peggy Boakes 16 years old again.

The story doesn't end there. The promoters are flying Peggy to Coolong-atta to see the house which she has won …a real surprise because Coolongatta is only about 20 minutes from my property. Who do you think will be presenting Peggy with her cheque, the keys to her new house and the car ignition etc etc?

"Moi!" as Miss Piggy would say.

Peggy Boakes knows nothing of this so, if the *Gold Coast Daily News* and the TV channels record: 'Lottery winner has heart attack!' — you'll know why.

March 4th 1997

I arrived at the doctor's surgery to have my dressing removed and had to sit in a crowded waiting room with a lot of sick people. By 11.30am, half-an-hour after my appointment, I began to feel a little uptight. A teenage girl was coughing and coughing without putting a handkerchief to her mouth, a baby in a push-chair with a runny nose was also coughing. A group of sorry-looking elderly people with dressings on their legs made me think that maybe I shouldn't be there. In a couple of days I had to leave for a series of nine concerts in Sydney. I figured that if I stayed here much longer I would end up coughing and spluttering like all these other people around me. By 11.35am, and still with no attention, I decided to leave. I made my apologies to the receptionist and told her that I had an appointment.

I couldn't help wondering how the doctors and nurses managed to stay immune from all that disease that must pollute the air in any medical centre with all the different cases that come in daily.

When I got back home I got Bloss to remove the dressings, bathe the wounds in some Dettol and then put on some antiseptic cream. I don't know if I'm doing the right thing but I would rather take my chances with a little common sense than risk picking up the flavour of the month in the doctor's waiting room.

We decided to go and see the film *Evita* this afternoon. Having heard many mixed comments about it, we decided to go and see for ourselves. The first unfavourable thing about it was the price of admission. That doesn't worry me too much because apparently, according to the publicity, the film cost many millions to make and we will be able to watch it in air-conditioned comfort for the best part of three hours. My seven dollars for a ticket seems to be pretty good value — and if I owned up to being a pensioner, the admission would have been cut by half. Also we are watching the work of some very skilled people. Alan Parker knows his way around a movie camera. Madonna *may* be a good choice, and both Sir Andrew Lloyd Webber and Tim Rice have a pedigree that is envied by many.

I remember, back in June 1978, seeing the opening night of the stage success *Evita*, and dropping a line of congratulation to Elaine Paige for her superb performance. If the film has only half the effect of that night in London, I will have had a great evening.

Incidentally, on that particular night I sat next to Cliff Richard. After the standing ovation I asked Cliff what he thought. He said: "Wow!" Which, of course, is pop-talk for "WOW!"

So we are off to see a movie!

As we made our way to the cinema, my mind went back to the early 1970s. I was getting gold discs for my albums faster than they could be framed. It was about this time that Norrie Paramor brought a song to me which he thought might make a good single. I read the lyric but could not make out what it was all about. Norrie told me that it was from a musical called *Joseph And The Amazing Technicolour Dreamcoat*. The song, *Any Dream Will Do*, was from the show and Norrie thought that I could do a decent job of it.

I recorded the song and guess what? Nothing happened!

The British public were more interested in buying my singalong albums that were selling like crazy. At one time we had no less than four albums in the Top 30. Then came the news that *Any Dream* ... had become a big hit in this part of the world. A disc-jockey in New Zealand liked it, played it and as a result it became successful. It happened just as I arrived and so I wired Norrie that Lloyd Webber and Rice would soon be collecting some very nice royalties.

Norrie later told me that my success with the record throughout

Australasia had inspired them. He said that they were seriously thinking of giving up.

I cannot complete a performance here without including *Any Dream Will Do.*

The movie *Evita* was magnificent. I read a few critiques after the premier in London, not all favourable, but I thought it was great entertainment, more especially as musicals nowadays tend to be of the *Hair* and *Grease* style with which I cannot identify.

Evita, because it was set in my teenage years, was different. I could think of the goings-on in the 1940s and '50s. Alan Parker, the director, captured those years vividly. The way he allowed the camera to dwell on the faces of the peasants and of the elite of Argentina, made Parker the star of the movie for me.

Madonna must have taken direction very well and turned in a performance I would have given eight out of ten for had I been the reviewer. Jonathan Price rarely showed what a strong man Peron must have been, but it wasn't about Peron. It was about Eva, and that was probably why he wasn't allowed to dominate — the voice was a little thin.

Antonio Banderos as Che stole the acting for me — he lit up the screen. Jimmy Nail turned in a good performance, too, but seemed a bit inhibited by the surroundings. Seeing it on the big screen was a bonus. It will be sad for those that have to watch on video or television. I loved the movie and I'll go again soon.

Wednesday 5th March

The Bulletin is a weekly magazine to which I subscribe. It seems to cover everything and the moment that it arrives there is a rush to get at it first. Among its contributors in the past were Kenny Lawson and 'Banjo' Patterson. The column, '100 Years Ago', featuring items that appeared in the magazine a century earlier is always interesting.

A piece that caught my eye today was about a 'greenhorn' law student in New South Wales: 'When he entered law school he was told, and seriously believed, that the Great Seal of England was kept in a tank — and that the Keeper of the Seal was the man who fed it every day.'

That reminded me of the 'oxometer' that I once sent for!

Another piece that reminds you that things haven't changed all that much concerned a doctor of a century ago: '...a young doctor hung out his sign for a week in a certain township to spy out the land. He had 14 applications for criminal abortion in ten days ….' To think we are led to believe that in those days they were all working hard up a t' mill.

Today was the day for presenting the cheque, car and house keys of the fully furnished luxury house with a swimming pool and 'room for a pony' to the previously mentioned Peggy Boakes from Adelaide.

I was at the site at 10am, safely hidden behind the front door when Peggy arrived to find out what she had won. Her whole family was with her, husband, sons, daughter and in-laws.

She seemed a little in awe of the TV cameras and media crowd and was totally struck dumb when, at a signal, I stepped out of the front door and demanded: "What are all you people doing, trampling on my front lawn?"

Her face was a picture. We hugged and kissed for the cameras. It was rather like a scene from *This is Your Life* except that the tears were joyous. Her lovely family enjoyed the moment as much as I did.

It will be on the TV news later on. I hope they've got the story right. I hope the interviewer is not some cynic who wants to turn a genuine fairy story into some sort of 'message'. I've learned not to trust these people who have the approach 'anything for an angle'.

I had to leave early to get packed ready for my series of nine concerts in Sydney. Bloss still asks: "Why do you do it?" It's like I told her earlier: "It wasn't me that won the lottery!"

March 7th 1997

After almost ten weeks in the serenity of Murwillumbah, Sydney seems like a Grand Prix circuit. We took the Quantas flight from Coolongatta, which touched down right on time. The passengers spilled out at an alarming rate, leaving us bewildered — perhaps they knew something that we didn't! At the baggage claim, the suitcases went round and round until they had all been picked off, but of our three cases there was no sign. The other passengers had all gone and I felt that awful feeling of 'lost luggage' coming over me. I thought about the band parts, the stage wear and the make-up and so on, all packed neatly in one case so that I could take it straight to tomorrow night's venue.

Tom Spencer, the agent, had gone for the car and was meeting us outside. Casually, at least I tried to sound that way, I asked a porter what had happened to Flight 465.

"You're at the wrong place mate!" said the porter. "It's up at the other end."

Hong Kong in
1959 – no wonder they asked the
British to leave.

Tulips From Amsterdam gave
me a lot of financial pleasure.

With Sir Bernard and
Lady Docker at
Claridges in 1959. I
told them my father
was a docker… "How
interesting," they said.

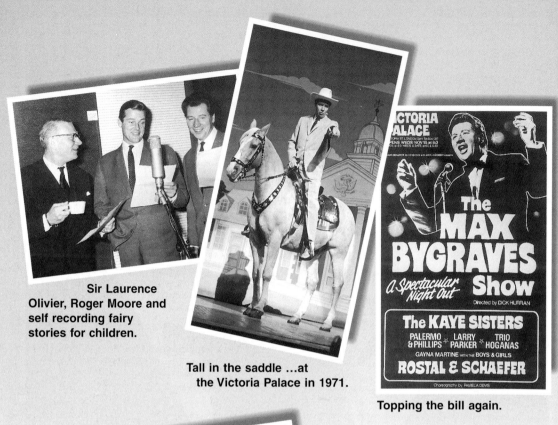

Sir Laurence Olivier, Roger Moore and self recording fairy stories for children.

Tall in the saddle ...at the Victoria Palace in 1971.

Topping the bill again.

The year is 1974 ...when everything turned to gold.

Love was a many splendoured friend – my old pal Geoff...

Sure enough, there were our cases, looking very lonely and dizzy as they went around on the carousel for the umpteenth time. With sighs of relief I looked for a porter, but, of course, there wasn't a single one in sight. Hoping that traffic control had not moved Tom on, we were forced to struggle with our cases and hand baggage to where we guessed he would be waiting for us. Tom was there all right, and the first thing he said was: "Why didn't you get a porter?"

With a determined-looking traffic warden ambling toward us I thought it better not to try to explain. "I was saving money. I've got a hernia, but I saved five dollars!"

We loaded the cases as quickly as possible. Two were quite easy, but the other was so heavy that I worried about the handle breaking: it was Bloss's personal case.

"What on earth have you got in there?"

She replied that as we were there for ten days she had packed everything that she would need. (Who needs six pairs of shoes?)

"Why didn't you pack the ironing-board and iron?" I was sarcastic enough to ask, but she was so happy to be in the metropolis that it went down like the proverbial lead balloon.

We checked into the hotel in Double Bay that we have used every year for the past decade. At one time we knew most of the staff by their first names, but this time there was not one familiar face. We went to bed rather exhausted and had no need of counting either sheep or Blossom's shoes, which would probably have outnumbered the sheep anyway.

March 8th 1997

It's good to be alive this morning. The sun is shining, the birds are singing, the view of the Bay is breathtaking and there is no doubt that Sydney has the most enviable situation of any city in the world. I think that one of Australia's biggest mistakes was in making Canberra its capital.

We get up singing and go down happily to breakfast. That's when the disappointment arrived! It's a long time since we have eaten, at least lunchtime the day before. I thought I would try some pancakes from the hot plate — cold! I tried eggs and bacon — colder! I asked the chef for two fried eggs, which were hot but watery. In the end we finished up with two slices of toast and coffee — lukewarm! And all this was followed by a bill for 53 dollars. We could have gone to at least four cafes just 50 yards away and had the same for six dollars.

I told the manager how disappointed we were and asked what had happened to the place since last year, but all he said was: "I'll see to it sir!"

We went across the road to the Roma Cafe — if you're ever down this way, keep that name in mind, it's really good — where we were served by two young students from Glasgow. One of them recognised me and asked for an autograph for her granny! That's when you come to realise how time is passing: once it was for themselves, then their mums, but now, they want autographs for their grannies.

I paid the bill to the wee Scots lass and in the background a tape was playing one of the songs from *Evita*. I joined in, but with my own selection of words:

"Don't cry for me Glasgow Rangers,

The truth is, I still love Celtic …"

She brought me a menu to sign, asking if I would write down the words because her granny had always been a Celtic supporter.

When I see Tim Rice again, I must tell him that I've altered the lyrics and hope that he doesn't sue me for plagiarism. If he does, then I'll never sing *Any Dream Will Do* again …not ever!

The first of this run of concert dates was soon under way and the audience became receptive after about ten minutes. I had worked out some new material on how nice it was to be back in Australia. Some of it is OK, but it didn't come up to the stuff that I have been working. It's not because the audience wants new material, but I try to replace some of the old for my own good, otherwise I feel like a talking robot.

There were some pros in the auditorium. I introduced Frances Yip, a beautiful Chinese entertainer who interviewed me on Hong Kong Radio more than 20 years ago. She hadn't aged a day. I hear that she lives in Eltham in Kent, when she is in England, and that she plays golf at Blackheath. A lovely lady!

Another personality, well-remembered by the crowd, was Ronnie Ronalde, a whistler-yodeller and a big name before he left to take up residence in New Zealand. He is still working and still 'wowing' them in the aisles. When I introduced him he stuck two fingers in his mouth and, turning to the audience, gave the most wonderful imitation of a blackbird call that you could imagine. The audience applauded, especially when I told them that it was the first time that I'd ever got the 'bird'!

Ronnie and I once shared top billing in a record-breaking summer show at Great Yarmouth back in 1951, the year my daughter Maxine was born. We had a Silver-Cross pram in lilac and lavender — the baby, not Ronnie and I! With the baby in the Rolls-Royce of baby-carriages, Bloss would stroll along the promenade as if she were the nanny.

One day she took Maxine out of the pram to go into a shop. When she came out, the pram had vanished. Ronnie reminded me that it was found the next day outside a fish and chip shop, but we never found out who had pinched it. After a few more reminiscences, Ronnie had to leave with his wife. When he got outside it was to find that his car had been stolen and he had to go and report it to the police. I haven't seen him to speak to since then, but I'm sure his car will turn up — probably outside a fish and chip shop!

March 9th 1997

What a contrast! I've just looked out of the window and there it is — heavy rain! The harbour is deserted except for two ferries passing each other en route to Manley. I had found it difficult to sleep and wondered why I was so restless. Eventually I put it down to last night's second performance at the club.

Theatre audiences are totally different to club audiences. In the theatre, a performer gets rapt attention but that is not the case at a club. Waitresses are still serving and in my case the audience had been imbibing for more than an hour while the dancing girls, the female singer and the magic act had been performing in the first half. There wasn't the 'live' feeling of a theatre and that second show had the feeling of a bridge too far. The audience were tired.

From the moment that I walked on to the stage, a customer right under my nose kept toying with a table mat, continuously turning it over and over. The rest of the audience appeared to be enjoying me, but this white-haired fellow in front of me kept looking round all the time. He didn't smile, he didn't applaud, and he kept looking at his watch. It's strange how, even though I had the attention of several hundred people, this one distraction from Snowy was making me feel uncertain. I found myself working to impress him, which is fatal, because your timing suffers in other directions. I finished to strong applause and I should have been satisfied. My sister, who had been in the audience, came backstage to tell me that she had never seen me better, but I could not get that clock watcher out of my mind. I hope he slept better than I did!

We went to a Chinese restaurant near the hotel with Lionel Abrahams and met his lovely wife, Nicky, most of his in-laws, his two daughters and the grandchildren, Indiana and Jake. When I first started coming to Australia, I would bring Lisa and Gina — Lionel's daughters — presents from England (how they loved the Harrod's logo!), but now it is their children to whom we bring presents. Bloss had found a shop that dealt in exclusive baby wear which she had had boxed and tied with pink and blue ribbons. The 'oohs' and the 'aahs' that came from the relatives made the rest of the diners applaud, and cameras were produced to catch the special moments. Funny how a couple of kids can weld a bunch together so strongly.

Because of the dismal weather we were taken on to an English pub, which Lionel thought would be a treat. It happened to me once before in Hollywood. Jack Benny took me to an English pub on Sunset Boulevard. I hadn't the heart to tell him that, back in England, we've got thousands of English pubs, and they're not all that great a novelty!

The Lord Dudley in Paddington was packed with young shaved heads and ear-ringed ladies. In no time I had two steaming hot Irish coffees put in front of me while two TV screens showed the Grand Prix which was being run in Melbourne. I could see Jackie Stewart on screen with two huge headphones covered on Australian Wool. Those advertisers don't miss a trick. Neither does Jackie. He hasn't been in a race for years but still keeps his name very much alive. Good luck to him, he works hard at it.

Back at the hotel Bloss and I had a serious talk on whether we should stay the week or not. The rain showed no signs of stopping which meant that we could be cooped up in the hotel room for the next seven days. I didn't fancy paying out 3,000 dollars just to be miserable so, eventually, we made up our minds and called Quantas, booking the 4.15pm flight from Sydney to the Gold Coast tomorrow. I will have to return on Friday for three more concerts but so what? At least I can roam about in 84 acres instead of being cooped up in a 16ft x 20ft room!

March 10th 1997

Having made up our minds to return to the Gold Coast we walked the short distance to Lionel's office to say goodbye. We were walking down the grassy central reservation of the road when we were stopped by a traffic warden who had been putting a ticket on a car. She asked if the car was mine. "I can't afford that rust-bucket," I said and, with my attention completely diverted, I stepped into the biggest pile of dog's pooh imaginable — soft and fresh. I tried to wipe my foot on the grass. No use! In Lionel's office I borrowed a loo-brush to try to remove the awful smelling mess. I used newspaper to remove the worst but the smell was terrible, a pong that followed you everywhere. I sat down for a coffee with Lionel but the smell stayed under my nose. I had to do something.

Double Bay has at least half a dozen men's shoe shops. I went into one and asked for a pair of black dress shoes. The assistant found the perfect fit at the second attempt. "Would you like them in a box?" he asked.

I told him no, I'd wear them.

He then asked if I would like my worn shoes in a box.

I told him no, he could burn them.

I don't think that he'd ever had a fellow leave a fairly good pair of Bally shoes to be burned and walk out in a brand new pair. I paid him 189 dollars and walked back to Lionel's office. On the way I met the traffic warden again. I told her what had happened and said that she should be giving out tickets to irresponsible dog-owners. All she found to say was: "It's not been your lucky day has it?"

Don't you ever believe that old adage about stepping into dog's pooh bringing good luck!. We got to the airport and missed our flight. Two hours wait in the Club lounge in new shoes isn't my idea of good luck.

Bloss did try to cheer me up: "Just think, it could have been elephant's!"

March 11th 1997

My time for writing these pages is after 9pm Australian time. That way, London is awake and I can talk to Jennifer about enquiries and go through the day's events. There is usually something worthwhile to jot down. Jennifer is on vacation in Barbados for two weeks with her husband, Paul. During her vacation we have diverted phone calls to Anthony down in Cornwall. He faxed me that there was an enquiry for a cabaret show at Gleneagles on June 30th, which reminds me of the last time I played golf at Gleneagles.

It was in the Bing Crosby Open Classic and, on the last hole, after playing a reasonable round, I took five to get out of a bunker. Crosby was watching. He walked over to the putting green, shook my hand and softly crooned a couple of bars from *Sand In My Shoes*. I was covered in it!

In that same tournament, a well-known Hollywood star discovered that Burt Lancaster had a better room than he did. Just to show his annoyance he threw a period clock at the wall. Some time before, I had written a song for Burt and Kirk Douglas to sing at a *Night of a Hundred Stars*. It was called *That's*

How Close I Want To Be To You. I knew Burt quite well to talk to. I asked him what made a star of X's calibre throw a tantrum like that. Lancaster smiled in that all-teeth-showing way and said: "He was just passin' the time, Max!"

It was at this tournament that I partnered Tony Jacklin, Johnny Miller and Phil Harris. Just before we teed off, Phil Harris introduced me to his wife, Hollywood legend, Alice Faye. As a teenager I adored Alice Faye, loved her looks, her sultry voice and the way she lit up the screen. As a young man I had read fan magazines and could tell you her career moves from the age of 16.

Born in New York, the daughter of a cop, she had dancing lessons and she also had this sexy singing voice which led to her being discovered by a well-known band-leader of the day, Rudy Vallee. He took her on as female vocalist and they toured the States. When they pulled into Hollywood, the band was asked to take part in a movie. The female lead was the mother of that great modern vocalist, Jack Jones, the son of Alan Jones of *Donkey Serenade* fame.

Alice Faye had a small part, but when the leading lady had an argument and walked off the set, the only other female capable of singing the songs was Alice. The rest is history: Alice Faye became a Hollywood superstar and, on that morning of the tournament, knowing all that I did about her, all I could say when I was introduced to her was: "Er, ah, ah, er, er, ah, ah ...!". She must have wondered who on earth this English moron was!

One day I must send her the song I wrote about her when I was in uniform during the war. I sang it a few times at troop concerts and also featured it on one of my television shows:

"Alice Faye — Alice Faye
If love could find a way
I'd hold you in my arms tonight
Alice Faye — so serene
How you light up the screen
No wonder I fell at first sight
If your love for Tyrone Power
Should fade just like a flower
Or if Don Ameche ever makes you blue
Just remember Alice please
Somewhere in the one and threes
Is a heart that belongs to you."

If our paths should ever cross again, I am sure that I could manage a little more than: "Er, ah, ah, er, er, ah, ah ...!"

CHAPTER FIFTEEN

Where Are My Shoes?

S INCE I was a kid, the silver screen has been like a magnet to me. Watching a video at home is great, but there is something special about the cinema. There is the unique picture house smell, the rustling of crisp packets, the creak of the tip-up seats, the pitch darkness except for the defiant 'Ladies' and 'Gentlemen' and 'Way Out'. When we watch a video at home, I get Bloss to walk in front of the screen a few times after it has started. It's never the same unless someone arrives late!

March 12th 1997

The movie entitled *The English Patient* is being highly acclaimed by the Australian press. One crit in *The Bulletin* advises everyone: 'Go and see it now, because you'll want to see it again!' He then adds five stars.

This afternoon we went to a comfortable cinema in Coolongatta where it was showing. There was a very healthy attendance for a Tuesday afternoon and not a lot of time wasted on forthcoming attractions. After an ear-shattering preview of a coming Harrison Ford and Brad Pitt event, the screen settled down to a sepia desert vista.

A bi-plane fell from the sky and we were into a story that unravelled slowly, unlike the three seconds we had just witnessed of Harrison Ford blasting away. It was so unusual to see in the modern cinema that it was a real pleasure to watch as the story unfolded.

One of the dangers in the direction of a great film like this is that in searching for some tranquillity, the director falls in love with the peacefulness and aims to lull us, then suddenly shake us out of it when the big drama comes. After about an hour into the story, Bloss and I were on the verge of falling asleep, but not from boredom. The film was far too good to miss even one frame, it was simply because of the peace and quiet that the story brings.

No big star names are featured and, watching the credits at the end, I could see nobody that I knew on the epic-making scene. *The English Patient* is a well-crafted, well-acted film. The only fault that I found was that the makers assumed that everyone had read the book, which I, for one, hadn't. Some of the flash-backs were not in chronological order and for me that made some scenes confusing. Nevertheless, as the critic said: 'You'll want to see it again.' And I will!

No wonder that the film stormed the Oscars!

March 14th 1997

I received a package from London containing a set of CDs. This was as a result of a request I had previously received to promote a good idea of the *Reader's Digest*, the launching of a five CD album of comedy songs. Three of my recordings are included in the album: *Cowpuncher's Cantata, Fings Ain't What They Used To Be,* and a duet I made with Acker Bilk, *Who Wants To Be A Millionaire?*

I feel rather chuffed with the illustrious company I keep as I share the album with names like Louis Armstrong, Danny Kaye, George Formby, Nat King Cole, Jimmy Durante and so many of the comedy names that made it into the Top Ten during the 1950s and '60s. From then on, the humour seemed to disappear.

Reader's Digest really do their research on things like this. I hear that they are planning Volume Two, and this before Volume One has yet made its appearance. I remember that they brought out a boxed set of my *Singalong* albums. People living in remote parts obtained them by post and I enjoyed the sales that were achieved by the clever marketing and presentation of *Reader's Digest*. You'd be amazed how many people of my vintage are afraid — yes, that's the word, afraid — to venture into the unknown realm of the record stores that always seem to have a heavy metal soundtrack going on quadraphonic. It frightens them away. Being able to purchase by post is a good way of getting the product you want without the fear of entry into an ear-blasting store where the salesperson is forced to communicate in sign language.

By the way, just in case you may be interested, the new CD package is entitled *Bring Me Sunshine*, and includes almost every humorous recording you can remember. This is not a sales pitch, honest. It's just in case …!

March 15th 1997 — Sydney

I took a stroll around Double Bay, known locally as Double Pay because of the expensive shops and restaurants. We lived here for five years and got to know the shopkeepers and some of the head waiters quite well.

I was alone on this trip. Bloss is staying up at the Gold Coast with Christine, our elder daughter. They get on like a burning haystack, forever laughing and talking. I thought that they would run out of conversation, but they never do. Today they have talked non-stop about a kangaroo that they saw outside our back door yesterday. In 30 years of coming to Australia, that was only the second wild kangaroo that we have ever seen. I told some people at the theatre about it. All they said was: "Is that so?" Yet Christine and her mother are able to chat about that stray kangaroo for hours on end.

I think that the 'roo' must have got hungry. We put food out for the birds and animals, so I guess this one must have hopped up to 'suss' out the menu. If you've never seen one hopping long distances, it is a sight to behold, so graceful. That awkward bottle-shape seems to disappear and you suddenly have Nureyev in full flight. I do hope that 'Jacko', as he or she has been named, comes back again.

The stroll around Double Bay was a pleasant experience. I was stopped by many smiling faces that I knew when I lived here. One of those faces belonged to Dean, who is the son of an old friend known as 'Hollywood George'. He died a couple of years ago with the Big C. He got his nickname from his stylish way of dressing. George was handsome and had a lot of style. He got his living at the racetracks and had a very attractive wife, Anne. Together they had three of the most beautiful children in the area. Dean, now 6ft 2ins, is due to be married in a few weeks and he was with his fiancee when we met. They'll make a gorgeous couple on the day. Dean filled me in on the local gossip as we sat outside a local cafe. I couldn't believe that I was talking to the same little blond kid that I used to watch going off to school with his satchel on his back.

The talk drifted to some of the racing fraternity and the Damon Runyon-esque characters that George, his father, had introduced me to.

One of these characters was called 'Verbals', and there is a true story that is always told whenever his name is mentioned. 'Verbals' was in a pub one evening when some officers of the Consorting Squad came in and saw him chatting with a convicted felon. This gave the officers the power to question, not only the felon, but also the person to whom he was chatting. When questioned, 'Verbals', who had a bad stammer, gave his address. "I l-l-l-live at t-t-twenty t-t-two P-P S-s-street. When the cop asked what he did for a living 'Verbals' responded: "I-I'm a r-r-radio sp-sp-sports c-c-commentator!" Even the policemen dined out on that story!

Liz, Dean's attractive sister, who I would have betted on finishing up as a model on some international catwalk, joined us together with her three children and her mother, Anne. I remarked to Anne that I thought that one day Liz would be famous. Anne replied: "She is famous. She's known as the woman with the three screaming kids!"

It was nice to see a happy family, still with that magic ingredient of 'togetherness'. George would have been proud.

March 17th 1997

Today is St Patrick's Day and suddenly the city is filled with Ireland's biggest export — people! Guinness signs have popped up all over the place and rosy-cheeked Irishmen in papier-mache green bowler hats are leaning on lamp-posts attempting to focus their eyes on the other side of the road.

Bands can be heard playing choruses of *McNamara's Band* and the pubs down at the Rocks are filled with young fellows trying to remember songs that their mothers taught them. Once upon a time the airwaves would play Irish melodies all the year round but, since 'The Troubles', we rarely get any of those lovely songs.

You would have thought that *Riverdance* would have united some of the 'rebels', but I don't think so. Even outside a pub one can feel a punch-up just waiting to erupt.

Christine came back from Dublin last week. She went to the same theatre that I had appeared in seven years ago and told me that she had seen two of the best comedians that she'd ever seen, but, like most people who have made a wonderful discovery of hidden talent, she'd completely forgotten their names.

Talking about names, my agent, Jock Jacobson, had a favourite story about a tailor's shop owned by Cohen and Kelly. A visitor remarked that it was a strange combination. "Oi Vay!" said the one partner in a strong Yiddish accent. "And by my life you wouldn't believe — I'm Kelly!"

The several times that I have been to that green and pleasant land, I enjoyed the chat, the blarney, the real hospitality and the surroundings. If only they would get their act together so that we could come and go and be able to spend more time with these lovely people.

The world knows that to walk down a Belfast shopping centre — as I have done on many occasions — is a lottery. The soldiers, guns at the ready, make a pedestrian wonder whether or not he will reach the end of the street safely. You do your shopping as speedily as possible and thank heaven when it is over.

I have friends who live in Bangor, just a few miles from 'The troubles'. They are a truly wonderful loving family, and I have spent many happy hours in their company. On my last visit, Maureen, the mother, asked me why there were so many Irish jokes.

"Surely we aren't as dim as the comedians make us out to be, are we?"

I assured her that they were not.

The following day I left to make an appearance down south. While in Dublin, I went into a large store to make some purchases. In order to pay I handed over my credit card. The young lady assistant looked at the name on the card, looked back at me and murmured" "Excuse me." She went over to the manageress and I heard her say: "It's himself!"

Soon, assistants were arriving from all over the store with scraps of paper to be autographed. I was flattered but quite embarrassed, too, and was glad when the manageress called a halt, with the words: "Come along girls, leave the poor devil alone!"

The concluding part of the story I still find hard to believe. After signing dozens of autographs, I was eager to take my purchases and make an exit, but the assistant, still holding my credit card, said in all seriousness: "Do you have any identification sir?"

When I returned to Bangor and told Maureen about it, she, equally seriously, said: "I hope you had your passport or something ..."

March 18th 1997

Things have got on top of me this past week. Apart from my trip to Sydney for more concerts, I have had an Australian accountant breathing down my neck for facts and figures concerning an apartment in Sydney that I lived in for several years and sold almost seven years ago. The flat had been in bad condition and Bloss had had it gutted and refurbished. She made a wonderful job of it before we finally sold up and moved here to Attunga Park.

We actually lost quite a bit on the transaction, but that's not enough for the tax authorities. They want bills, receipts and so on. I managed to trace most of them and suddenly the boot is on the other foot — I can now make a claim on the losses I incurred. Of course, the acknowledgement of that fact doesn't come as speedily as the original demand. I called the inspector at the tax office in order to clarify my position, but I am still no wiser. I'll let my man in London work it all out.

Tax and bank authorities worry me with 'money-speak'. I aim always to be free of that kind of worry and pay accountants handsomely to keep me 'worry-free'. I can never really understand why I have to pay tax here in Australia *and* in the UK!

I puzzle, too, over why it is that I have never been able to get a resident permit. How do people like Clive James, Rolf Harris, Germaine Greer and others, live in the UK and make most of their living there? Whereas, the moment my visa is up I have to leave these shores. I told my Australian agent that I would be better off in the Isle of Man. "Where's the Isle of Man?" he asked. I couldn't resist the old music hall joke: "The Isle of Man? It's nowhere near the Virgin Islands!" (boom-boom!)

March 19th 1997

A trip to Oasis — no, not to see the group — a collection of shops at the south end of Surfers' Paradise. There is a one-hour time difference between New South Wales and Queensland and very confusing it is too. I am appearing there over the Easter holiday for four concerts. The walk to the venue from the hotel is barely 100 yards but, on the other side of the road, you add an hour!

The people who travel from Queensland for the show are invariably late and in the past, the manager has often asked to delay the curtain because a coach was on its way. Nobody seems to mind, it just creates more merriment. When the late-comers finally file in they usually get a good-hearted round of applause.

In Oasis stands the most wonderful sculpture of *The Man From Snowy River*. On a downward slope, surrounded by opal, the rider is guiding his horse down into the water. There is also the full poem, by 'Banjo' Patterson. It is a magnificent work of art but it has one fault. The piece is set among an alley of shops so that the farthest one can get back to admire it is about six or seven feet. It should be viewed out in the open so that the eye can take it all in from several yards away.

Bloss noticed a poster of the bronze for sale and, as she looked at it, the shopkeeper agreed that the public do not get the real beauty of the piece. He said: "Not only that, but it's only in black and white on the poster. I wouldn't pay 12 dollars for it!" Bloss agreed with him and asked the shopkeeper how many he'd sold. He told her: "Only two."

"What? In a week?"

"No mate, in six months!"

I wonder if he ought to alter his sales pitch!

March 20th 1997

Today we went for lunch at Banorra, a golf club on the Gold Coast. For ten dollars — that's five pounds — we had a selection of three soups, a salad bar, hot or cold roast beef or lamb, dessert, cheese and coffee. Wine was £1.50 a glass.

I took four others and it cost less for the six of us than it would have cost for lunch for two at my club in London. Many retired people among the golfers told me that there were at least half a dozen other clubs in the district that supply meals at the same price, sometimes even cheaper. Now, if the British Prime Minister would only nationalise golf clubs and provide the elderly with this sort of bargain he would be sure to ride on a crest of popularity right up to the next election.

To become a member of these clubs costs about five pounds per annum. This gives the member free golf, free snooker, free table tennis, free dancing in the evenings, and free musical entertainment. If a person likes a flutter on the horses, the lottery or on football, there are also facilities which are no more than ten paces from your armchair.

It all works wonderfully well and, to prove the point, there are more than 1,800 of these clubs in New South Wales alone. There is also the grand opportunity of watching one of the world's greatest entertainers, but book early won't you? After all, I only come once a year!

March 26th 1997

Sometimes when I leave home to do a concert, I feel like a small boy going off to school for the first time. My wife usually accompanies me to the door and does a check: "Make-up? Suit? Socks and shoes? Contact lenses?"

I feel that I should be responding with: "Yes Hyacinth," in the same way that poor Richard does in the TV series *Keeping Up Appearances* .

Today, before leaving for a concert at the Gold Coast, it was: "Music? Straw hat? Towel? Soap?" After a series of resigned "Yeses!" I was on my way, thinking that I had bags of time. Roadworks at a place named Tubulgum held me up for 15 minutes and took away all that spare time.

When I finally arrived in my dressing-room I really had to get a move on. A quick dash of Max Factor, a quick brush of the tuxedo, a brief brush of the patent shoes ...er, the shoes! Wait a minute, where are my shoes? Ah here in the shoe bag, here we are ...erk! Panic! The shoes are white! They belong to the outfit that I wore last week. No way can I wear white shoes with the tuxedo for tonight.

A quick trip to the bandroom turned up no black shoes at size ten and a half — the nearest was eight and a half! Eventually Russell Roylance, the managing director of the venue, turned up trumps. "Here," he said, "Use mine. I take ten and a half!" They were a bit tight, but I thought that I could get by.

My act goes on for one and a quarter hours and, halfway through, the shoes were killing me. I had to explain to the audience what had happened and ask if they minded me taking off my shoes. They were a good audience and they didn't mind, we even had a few laughs as I carried on in my stockinged feet.

In the middle of the *Straw Hat*, I go into a soft shoe dance. Halfway across the stage I stepped on to a sharp nail and had to stop to remove it from my foot. The audience enjoyed all this, especially when I held up the tack and let it drop on to the microphone, showing that it really was a piece of metal.

When I arrived back at the house, Bloss enquired if everything had gone all right at the concert. I said it all went fine and walked into the bedroom to find my black patent leather shoes which I needed for the remaining three concerts. Tucking them into my shirt, I made a quick dash for the car to put them into the boot. After all, I didn't want to forget them tomorrow.

On coming back into the house I answered the quizzical look that I got from Bloss with: "Just checking to see if I'm OK for petrol tomorrow!"

March 29th 1997

Because of an eye operation on the previous Tuesday, Bloss found it difficult to thread a needle and so she gave it to me to do. I found that the eye of the needle was much too small to allow the cotton to pass through. She sighed that sigh which said: "What a jerk!", took the needle and cotton and walked over to the window. In one movement, she turned and walked back toward me with the needle threaded and knotted. "Where's that shirt you wanted altered?" she asked.

The dress shirt was one which appeared to have shrunk around the collar, or maybe it was because I had put on too much weight, I could never decide which. Whatever the reason, it needed altering before it strangled me while I was performing. Deftly, Bloss worked on the collar, finally throwing it to me. "Try that. It's much looser now!"

"How much do I owe you?" I said jokingly.

She gave me a kiss and said: "Can I have a receipt?"

I kissed her back: paid in full!

On the back page of the *Sydney Morning Herald* is an article about a gentleman named Ron Casey, a well-known name in the Sydney area, always in some sort of trouble or other. On one occasion he had a stand-up fight with a pop singer named Normie Rowe, 'live' on television. Casey regularly opened his mouth and put his big Irish foot in it. On the one occasion that we met he gave me a hard time of it. He is a clever and controversial broadcaster but, whatever is said, Ron will twist it to get extra time out of it. Unless you tell him to 'sod off!' you can find yourself embroiled in arguments that, with his quick brain, can tie you up in knots. It's best to get up and leave, like I did one night several years ago.

I had just finished a show in Melbourne and was sitting in the hotel lounge with Tom Spencer, having a quiet gin and tonic, when Casey, quite uninvited, sat down beside us. In a joking voice he said: "So, you're the great Max Bygraves?"

I knew that we were in for some heavy ear-bashing from this individual, who was finding it quite difficult to focus. In no time at all he was telling us why the British had no right to be in Northern Ireland, or that I should not be in Australia earning money and then taking it back to the UK. It was no use trying to explain that I paid taxes in both countries, or that, after all, wasn't he from Ireland and doing exactly the same. It was like arguing with a brick dunny, which is why I got up and left.

Today's article was about Casey shooting off his mouth yet again. This time his beef was with a mobile phone company named Nokia and he was having a go at 'that Japanese firm' for taking over more Aussie assets. On Radio 2 GB he ranted: "Look, I'm a PoW. I'm under the Geneva Rights. Oh don't hit me over the head with your rifle butt, you little Japanese PoW guard bastard …!"

There was even more reprimand for this 'Japanese' phone company Nokia. Only trouble was, Ron didn't even bother to check properly. Nokia is the world's third-largest manufacturer: only it isn't Japanese, it's Finnish! Oops!

March 30th 1997, Easter Sunday

Last night we put the clocks back one hour, stayed at some hotel in Coolongatta and hardly slept a wink. The air-conditioner was controlled by some digital thing like a TV remote control and we must have done it wrong. At 2.30am we woke up shivering and couldn't find the secret of turning it up. After several attempts we turned it off altogether, then couldn't sleep because it was more than 80 degrees Fahrenheit. By 5am we decided to drive back to our own place at Murwillumbah. All this was due to the fact that I'd booked the hotel to save a journey back after my concert. Things rarely work out the way you planned do they?

I was due on stage at 9pm, so, at around 7pm I ordered a sandwich from room service. Just as I was leaving at 8.30pm, the sandwich arrived. I was hungry and so I gulped it down and arrived at the theatre wishing that I hadn't.

I tried a few scales in the dressing-room to loosen the vocal chords and wasn't very pleased with what I was hearing. I walked on to a warm and enthusiastic audience, but I had the feeling that this wasn't going to be a good show because of that sandwich which felt as if it was stuck in my gullet. However, I went off to a standing ovation and was told by Paul, the stage manager, that I had been on for an hour and 40 minutes when it should only have been 60 minutes. Paul's darkened face told me that he was far from pleased. Forty minutes overtime with almost 1,000 people in the auditorium meant that I had robbed the club of 40,000 minutes of potential gambling time. It's my last show today, so I said to Paul: "Never mind, I'll only do 20 minutes tomorrow to make up for the time I lost you!"

He didn't seem to see the funny side.

March 31st 1997

We hit the road at 5.30am and I stopped for petrol at a garage with a sign reading: 'Five-minute car wash'. The car wash seemed like a good idea so I bought a ticket and went through, then returned to the forecourt to pick up Bloss who will not sit through a car wash because it makes her claustrophobic.

She screamed as she sat down in the passenger seat: "The seat is soaking wet!"

I looked at the offside window and it was down about half an inch. Not far, but far enough to soak the nearside seat. "I'm wet through!" she wailed. I told her that she'd have to ride in the back. She agreed, saying that she would have to change out of her wet things.

In the driving mirror I could see her dress down to the bare essentials.

"I hope nobody sees me," she gasped as she struggled out of her shorts. I slowed up and pulled over to the side and she asked me why I was stopping.

I kidded her that we had just passed an old hitch-hiker and that I was going to offer him a lift. That got me a swipe around the ear and a scream of: "Don't you dare!"

When we arrived, she told the story to Christine who collapsed with laughter, especially when I added that, somewhere on the Pacific Highway, was an old hitch-hiker who had reported to the police that he had seen a naked woman beating the head of a Mitsubishi driver as he careered down the highway. I added: "I hope that old fellow didn't get our number plate!"

We will have to seriously consider returning to the UK in a few weeks, something that we have managed to put off so far. Now that it is almost April, it becomes a serious thought.

A couple of days ago we had visitors for lunch and among them were those very nice Scots, the Krankies. Little Jeannette, who plays the naughty boy in the act, with Ian, her husband, warned me that a certain airline of which I had been fond had 'gone off'. They recommended Singapore Airlines, so I planned to make some more enquiries. Ian and Jeannette are well-seasoned travellers and know all the best carriers, so it may be good to have a change.

Jeannette, who only comes up to my waist, keeps threatening to give up the little boy character and retire. When I asked why, she replied: "I want to feel what it's like to wear a dress!"

CHAPTER SIXTEEN

April Fool

A NEW month begins, our last weeks in Australia and we mean to enjoy them, starting right now!

April 1st 1997

Ever since Richard Dimbleby hoodwinked the great BBC audience about the spaghetti famine, where the trees were suffering and there was little hope of the harvest coming up to expectations, there have been many attempts at April Fool's jokes. Most fail miserably, but one joke that was carried out here in Australia fooled many, and it didn't even happen on April 1st

I got just the gist of it from some of the musicians with whom I travelled. They told me that it was put together by a radio presenter named Ian MacRae. I have heard him several times and he has a certain style and humour that many of his colleagues appear to lack. MacRae held a competition in which the prize was a trip in a Jumbo jet that would go UNDER the Sydney Harbour Bridge. During his show he even rang Boeing in the US and discussed the possibility of a Jumbo being able to make a flight under the bridge. Boeing's spokesperson assured him that, with the right weight and no cross winds, the wing span could just make it. Ian also talked to a pilot and an air stewardess live on air. The joke was elaborate, it deserved to succeed.

On the morning that the stunt was due to take place, thousands of people lined either side of the bridge to watch. The TV crews were all there and sightseers had their cameras all pointing up into the sky. Six listeners had won seats to be aboard the Jumbo. You can just imagine the groan that went up when a barge came into view, carrying a huge model of an elephant with the six winners perched happily on it sipping champagne.

April 2nd 1997

I received the collection of *Bring Me Sunshine* CDs from London today. It is due to be released to the British public with more than 90 tracks of songs associated with some of the classic humour of the 1950s and '60s. They bring back so many memories. Apart from the artistes like Danny Kaye with *Tubby the Tuba*, Joyce Grenfell with *Nursery School* and Bernard Cribbens' rendition of *Right Said Fred*, it is filled with nostalgic comedy that will endure for ever. I'm honoured to say that there are three tracks by myself which I didn't expect to be included and I was pleasantly surprised by the choice. One came from the album *Max Bygraves and Acker Bilk Twogether*, which I thought had been lost for ever when Pye Records was taken over just as we finished making it. However, there we are, giving out with *Who Wants To Be A Millionaire?* on this *Reader's Digest* package and, pardon the modesty, it sits in comfortably with names like Jimmy Durante, George Formby, Arthur Askey, Louis Armstrong and others.

The week that we spent in putting that album together is indelibly printed in my mind. Acker and I met for the first time with the music arranger, not knowing each other's sense of humour. After a few hours I felt that I had known Acker most of my life. I loved his country bumpkin style of West Country humour, and he had a wealth of stories that had me helpless with laughter. He. in turn. enjoyed my Cockney stories and we got on famously.

It is almost impossible to travel anywhere in the world without hearing Acker's *Stranger On The Shore*. Everywhere that music is played, that tune will be heard. On this session, it was decided that I would sing the vocal and then Acker would play his solo, which is like a thumb-print.

I was curious to see how he got his unique tone, since many clarinetists have tried but few can get near to it. The only trick that he appears to use is that he allows the bell of the clarinet to almost slide over the microphone, playing with such feeling, eyes closed, and with the slightest variation on the melody now and then. It all comes out so right. There was no effort, no swanky energy, just feeling and concentration. Once again *Stranger On The Shore* was beautifully played.

A couple of years later I was in Auckland, New Zealand. Early one morning I got up to take a stroll along the beach near to the hotel. There was hardly a soul in sight, just one chap strolling toward me, throwing occasional pebbles into the sea. He was a good half-mile away, but as we drew closer together we both stopped in disbelief. Neither of us knew that the other one was in New Zealand. At 5.45 on a beautiful morning we were like two strangers on a shore. I couldn't believe my eyes.

"Acker, what are you doing here?"

Without missing a beat he said: "I forgot the ending of that joke about the shark and the squid!"

April 3rd 1997

Yesterday we were invited to lunch with our neighbours, the Bedsers. Shirley and Bill are our nearest neighbours and live about a half-mile from us.

They claim relationship with the famous Bedser twins of Surrey and England cricketing fame and, back in London a couple of years ago, I asked Alec, one of the twins, if he knew anything of them. Although he was aware that he had relatives in this part of the world, he had never met them.

Over lunch, we talked about our forthcoming trip back to England. I have 24 shows booked from May 3rd, when I open at Eastbourne, right the way through to September 27th. I told Bill that when I return to London, I invariably finish up with a cold for the first few weeks. That was when Bill talked me into getting a 'flu jab.

Bill is in the aeroplane business and spends half his time in Arizona. He is a keen pilot and before we left his house yesterday, he asked me to tell him truthfully, if his landings and take-offs bothered me at all. I could honestly say that they did not. In fact, I found them quite comforting. The reason he asked was because another neighbour, further out, was complaining because they were in his flight path. Had he been in the flight path of Heathrow or Sydney Airport, that neighbour might have had something to complain about, but Bill comes and goes rarely more than twice a week. Most of us in the vicinity of his private runway have the feeling that, in an emergency, Bill's plane would be a godsend.

I arrived at Dr Noble's today for the 'flu jab. Dr Noble, also a keen pilot, seemed not too friendly at first. Hardly looking up at me, he wrote out a prescription and sent me off to the chemist for the vaccine. When I returned to his surgery he asked for various particulars. I told him my name, address, and date of birth.

"You are over 60?" he asked in a disbelieving voice.

I corrected him: "I'm over 70!"

He put his pen down and gave me a long, hard, look.

"You look absolutely great, Max!" he enthused.

I thanked him for the compliment and then had to give him a brief run-down of my family history, which seemed to interest him. He asked me how I stayed so fit.

"I keep away from doctors," I told him.

He gave me the jab and I paid him 30 dollars. Hopefully, I will now be able to stay ahead of any colds or sneezes that come my way on my return to the UK

When I arrived back at Attunga Park I proudly recounted how impressed the doctor had been with my health. Ever since then I have had to put up with them all taking the mickey. There are jokes about Peter Pan, Dorian Gray, the painting in the attic, and how unfair it was for me to be holding a senior citizens card. Secretly, I enjoy all the ribbing.

At 74, with appearances throughout the UK in the coming months, a series for BBC, running around plugging this book, and so much more, I am not complacent. I just thank God — and I do so often — that I am allowed to carry on in a profession that I enjoy so much. I will let you know if the vaccine works.

April 4th 1997

There is a great excitement and much twittering around the house today. The reason? A new car!

A few days ago, we stopped at a service station and sitting on the forecourt was this eye-catching, automatic, power-steered, air-conditioned Mitsubishi estate. Christine could not take her eyes off it.

"Wow! That's the car I would love to own!" Her voice was wistful.

The reason she would like an estate is because Barry regularly delivers completed paintings to the galleries in Surfers' Paradise. At the moment, Christine has a small Ford saloon and Barry has a 1960s Falcon.

As the paintings get larger, so the cars seem to get progressively smaller and they have great difficulty in transportation. Bloss and I had been racking our brains for a birthday present for Christine and decided that the estate would be appreciated, and how! Off she went to trade in the Ford and today she becomes the proud owner of the Mitsubishi.

A few years ago, I could not interest myself in foreign cars. Having had a

Rolls-Royce in the garage since 1954 and owning several since then, I have always driven the world's supreme automobile. However, I must say, that having hired and driven foreign cars over the past few years, especially the better Japanese models, I am more than a little impressed.

My present Mitsubishi feels as good and as luxurious as my Rolls back in England, and only a quarter of the price. I am so impressed that I am considering getting one as a second car when I return. That's how I feel today. When I'm standing on British soil in a few weeks I probably won't be so unpatriotic. We'll see!

Now that they've gone off with the car-dealer, perhaps I can get on with some work.

There is a fax from Buckingham Palace, politely turning down my son's suggestion of a song to be sung at Her Majesty's Golden Wedding Anniversary in June. The song, a joint composition entitled *The Golden Years*, is a very beautiful love song that Anthony composed for our golden wedding. He did it as a present for Bloss and myself. I sang it for most of the year and dedicated it to anyone in the audience celebrating an anniversary. The words that Anthony wrote suited most anniversaries:

> The Golden years — each precious day I will remember,
> I'll hold on to the memory of days gone by,
> The laughter, every smile has made it all worthwhile,
> Life's carousel has turned around and left me dizzy,
> But you're still here — the way you were when love was young ...
> Here's to more Golden years — here's to you ...

One day I will record it and then perhaps it become popular. If it does, I hope Her Majesty rucks the Lord Chancellor for turning it down: "See what you've done? We could have been on Top of the Pops!"

6th April 1997

I spent most of today studying the racing from England. Anthony knows that I like a bet on the Grand National so he faxed me the runners and riders for today's big race. It caught on with the rest of the family, too, and they all wanted to pick a horse. After much deliberation, we selected seven 'winners'. I phoned William Hill and spent quite a lot of time on an overseas call relaying my fancies to the receptionist in Leeds. The girl with the Yorkshire accent read back my selections, all 'each way' bets, then told me my bets came to £146 and said: "Thank you for calling William Hill."

I then told the punters that they would pick up their winnings in a few hours time when the race was run. Some hopes! Five of the horses bet on were 100-1. In a race like the Grand National you never really know, do you?

Just after 1am the phone rang. I thought that it just had to be good news, Anthony calling to tell me that one of our 100-1 selections had just romped home. It wasn't! It was to tell us that the bloody IRA had been at it again. Sixty thousand people at Aintree had been herded from the course because of the threat of a bomb. I didn't know whether, on an occasion like this, all bets were off. But I did know for certain that the IRA had made another dastardly effort to bring attention to what seems a totally fruitless crusade.

When will they learn, when will they ever learn?

Since I was a kid in the '30s, this same fiasco has been going on. My aunt, Mag Murphy, would sing defiant rebel songs about Bold Robert Emmett, while at Sunday morning Mass, where I was an altar boy, the congregation at St Peter's and the Guardian Angels would sing *O Salutoris*; and an hour later half of them, including the women, would be in the 'Adam and Eve' pub singing more rebel songs. Soon Mag Murphy would ask my father, her brother, why he wasn't singing. My father would make some excuse and, in no time at all, Mag had got a glorious punch-up going.

My grandfather from Limerick, and proud of his Irish ancestry, was, like my father, unbiased about the 'Cause'. There is much Irish blood in our family as the names of my sisters testify. It was fashionable then to claim Irish ancestry but, in my teenage years, what remains uppermost in my memory of living in South London were the constant fights that the Lynchs, the Dempseys and the Murphys became involved in — and even seemed to enjoy.

That's why the Prime Minister always brought a smile to my face whenever he mentioned the Irish situation, looking like a beaten headmaster. He meant well, but it has to be frustrating trying to bring an end to this puzzle. As my father often said about political leaders: "What chance is there of peaceful co-existence in the world when even next door neighbours can't get on together?"

April 8th 1997

Today is the first time that I have felt cold in Australia. The temperature in Sydney was an unheard of nine degrees Celsius. I decided to wear the only sweater that I have here, but by nine o'clock I had to take it off again. We were back to the clear blue skies and birds, dozens of them, singing wonderful notes that can only otherwise be reached by the Spice Girls!

I got the tractor out and went to work on the grass. This isn't grass like we have in Bournemouth, this is 'grass-grass', acres of it, 84 to be exact. It usually takes more than two days to get it all cut and then the sun and the rain work their magic and suddenly we are knee-deep again.

The field that I was working on has many young trees, so it is not possible to make a cut like the Wembley football pitch, it has to be cut in small circles. The last person that I employed to do this was an absolute hooligan who just bashed into the trees that got in his way. The tree-surgeon helped to patch them up and now they are blooming again, although we did lose a few. I'm glad that I planted, with a lot of help of course, seven acres of hoop pine trees down in the lower field. I planted them four years ago when they were just 18 inches high, now, most of them are eight to nine feet tall. We presented each of our six grandchildren with an acre, all producing about 400 trees to each acre. I had it done legally so that, when they are all grown up, they will each own a small part of Australia!

April 9th 1997

I got a call from Keith Potger in Perth, telling me that the wonderful quartet, The Seekers, were banding together again for a return to the recording world. He told me that Judith Durham, the lead female singer, was singing better than ever and that the group now sound far more mature than when they were the world's best sellers with songs like *Morning Town Ride, Georgie Girl* and *The Carnival Is Over*.

The Seekers first came to Britain in the mid-60s when they appeared as a supporting act to me in *Music For The Millions* at the Winter Gardens, Bournemouth. Harold Fielding produced the show and it was obvious, even then, that their harmonies and fresh-faced approach labelled them as a group with exciting prospects for the future.

When we lived in Leatherhead, I once invited them to a fancy-dress party at our home. Judith and her husband came in one large pillowcase with just their heads and feet sticking out. They said that they were 'togetherness' and they certainly maintained that quality until recently when, sadly, Judith's husband passed on.

Keith had called me because he had heard a woman on the ABC Radio, enquiring about a song entitled *The Golden Years*. She explained that she had seen me perform it at a concert in Perth, had tried unsuccessfully to trace the record and could the ABC help? Obtaining the lady's number from Keith, I called her in Perth.

A warm voice answered the telephone. I told her my name and the lady, Mrs Ford, was in ecstasy. She didn't even bother to check if it was a hoax call because she said she recognised my voice right away. She told me how much she enjoyed my work and I told her that I would send her the record she was asking about. As the song says: "Make someone happy — make just *one* someone happy, and you will be happy too!" I was happy all day long after that call.

I also sent a copy to Keith Potger to use in The Seekers act. I think that they have enough old material to fill an hour, but it is wise to include some new songs too and *The Golden Years* is a well-crafted composition written by my son and Gary Forse. Who knows? It could be another big hit for them. I certainly hope so.

April 10th 1997

Suddenly the airwaves, the newspapers and the magazines all seem to be obsessed with protests. In Sydney there is a large student demonstration against paying for education. In Tel Aviv, rock-throwing youngsters are giving police a hard time. The one that surprises me most, though, was a 40,000-strong protest march by Hawaiians, objecting to the US occupation of their islands. One irate female islander was in despair over the way that the Americans have dumped 3,000 nuclear warheads on them. "Yes," she said. "You didn't hear wrong — *3,000* nuclear warheads on our islands!" That's why 40,000 people were marching to protest to the American President. They also wanted to return to the way that they lived before they became just another state to the USA, before their culture had been eroded, before the loud-mouthed tourist dominated Waikiki Beach, and before the simply strummed music of the islands had to be played with a heavy metal beat.

The last time I was in Honolulu to join the QE2 was three years ago. My hotel room was on the 24th floor and the only view of the ocean was through other high-rise hotels that looked like a row of rotten teeth on the skyline.

I can really appreciate the islanders' concern because I lived among them for a while. It was more than 30 years ago and only for a couple of months, but I got to know them all fairly well where I lived in Kanehohe, which is about a dozen miles from Waikiki. One of my dearest friends from those days was Aku, a radio broadcaster with Station KGMB. It's easy to remember because Aku was very fond of my recordings and played them so often and regularly that one listener felt obliged to write in and ask if KGMB stood for 'Keep Getting Max Bygraves'.

Aku passed away a few years back but even then, in those days when he referred to his radio station as the 'coconut wireless', islanders used to phone in to complain that warships, planes, soldiers, marines and sailors were turning Hawaii into a dump.

Ever since Captain Cook and his men first passed this way and brought sexually transmitted disease to these lovely islands, the Hawaiians have been wary of who, or what, comes there. After the Pearl Harbor attack of December 1941, they were lulled into the sanctuary of the USA, but now in 1997, they are beginning to think that it would be better to go back to the way they managed themselves, without US tax, without US dominance, and without feeling obliged to say: "Have a nice day." If you can't have a nice day in Hawaii and smile at each 'Aloha' then you'd better see a doctor, you're either dead or dying!

April 11th 1997

As I walked out of Cazzie's restaurant today, I saw a walking picture gallery. It was a chap of about 45, in swimming trunks and strutting his stuff. He had a wonderful physique and was covered from head to toe in tattoos. Totally unashamed by the gasps of passers-by who gazed open-mouthed at his torso, on which you could not have found a postage stamp space that had not received the attention of the tattooist, he strolled down the street.

This chap had pictures of snakes, sunrises, naked ladies, devils, the sort of angels depicted in Bible paintings, in fact, almost everything you could think of and probably a lot more! He was gone before I could get a really good look, but I found myself thinking about him for the rest of the day. I kept wondering what would make someone go in for that sort of graffiti on their body. There must have been a certain amount of pain and discomfort involved. And for what? Where does he get his kicks from?

Tonight I looked into my favourite magazine, *The Bulletin*, and at the regular article, '100 Years Ago'. Lo and behold, it had a piece about tattooing in the past. The article claimed that it was the practice of certain criminal types and, I quote: 'But it is also the characteristic of seamen, whose criminal average is only ordinary. The truth is that anybody will start tattooing as a pastime if there is nothing better to do. Tattooed people are idle people, and idleness leads to crime.'

It reminds me of the joke about the man who rushed into a tattooists and shouted: "I'd like my testicles tattooed!" The man who did the tattooing looked up and said: "Hang on a minute, I'll go and get my ball-pen!"

CHAPTER SEVENTEEN

Max The Gravedigger

THE tabloids have slipped up. Can you imagine the headlines? 'Max Bygraves becomes gravedigger in Australia.' I couldn't have sued them because it was perfectly true. I had indeed travelled thousands of miles and my circumstances forced me into becoming a gravedigger!

You see, it was like this:

April 12th 1997

We have very large windows and every so often there is a sound which reverberates right through the house. It's a sound that we hate to hear. A bird, flying full pelt, hits the glass, obviously thinking that there is nothing in its way. I wish there was something that we could do about it instead of seeing the poor things lying there.

It's the sound that is so unforgettable. As it hits the glass it sounds like a professional full-back taking a free-kick at the window. The whole place shudders and we mount a search to see which of the many windows has an unconscious bird lying outside it. Sometimes there is a sign of life and we are able to nurse the little bundle of feathers back to life, but more often it is the other way.

It depresses us all so much when we have this sort of accident, and it happens once or twice a month. At Christmastime, when the grandchildren were here, it happened. The tears flowed quite freely. I dug a little grave and we put some stones around it for the small bluebird, and that pacified the little ones. That is how I became a gravedigger and, as I said before, I wish there was an answer. We have tried most ideas. Any suggestions?

One very good tip that I saw on ABC's TV gardening programme, was to keep the inside of a boxed wine, which is very popular here. When the wine has been finished, blow into the tap to inflate the silver container, leaving it slightly under-inflated, then hang it near the house. The breeze moves it slightly and the mirror effect seems to act as a warning to birds in flight. It doesn't always work, but it does cut down on the amount of accidents. We have several of the boxes hanging up, and when visitors ask what they are for we tell them that we are drying the wine: "Would you prefer medium or dry wine?"

Back to my newspaper. There is a page with pictures of Julie Andrews featured in some Rodgers and Hammerstein hits. Julie seems to have been in the news quite a bit lately.

Last night the years melted away as we all watched *The Sound Of Music* on Channel 9. Watching Julie, I was reminded of her as a 13-year-old — all pigtails and innocence — in the radio show *Educating Archie*. Later, she became my leading lady when we did *Cinderella* at the London Palladium. It was Christine who reminded Bloss that she had bought an Elna electric sewing machine from a salesman, who turned out to be Julie's father, Ted. She still uses that machine today and it must be over 40 years old.

Earlier in the day I had been reading a piece in *Variety* that told of Julie having to back out of her Broadway show *Victor/Victoria* because of poor health. Customers had been asking for refunds when they discovered that she would not be appearing, and that her place was to be taken by an understudy. Liza Minelli had stepped in for a month, but the show was into losses, the insurance company was reluctant to pay up because of some technical hitch. With a lump in my throat, I watch little Julie singing *Climb Every Mountain*, and I hope that she is able to 'ford every stream'. It is a tough business when things go wrong but, when your health is good, you are usually able to surmount most things. So, Julie, here's wishing you lots of good health! Cheers!

Last week, as I previously mentioned, there were protest marches galore, but the one that takes the cake today is the one that took place down at Byron

Bay. Thousands of people turned up to see the nudists up in arms — among other things — to stop the authorities banning their use of a beach where, for most of the year, they sunbathe in the niddy nod.

To entice the public to come and support them and sign the petition, they have advertised singers, jugglers and a rock group — all naked — plus 'a comedian doing a stand-up spot'. As Eric Morecambe would have said: "Follow that!"

April 14th 1997

Peter is the electrician who looks after all the electrical technicalities of the property. There are quite a few items to be checked: security lights; that the quarter-mile drive is lit up; all the lights in the main house; the two refrigerators; plugs; electrically-assisted curtains; TV, hi-fi; and also the four chalets and cottage at the lower end. There must be more, but I dread to think.

Peter is here today to check and repair one of the drive lights which I brushed against with the tractor, fusing all the lights along the drive in the process. We always chat and set the world to rights, and today our discussion was about Tiger Woods, the 21-year-old who has rewritten the book of golf. It has shaken the golf-world which has become bogged down with the same old champions winning everything. Suddenly, along comes this young tornado and makes names like Nicklaus, Norman and Faldo fade into the bunkers. Tiger Woods has just won the American Masters by strokes.

Although we've had golf aspirants come and go in the past, this likeable youth seems set to stay for quite some time. Black athletes have won almost everything in the sporting world, but never before in golf. There are a few good players but from now on, just watch the golf courses around the world becoming inundated with young black golfers hoping to join the various clubs. I hope they do. Golf is the last gentlemanly game left, quiet and respectable with nothing of the yobbo element that has invaded other sports such as soccer, cricket, rugby, even snooker.

Peter and I agreed that perhaps that non-violence in golf was caused by the realisation that any golfer can reach for a metal club to protect himself. The yobs are never too fond of a fair fight, so a reasonably fit man wielding a number-four iron would be a bit too daunting for them.

The autumn has arrived here, and the trees are shedding leaves everywhere. The mornings are chilly and the nights call for an extra blanket, but the days are still superb. The air is so clean and pure. The house agent called on the phone to ask if a prospective buyer could come to view. Apparently it was a lady who wanted a property to turn into a health farm. Suddenly I felt quite crestfallen: I didn't want to sell. It will mean giving up the trees, the meadows, the creek for fishing and, although it needs a lot of looking after, the plusses are far too numerous. I wonder if I'll like the prospective buyer. If I don't ...we'll see!

To give an idea of the love I have for this place, think about this. Blossom has just told me that we are out of lemons. We have visitors who like a slice of lemon in their gin and tonic. So, I put my pen down, walk out to the lemon tree and cut off a small branch holding half a dozen fruits — Voila! If we needed lemons in England, I would have to get the car out, drive to Tescos, find a parking spot, queue to pay and then drive home again. Here, I walk two metres — and Cheers!

April 16th 1997

I saw the film *Jerry McGuire* from 10.30 this morning while Bloss had a hairdressing appointment. The movie ran for two hours and 35 minutes. When I came out she was still in the hairdressers. What on earth do they do for more than two and a half hours?

All this is in a large shopping mall, so I decided to have a cup of coffee at the cafe where we had arranged to meet. Bloss soon arrived, complaining that the new girl had used hair lacquer, which she dislikes.

As we sipped our coffees and feasted on excellent cakes, two teenagers arrived and sat at the next table. They were quite pretty girls, but both had rings through their nostrils and wore earrings that looked as if they weighed a couple of kilos. One of them even had a gold ring through her lip. They were wearing long black dresses, no make-up and had multi-coloured hair. One of them bent to pick up a paper serviette and, as she did, a young fellow zoomed past on a skateboard, missing her by inches. She straightened up and turned to her friend, saying, and I swear that this is true: "Jeeze, there are some freaks about!"

April 17th 1997

We're going to the Gold Coast Arts Theatre this evening. It is one of the classiest theatres in Australia and we are going for two reasons. One is to see and hear the maestro of the harmonica, Larry Adler, and the second is that I have been offered an engagement there for next January.

I would like to appear there but, at the same time, I want to size up the auditorium. I am at the stage in life where I don't want 'worries'. I want to see if the sound system is OK, if the lighting works, if the seats are comfortable and if the management is good with box office, publicity and PR. I also want to check if the audience is of the type that would find my sort of entertainment to their liking. Throughout my career I have managed to adapt to audiences and, although some are harder than others to win over, I have never yet failed. Or, perhaps more to the point, I have never lost money for the promoter. Yes, I would like to work there. After all, the rain is warmer there than in the UK!

I have never before seen Larry Adler in action on stage, even though we did work together in the movie that I starred in entitled *A Cry From The Streets*. I know that he is a superb musician and a first-rate raconteur with a wealth of anecdotes. This is the sort of entertainment that I really enjoy.

I will probably meet with him after the show and ask him about a certain story. I want to know if it is true or if it has been embellished over the years of telling. The story crops up now and then and it makes me curious.

The story is that, many years ago, when Larry was appearing at a certain theatre in London, the queue was long and paying high prices to get in and see the virtuoso. As a stunt, Larry dressed in an old raincoat and cap with a woollen scarf to hide his tuxedo. Then he went out to the queue playing several popular melodies as they shuffled along. Then he went around with the hat. The people paying top prices to get in to see one of the highest-paid performers in showbusiness dropped a few coins into the 'old man's' hat. When Larry got back to his dressing-room he counted out his 'take': it came to sevenpence.

We got to the Arts Theatre where four seats had been left at the box-office by promoter Andrew McKinnon. We settled down for an evening of rare entertainment.

The lights dimmed down for the entrance of Bernard Walz, a young 6ft 6ins pianist who fools the audience with a classical 16 bars and then segues into an arrangement of piano pops, ragtime, boogie and honest-to-goodness piano playing. Thunderous applause acknowledged his tremendous playing and he left the stage with a winning smile, re-emerging from the wings, moments later, with the star of the evening, Larry Adler.

Larry was never a big fellow, and standing beside the giant frame of Bernard Walz he seemed even smaller. He acknowledged the warm applause and informed the audience that he was: "Happy to be here — at my age, I'm happy to be anywhere!"

Larry didn't mention his age, but most of us have known him all our lives and knew that he must be in his 80s. After some good-natured patter, he sat down in an armchair and filled the evening with classics from the great composers: Irving Berlin, Duke Ellington, Hoagy Carmichael and a generous helping of Gershwin, all broken up with chat from his long experience in showbusiness. He told us of his meeting with Ravel, and how he was permitted to include the *Bolero* free for perpetuity; and of his black-listed days in the USA. He had so many anecdotes, all delivered with economy and, almost all, with a big laugh pay-off.

Genevieve Davis, a very experienced vocalist, broke up the music and chat with a series of songs which Larry filled in with. Her rendition of *I Get A Kick Out Of You* got a tremendous reception.

With Craig Scott on bass and David Jones on drums, the crowd really enjoyed the programme, but saved their standing ovation for Larry's penultimate offering of Gershwin's *Rhapsody In Blue*. It was quite moving to see this octogenarian shuffle modestly from the wings to take his bow for this fantastic accolade.

Then came the unexpected finale: *The Gettysburg Address*, with words spoken by Ingrid Bergman, Larry accompanying the words with a powerful *Battle Hymn Of The Republic*. The lights were slowly dimmed to a final blackout — sheer magic!

The evening's entertainment was over and every one of us in that audience knew that we had just witnessed a culmination of talent that had been welded together wonderfully and professionally for our entertainment. It will remain a memorable experience for all of us.

We were treated to even more stories in Larry's dressing-room after the show, not to mention the generous vodkas and tonic! One story, well, not a story really, more of an aside, was that when Larry had been appearing at the Sydney Opera House a few nights previously, his daughter had flown out from London to attend. Larry was quite moved by this and thought that it was one of the nicest things he had experienced in his lifetime.

Before we left, I asked Larry about that story of him playing the queue and earning sevenpence. He said that it was perfectly true and that it happened outside the Holborn Empire in London. I might have guessed that it would have to be the Holborn Empire! There was only one thing wrong with the version that I had heard. Larry told me that the 'take' was more than seven-pence — it was ninepence. Just like a pro, pushing his salary up, even in those days.

Good health Larry, and thanks for a great evening ...Cheers!

April 18th 1997

My son-in-law Barry and I decided that we would have a game of golf, so I called the steward at Banorra who made us most welcome. He told us to be on the course at 1.45pm and we arrived promptly. The club pro, also named Barry, lent us his golf cart and off we went to the first tee.

A full round in a golf cart usually takes about three hours. Not today it didn't! Two games of four players each were already waiting to tee-off when we got there. Twenty-five minutes later we managed to drive two straight balls up the fairway, then we had to wait again for the chaps in front as they searched for a lost ball. To make a long story even longer, by the time we reached the ninth hole we had been 'playing' for two hours and 40 minutes. It was very hot and so we decided to call it a day, put the clubs in the car, have a cold beer, and be happy to have played nine holes instead of the 18.

It will be my last game in Australia. I leave here next Wednesday and, with a four-day stop-over in Singapore to see Alex McColl and Marie, we head for London. A few days after that I start my lengthy tour of the UK. Some of the dates I have played and enjoyed before, like Bath, Sutton and Eastbourne, but at least half are new to me. Let's hope that they are decent venues. I say this because as a visiting artiste, these 'inexperienced' dates can be a nightmare. I have been through it all before. For instance, the first smack in the eye can be that there is no parking space reserved. Then Bert, our driver, will have to scout the streets hoping to find a convenient spot. And that ain't easy folks. Not for a Rolls it ain't!

The musicians and the supporting acts have taken all the best parking spaces, the band rehearsal has been cut short because the lads want to go and have a meal, somebody has forgotten to turn on the hot water in the dressing-rooms, the stage manager doesn't have a stool for me to sit on during my act, my pianist isn't happy because the piano has not been tuned, the lighting technician asks for a lighting plot — and when you give it to him you know that there is 'nobody at home' when you look into his eyes, and so you settle for 'keep it bright when I'm talking, fade down for the songs, and then snap it up at the finish'. It invariably turns out wrong.

The worst nightmare is to walk on stage to a generous reception and say: "Good evening ...", then realise that you are speaking into a dead microphone which a technician has forgotten to switch on. Instead of a smiling entrance, your face shows the panic. You tap the microphone, hoping that the sound man will hear and hasn't left to have a cigarette.

It has happened to me so many times in the past and is bound to happen a few more times yet before 'I face the final curtain'. Once it happened at the Philharmonic Auditorium in Los Angeles where I was appearing with Judy Garland. It was 1951 and I wasn't as experienced in those days. I had received a few compliments in the daily press and so there I was, with a big smile, in this gigantic auditorium all ready to turn it on for the expectant American audience, expectant for Judy Garland that is!

As far as most of them were concerned, they could have done away with all the supporting acts. It was a matinee performance and as soon as I said: "Good afternoon," I knew that the amplification wasn't on. I tapped the microphone and a gleeful voice from the front row shouted: "It ain't on, we can't hear ya!" Luckily I am endowed with a good set of lungs and, even without a mike, can make myself heard. Not for long, but enough to let the packed audience know that it wasn't my fault. I picked up the lead and walked toward the wings; when I got to the corner, I held it up to the unseen stage manager and shouted: "Can somebody put a quarter in the meter?" Then, still holding the lead, I walked back to centre stage, leaned into the mike and said: "Hello, hello ...!" It was on and the audience applauded.

I have often wondered what I would have done if it had not come alive, because for an unknown performer with an English accent, trying to get across to an all-American audience is no easy feat. I saw it happen to Danny Kaye at the London Palladium, but he had a good idea that amused the packed house. He walked to the wings, picked up the stage manager's cup of tea, sat on the front of the stage and quietly sang *Minnie The Moocher*. The audience replied with: "Hi de hi de hi," and so on. When he was through the sound was on once more.

It takes years to learn these tricks and, nowadays, I have quite a few up my sleeve in case of emergency. The one that I don't use is the one that one exasperated female American star, who shall remain nameless, used when confronted by a dead microphone. She shouted: "Shit! The f****** sound is off! And so am I!"

She then left the stage and didn't return until it was fixed.

April 22nd 1997

I must have used dozens of writing pads, and refilled my pen countless times, but this is my last day in Australia and tomorrow, when I leave for Singapore, will be the first day that I haven't sat down to write out the jottings on those pages. I expect Jennifer will be relieved. I will be sorry in many ways because it has been good to make something out of each day's events. Jennifer received the faxes, sent from Australia at 11pm — Australia time — and then sets them up to make them readable. A fax from her yesterday warned me that it has turned wintry again in London — and that the IRA have caused more havoc which will probably go on until the General Election.

We ran out of milk today. When I drove to the local store, Geoff, the boss, said: "How come you blokes defeat the Germans, wrap up the Falklands, beat them down in the Gulf, and yet allow a handful of bloody rebels to dictate to you?"

I couldn't come up with any answers. I asked him what he would do if he were in the Prime Minister's place. Geoff, a Hungarian who came here when he was nine, said: "I'd shoot the bastards!" I suppose a lot of people on the mainland are thinking that way but it all takes too long to explain. "How much do I owe you for the milk?" I said.

Tomorrow I will make my way to Brisbane, then to Singapore, stop over a few days and, hopefully, arrive in Bournemouth on Sunday. This may be an omen: this is the very last page on the writing pad, so that's it folks!

CHAPTER EIGHTEEN

Max The Pilot

O H, to be in England, now that spring is here! I forget who said that — me I guess. With that in mind, Bloss and I took it in turns to sit on our suitcases. The trouble was that they only sank when I sat on them, and that means a prescription of salad for a week from Doctor Blossom!

After much huffing and puffing, and a lecture by me on the benefits of leaving behind the kitchen sink, we finally managed to set off on our last trip for a while along the Pacific Highway. I really wish it had been gloomy, or overcast, but the day gave us brilliant sunshine. We cruised along, with Barry driving and Bloss and Christine in the rear seats, chatting 19 to the dozen. Those two never seem to get tired of one another and they can get engrossed in any sort of subject. This time it was the behaviour of green frogs! As I gazed at the beautiful countryside, I felt saddened to be leaving on such a perfect day.

We were going to stay in London for a while. Knowing that with the approaching General Election, the place would be a target for IRA bombers, the weather turning to freezing conditions, and the thought of a Labour government who had already hinted that taxes would have to be raised, thoughts of the old home town were beginning to seem rather unattractive.

The new Brisbane Air Terminal is the best I have ever seen. I guess Olympics 2000 has a lot to do with the futuristic structure. It is breathtaking, roomy, airy, trees growing inside, shopping and cafes, all so bright and beautiful. I have already made my mind up that if, and when, we return, we'll give Sydney a miss and plump for Brisbane — magic! Christine and Bloss were unable to fight off the tears as the time approached for departure.

Chief steward Vic welcomed us aboard the 747 and informed us that he had been born in Dulwich and that, before his emigration to Australia, he had been a fan of the radio show, *Educating Archie*. He remembered my songs and even went into a chorus of *Fings Ain't What They Used To Be*. As we sipped a Bucks Fizz, Vic returned and said: "Compliments of the captain, would you like to go up front for the take-off?" Yes please!

Taking the vacant seat in the tiny cabin, I shook hands with Captain Dale, his co-pilot, Louise — yes, a lady driver — and Kevin, the flight engineer. Kevin strapped me in, handed me a headset and told me to watch the procedure — and if anything went wrong to follow him, "Cos I'll be off first!" Kevin was obviously the comedian of the trio.

I have been invited 'up front' quite often, but never before in a Qantas 747. It was exhilarating. Everything was double and triple checked and suddenly we were airborne. With a click the undercarriage was stowed away and then, smoothly, we circled the terminal for one of the most pleasant flights that I've experienced in 50 years of flying. I got the same buzz as I did on my first RAF flight in a Russ Moth back in 1942.

What seemed like ten minutes later, we were on the tarmac at Singapore. Our car wasn't there, so we got into the taxi queue and 40 minutes later arrived at the Tanglin Club. It was then that I realised that I hadn't bothered to get any Singapore dollars. Believe me, it's far from easy to get a native driver to accept a handsome tip in English money. Luckily I had some American currency. "Ah yes! American dollar good!" said the grinning cabbie.

See what Nick Leeson did for the English pound when he worked for Barings Bank in Singapore?

April 24th 1997
Having decided that there would be no shopping sprees in Singapore, after a hearty breakfast we wandered toward Scotts Road. We should have known better. The temptation is just too great to resist. The casual shopper finds the sales impossible to ignore. For block after block, the windows entice the gazers inside. Now if there is anything that I don't need it is slacks, pants or trousers — depending upon which part of the world you are from. Around the world I have bought more than a couple of dozen pairs, but I have only worn slacks about three times in the last three months, as the rest of the time I have been in shorts. Sure enough, into the Singapore store I went and came out with three pairs.

The reason for this trouser fetish is that I can never find that tailored fit in the UK. I like American-styled pants, so I think that when I find a stylish pair, I'd do better in buying two or three, which is what I did in Singapore. When I got them back to the hotel and looked at the label, guess what! 'Made in London, England'!

Outside the store the rain was coming down like stair-rods, so I went back in and filled another two carrier bags, hoping that Qantas would let us back on with all this excess luggage. I mentioned to Bloss that we had five bulging suitcases already. She replied: "So what? Elizabeth Taylor had 12!" It's hard to reason with a female shopper.

At the Tanglin Club, where I always stay in Singapore, was a St George's Day Ball with cabaret supplied by the Manfreds, a '60s group featuring Paul Jones. Like us, they had left Australia the day before. They were most unhappy with the sound system, which is tough on an act who only want to give of their best. A lousy audio system is a big let-down but, like true pros, they were prepared to try again for the second booking on the following night.

Today the Royal Navy invited us aboard HMS Fearless, a frightening war-ship equipped with helicopters, guns and all the paraphernalia of war. After saying hello and having a drink with the petty officers in their mess, we moved on to the higher ranks where we were served with fish and chips in a basket. We were told by some of the crew that they see so little light aboard this man o' war that the only way that they know it is Friday is when they get their fish and chips in a basket! I spent two hours aboard the ship and learned that they were in this area because of the handover of Hong Kong to the Chinese. They were standing by 'just in case'.

I heard one sad story about a young rating on jungle training. The down-draught of the helicopter rotor blades lifted a tree, which fell on him and broke his back. He will, most likely, never walk again. To have something like that happen — and in training, not actual warfare — is a real lousy deal.

April 25th 1997

The day started with a disappointment as a sports shirt I had purchased proved to be too small and would have to be returned. Then we found that the lunch we had planned, crab in chilli and ginger, was only available in the evening. Then, to crown everything, Alex McColl, who had arranged for us to have lunch aboard the Royal Yacht, Brittania, told us that it had to be cancelled.

With the whole afternoon to fill, I hoped that Bloss would not suggest another shopping trip. Alex asked if we would like to make a couple of people happy. When I asked how, he said: "Come up to the hospital and say hello to a couple of lads from HM Forces who are in a bad way!"

Fifteen minutes later we arrived at Gleneagles Hospital, one of Singapore's largest, and entered the room where Leading Aircraftsman Alex Greig was lying. Alex had fallen 15ft from a helicopter on to a metal deck during manoeuvres

We had plenty to talk about, especially as Alex comes from Cornwall where Anthony and his family are living. In the middle of our conversation, Alex's attractive young wife, who had been flown out by the Ministry of Defence, came in. Without looking around she walked right up to her husband's bedside and whispered: "Darling, Max Bygraves is coming in to see you."

Alex took her hand and tried to catch her eye.

"Max Bygraves is on his way here to see you," she insisted, oblivious of Alex McColl and myself standing just a few feet away. Her husband desperately nodded his head toward us and for the first time she looked round.

"Oh God!" She buried her face in her hands.

I always say: "If you're going to make a faux pas, make it a big 'un!"

The rest of the visit was a feast of fun with me reminding everyone that 'it was great to be recognised'. We stayed a while and then, after wishing Alex well, we moved on to the next patient in another room.

Lee Rowe was in far worse condition than Alex. Twenty years old and from Chatham, there was fear that he may never be able to walk again. He was the young man who had the tree fall on him. It was one of those accidents that are completely inexplicable.

His parents, Julie and Nigel, who had arrived from England only that morning, were relieved to find their son alive. He was getting the best of attention and, hopefully, the 50-50 chance that the doctors gave him will work out in his favour. He said that he was finding it hard to sleep. I joked that I'd send him some of my records: "That'll put you to sleep all right!"

All those trivial disappointments that I'd had earlier in the day vanished completely. I was thankful for chaps like Alex and Lee who spend their time sailing the oceans and keeping us all safe while we slumber contentedly. Make no mistake, we have the greatest navy in the whole wide world and, before I go to sleep, I have promised myself to offer some thanks for all the thousands of men like Alex and Lee, not forgetting the ladies that also wear the uniform. When those awful tax demands come through the door, I'll take some consolation in the thought that this peace of mind does not come cheap.

May 1st 1997

Our third day back in the UK and it was HOT! A wild idea entered my head and, surprisingly, Bloss agreed to it. I wanted to take a boat from Westminster Pier to Kew Gardens. A quick phone call informed us that there would be a boat leaving at 2pm, so we made a dash for a taxi and were seated on the boat at 1.55. Amazingly it pulled away exactly on time.

We passed the deserted House of Commons. Everybody had gone for the election. I couldn't remember seeing the Commons so empty. We were voting that evening — we had to since we had travelled more than 15,000 miles to be home for polling day.

The boat was fairly empty with no more than 30 passengers aboard a vessel which usually took 300. We sat up front to catch any breeze that might be about. Charlie Wyatt, the skipper, left the wheel and came up to say hello. He had already told us that the Thames was now cleaner than it had ever been. In fact it is now one of the cleanest rivers in the world. I told him that, when I was a kid, I swam across the river from Rotherhithe to Wapping. It was so polluted that, if you drowned, you were pulled out already embalmed!

Surprisingly the slow trip up the river takes one and a half hours, so we decided to stay on for the return journey. I chatted to a Cockney who told me that when he was a youngster visiting Kew Gardens, the entrance fee was one penny. Today it had cost him four quid. "Bleedin' robbery!" he exclaimed, reminding me a little of Steptoe senior.

We landed at Westminster in the rush hour, which made a taxi impossible, so we decided to walk to our flat in Victoria, cutting across St James's Park. The flowers in front of Buckingham Palace had been put in place and the blaze of colour looked magnificent. Those gardening chaps do such a wonderful job each spring. They should be given knighthoods.

On our way to the flat we passed the polling station and, luckily, we had our polling cards. It was still very hot and so, after voting, we decided to have a cuppa at the flat and then eat later. We were both so knocked out that we slept until 9.30pm and only woke up then because there was a suspected fire in the block opposite and three fire-engines turned up with their sirens blaring. It was all over quickly, but the noise and panic had removed all traces of tiredness.

It was still very warm, so I took a shower, had a sandwich and watched Election '97 on the TV, during which I fell asleep again with my face smarting from the sunburn I'd received on the boat. I awoke at 1am to hear that Labour was in for a landslide victory. I gave up and went to bed. Was this what I had flown halfway across the world for?

May 2nd 1997

We woke up to a new day, a new Prime Minister, and a new Government. What a victory for young Tony Blair. At 44, the youngest Prime Minister since Shirley Temple. The newspapers, depending on their politics, were trying to assess what went wrong. Why did the Tories go down the pan so completely?

Those shaken faces of Heseltine, Portillo, Jeffrey Archer and several other Tory stalwarts. They were trying to look cool but could give no reason for what was described as a landslide but, in reality, was more like an earthquake. I voted for John Major because I think that he is a decent bloke. I didn't like the idea that if he lost, he'd have to take even more stick. I never have liked the supporting cast he called his Cabinet. And there are some among Blair's that I feel could be hiding behind New Labour masquerade masks that will suddenly be removed at midnight!

We all know that looks can play such an important part nowadays. Portillo never had it and neither did Rifkind. David Mellor and those other plum-in-the-mouth politicians did not have the common touch that wins votes. Tony Blair, with a good sound marriage, three good-looking children and a wife who seems to have an inner wisdom, had such a good commodity to help the voting. If people are looking for something that Labour has, and the Tories had not, I can suggest in one word what it is: ENERGY! Mrs Thatcher had it when she romped home 18 years ago. Now, in 1997, Tony Blair and company have it too.

I wish him well and hope that his lack of experience doesn't hold him back from making Britain the country that he envisages. I hope that he can select the right team he needs to help him to do it, but watch it Tony! The ghouls of the Red Flag are right behind you!

May 3rd 1997

Another old acquaintance, Hughie Green, passed away today. I liked Hughie.

He was headstrong and seemed to enjoy litigation and would sue at the drop of a contract, but he was also responsible for unearthing some of the very best talent for television.

He once put on a show for the RAF from Victoria Palace and captured a real scoop to open. Richard Burton was to recite a poem that was about the Battle of Britain. Hughie asked me to take part but I couldn't make it as I already had a long-standing commitment elsewhere. When I told him that I would be in Spain, he even said that he would fetch me in his own plane and fly me back afterwards. It was important to him because it was being shown on BBC1 and he needed 'names'.

When I explained that it was just impossible, he wouldn't speak to me for over two years. He told me that the show was dedicated to young men who had risked their lives so that we could be free. I said: "I know Hughie, I was one of them!"

After a couple of years of looking the other way when we were both doing shows at Thames Television, I met up with him again in the Caribbean. It happened at the site where the *Island In The Sun* movie had been filmed. As I rounded the deserted colonial house with Blossom, I literally bumped into Hughie, who had a movie camera. "Hello," I said. "Aren't you Harry Belafonte?"

Now Hughie has left us to knock for opportunity up there in the big show in the sky. We finished up good friends again in the Caribbean: "And I mean that most sincerely folks!"

John Junor also left us for that big press reception up there, and also left a big void in my Sunday reading. He was a crafty writer who always threw the ball back into the reader's court by starting a column: 'Am I right in thinking ...?' It's a good technique and John was exceptionally good at it.

I never met him formally but had a chalet right next to his at a golf complex in Spain. From mid-morning he would sit at a small table with some of his cronies, among them Sir Denis Thatcher, and the table was always packed with drinks of all brands. When I wasn't playing golf, I could hear every word they discussed. I once heard them arguing for over an hour about whether a cricket ball should be polished on the bowler's trousers before delivery.

Since then I have got to know Sir Denis Thatcher quite well. Today, at lunch, just a few hours after the complete election result, I asked Denis how he felt about it. He replied in one word: "Gutted!"

I am off now to do two shows at the Secombe Theatre in Sutton. It must be nice to have a theatre named after you as Sir Harry has done. I don't suppose it will ever happen to me. As I told the audience: "You could never have a Bygraves Theatre. Going to the Bygraves sounds all wrong ...all right for a cemetery though!"

That is where I have to leave this diary account. I have tour dates all over the place, a radio show, some television, letters to write and a whole backlog of telephone calls and faxes to catch up on. Jennifer has been busy while I have been away, and so has Johnny Mans who handles much of my work these days. John is one of the busiest blokes in the business. He has been my pal Norman Wisdom's manager for a good number of years, and acts as manager and agent to a lot of big names. He is also a promoter and there is not a night that goes by that he does not have at least one show on in a theatre somewhere. He is a modern day Val Parnell.

The whole point of this section was to give you some idea of what we are really like, how we spend our time and what interests us. In short, it was an invitation into our sitting room. Thanks for coming in!

CHAPTER NINETEEN

Reflections

BLOSSOM has not been in the best of health recently and because of that I have been forced to help out in many of the chores that most men take for granted, especially when we come into a clean home, hot meals ready, beds made, washing up and laundry done and the 1,001 other jobs that go to keeping a household running smoothly. I know that I can afford help, but even that becomes the woman's worry. More and more I have become aware of this, especially when the 'help' wants holidays or is not available because of illness. Sometimes I have been the only able-bodied person around. At first it was a sort of novelty, but it's easy to have too much of the chores.

Shopping is an example. If I put on hat and glasses, it is sometimes possible to get around the supermarket unrecognised. I don't do this because of vanity but because, if some sharp-eyed person does detect me, they usually say one of three things: "Why aren't you ever on television?" "I thought you had gone abroad!" Or, and this is the worst: "I thought you were dead!" I often want to answer: "No, I'm not a broad, I'm a healthy macho!" But that's too deep for most supermarket customers. As to the last statement, it's just like Eric Morecambe said: "There's no answer to that!"

My usual thought is to get out of the supermarket as quickly as I can, but it's never that simple. I always thought that the original idea of the super-market was to cut the queues and give speedier service. Nah! I think that shoppers were in and out of the corner shop much quicker than any self-service store. Find a shopper with a trolley stacked as if they were off to feed the local scout group for a week, then find that they've forgotten their credit card, then watch the queue get longer and angrier as the sales-girl keeps ringing for a supervisor.

After 15 minutes, join yet another line for Lottery tickets. Why the Bygraves need Lottery tickets I'll never know. "It's fun," says Bloss. It's no bloody fun when a couple of yobs in front of you have turned up to purchase a combination for the local works, and require 780 permutations. Usually the Lottery tickets are on sale at the same counter that sells 'smokes', so they smoke, and smell, at the same time. And next week they could be millionaires.

I suppose that most people dream of winning that gigantic jackpot and stand there dreaming in the Lottery queue of what they'll do with ten million pounds. I do! I'd like to give half to some charities that I've been involved with in the past. And with the other half I would buy my own supermarket and close it, so that I was the only shopper!

It's good to talk, though. I like to ask people in the queue what they will do with all the money should they be lucky enough to win. Most answers are run-of-the-mill: pay off the mortgage, buy a new car, have a holiday and so on. One fellow did surprise me, though. He said that he would fly to the foot of Mount Everest, book a team of top sherpas and then try to make it to the top.

"Have you done a lot of mountaineering?" I asked.

"None! The highest I've ever been is to the top of the Post Office Tower!"

"What makes you want to get to the top of Everest?"

"'Cos then there'd be no bloody supermarkets, and no bloody queues!"

I have a friend, a comedy actor named Gordon Peters, and he told me the best Lottery story that I have heard up to now:

It's Monday morning and there is a knock at the door. A bleary-eyed individual opens it.

"What do you want?"

"Did you buy a ticket for the Lottery last week?"

"Yes!"

"Well, have you checked it?"

"No, I've been too busy working."

"Have you got the ticket with you?"

"Yes." He hands over the ticket and the caller checks it.

"Sir, I represent Camelot. You have won nine million pounds."

"Really … are you sure?"

"Yes sir, nine million pounds. That's a lot of money. Will you give up your job?"

"I certainly will."

"Will you travel?"

"I sure will. I'll go all round the world on the QE2, I'll fly Concorde, I'll sunbathe in Tahiti, I'll …"

"What about your wife, does she work?"

"Yes, she cleans the lavatories at the supermarket."

"I suppose she'll give up her job too?"

"Why? Has she won the Lottery as well?"

—oOo—

October 16th will mean another birthday. I don't like mentioning my age, not since I read a report in the *Daily Mail* a few days ago, headed: 'Old man in his 70s mugged.'

One of my friends, hopefully in jest, asked me if I found it embarrassing to be in my 70s singing songs like *You're A Pink Toothbrush* … and *Gilly Gilly Ossenfeffer* … The truth is, I find that my particular audience want to hear these songs. I could sing other songs but it's a long time since they 'wrote 'em like that'. I think the last one was *Tie A Yellow Ribbon Round The Old Oak Tree*, and that was 20 years ago. The only one since is possibly Stevie Wonder's *I Just Called To Say I Love You*. I have so much material, having recorded more than 700 songs for my *Singalong* albums, I guess that it's just laziness not keeping up to date. Somehow I can't seem to get my tongue around today's pop songs.

Last autumn I was a guest at a literary luncheon at Simpson's in the Strand. The host, Richard Ingrams, introduced me as: "Er …Max …er …er …" I had to prompt him with 'Bygraves', which got a big laugh from the audience, and almost a smile from Ingrams.

I mentioned to Anthony that I had been very impressed with a speaker named Ned Sherrin. At one time I had thought, quite wrongly as it happens, that he was one of those writers that lived like parasites off the hard work of others. Since hearing him, however, my admiration of him has increased.

I must have enthused quite a bit because among my birthday presents was Anthony's gift of Ned's latest book, *Sherrin's Year*. It is written in diary form and, as a diarist myself who has put together a diary on the war years, soon to be read on BBC2, I was most interested.

Ned Sherrin's book is quite a large one, but if you skip the interminable references to what and where he ate, plus the visits to the dentist etc, you can get through the book in half the time. There is no doubt about him being a busy body, which makes one wonder where he gets the time to write, especially as, like I am doing now, he writes in longhand.

Also, on page 130, he really shocked me — and at my age I'm not all that shockable — by confessing to going with a male prostitute 'rather than wooing a young actor'.

There were other presents too. Blossom had seen me looking longingly at a Callaway carbon shaft golf club. I dearly wanted it, but they are pricey at £300 plus, even though they are wonderful clubs to handle. It wasn't just the price that put me off. I have six sets of golf clubs around the world, and to embark on a seventh is plain stupidity. After all, it's how you hit a ball that counts, not what you hit it with. Bloss scored again, though, and the new club was there for me.

Barnaby and Oscar gave me half a dozen linen handkerchiefs, a simple present, but really appreciated. I am one of that rare species that still carries a pocket handkerchief and, next to freshly laundered sheets, a freshly laundered handkerchief gives me much pleasure.

When I arrived in Spain the day after the literary awards, Maxine, who was uncertain what to give as a present, got an idea when I mentioned that I had been cold in the night. She presented me with a set of winceyette pyjamas. I have worn them every night since and feel more grateful each night. I wondered how Maxine knew that I would wear winceyette pyjamas, but, of course, she had heard my complaint about the cold.

Maxine speaks very good Spanish, so I asked her to translate what was on the pyjama label. She told me that it read: 'Keep away from fire.' So if the fire alarm goes off in the hotel one night, I suppose that the first thing I should do is take off the pyjamas. I wonder what the press would make of that: 'British Streaker Breaks Olympic record!'

—oOo—

Blossom enjoys vegetables. I often get: "You don't eat enough vegetables, not for such a big man."

It's hard to make her understand, even after all these married years, that I am not all that fond of them. A nice juicy steak with a baked potato, or some chips with some plaice or halibut, is quite adequate for me. I know that she's right. I am aware that the vitamins from a bowl of fresh vegetables can be a blessing, but I just find them boring. A few years ago I decided to do something about my veggie intake.

One day the recipe for gazpacho soup caught my eye in the newspaper. I decided to find the ingredients, which we had, and set about cutting up the onions, tomatoes, cucumbers, putting them in the blender together with a teaspoon of olive oil, tabasco, salt, pepper, garlic and vinegar, add the stock and — Voila!. It came out just as the chef predicted. After chilling, I served it to the guests at dinner one evening. "Wow!", "Formidable!", "Delicious!", and "Please sir, can I have some more?" were among the slurps of ecstasy.

That was more than five years ago, and this chilled soup is now a must throughout the summer. I got quite cocky with my culinary skills. I experimented with pea and ham, cucumber and fresh tomatoes that I had grown myself in the greenhouse. I spent a lot of time last summer, nursing the plants and, when they were red and shiny, I picked them for adding to the soup. It tasted bloody awful! There's only one good way to make tomato soup I think — it's with tinned tomatoes.

What all this is leading up to is that the family are really hooked on my gazpacho. They don't care for any of the others that I make and if I serve these up, their first words on arrival are: "Got any gazpacho in the fridge?"

Now, I spend far too many afternoons in the kitchen. Anthony suggested that I bottle it and sell it in the same way that Paul Newman sells his salad dressing. The reason should be obvious. Making just a bit for the half dozen of the family is a big chore. If it caught on and I had to make it for thousands, what sort of time would I have left to write a masterpiece like this book?

—oOo—

One acquaintance of mine, who shall remain nameless, is absolutely football mad. His wife is as bored with the game as he is enthusiastic but, when the World Cup was played in Italy, she did not want to miss out on a holiday so she went along for the ride. On the way, my friend picked up a couple of tickets to see the live performance of the Three Tenors. Now, his wife, who knows even less about opera than she does about football, was quite unprepared for the reverence expressed for Pavarotti, Carreras, and Domingo. She thought that they were a juggling act! Because of the hype and the charisma that these three tenors had created, she gradually became aware that she was at the start of something really big.

Musically, she doesn't know a B flat from a bull's foot. She was also unaware that some shrewd impresario had launched the singers on the wave of World Cup fever and that non-music-lovers were learning to pronounce words like Luciano, Placido and José for the first time, even adding a few new words like: "Ah Supremo!" and Molto Bene!"

When friends and neighbours were later informed that she had sat just two rows back from 'Lucy' and 'Dom', she became, for the first time in her life, the centre of attraction.

"Did you touch him?" asked one friend excitedly.

"No, but he threw me his handkerchief!" she fibbed.

Her husband backed her by saying: "Yes, and it was soaking wet!" He, too, was beginning to enjoy this reflected glory.

Since the day of the World Cup she has become a fanatic. Every CD, every TV appearance, each video that floods on to the market, she has to buy. At the library she has read up on the lives of Puccini, Verdi and so on. And all this because she is convinced that one day she is going to bump into, if not all three of them, at least one.

My friend says: "Walking into that house is like walking into a bleedin' Covent Garden Opera!" Sorrowfully he shakes his head. "The worst bleedin' thing that I ever did was to take her to that World Cup in Italy. Before that she was so bloody stupid — now she's thinking of taking up opera!"

"Did you know that they are appearing in Melbourne next February?" I asked innocently.

Naturally, he had to book her a ticket on Quantas and front row seats. He is not a poor man, so expense was nothing to him. I managed to find out which hotel the tenors were staying in and so my friend booked the last single room for his wife, whom he loves dearly, even though he can't stand the scales that she practises most days and nights.

But now it is all over. No more operatic scales. No more mention of Big Lucy. Dom is cast to one side.

And so is José.

How did this happen?

With her window open she practised those ear-splitting scales until, one day, a lout on a motorbike shouted: "For Gawd's sake missus, you sound like a bloody cat being doctored!"

After that she became disillusioned and did the only thing that she could do. She gave away all the CDs, videos, programme souvenirs, the lot! She doesn't, ever again, want to listen to what the egg-heads call 'real music'. In fact, she became an Oasis fan!

—oOo—

It's been quite a while since we heard the patter of tiny feet in our household. Once upon a time there were quite a few: our own children, followed by their children. But, as they all grow up into men and women, that sound becomes rarer. The last time that I heard the patter of tiny feet was when a midget came to stay and went for a swim in the pool!

So Bloss and I were quite thrilled when three-year-old twins came to stay with us. Their father, Martin, is our handyman in Australia — and, to me, he is the best. Nothing in the field of maintenance can faze him. He's a great family man, too, and has a lovely family, including the twins.

Shy at first, the twins soon got over that when I showed them how to juggle three balls. When I allowed one of the balls to hit my head and I became 'groggy', they thought it was great fun and shouted for more. The diablo, too, was a success. They thought that I was a 'clever man'. I hadn't the heart to tell them that my eight-year-old grandson had taught me the diablo when he was staying with us the previous summer.

Personally I liked the diablo best — juggling those balls and heading them gives me quite a head-ache!

I got the twins interested in some tapes that I made many years ago. Titles like *Gilly Gilly Ossenfeffer* and *Changing Guard At Buckingham Palace*, were requested over and over again. It got me to thinking that there are not many songs that interest smaller children nowadays. Whatever happened to *Nellie The Elephant*, *Sparky's Magic Piano*, and *The Runaway Train*?

I know that EMI and one or two other companies still market a few, but Uncle Mac used to fill an hour on Saturday mornings with requests from the under-sevens. Many young mothers must have been grateful for the break as they sat their young children in front of the radio. I don't know if I'm going through a second childhood, but I get a big wave of nostalgia whenever I hear *A Four-Legged Friend* or *Mud, Mud, Glorious Mud*.

—oOo—

Before I came to live in Bournemouth I lived somewhere else! I won't tell you where because it could put an end to a very good source of revenue. Let me tell you a mice story ...

It must have been about 2am when my wife's elbow woke me from a deep slumber.

"There's a mouse," she whispered. "I can hear it squeaking."

"What do you want me to do — get up and oil it?"

"If it jumps up on the bed, I shall die!" she gasped.

Remembering how much I dislike funerals, I decided to put the light on. I was totally unprepared for what I saw. Not one! Not two! But three of the furry little rascals having a meeting in the middle of our bedroom. As I gave a great gasp of astonishment, they all made off in different directions, disappearing at different points along the skirting board. I threw my slipper at the slowest one. He went 'eek!' as he disappeared, and I thought: "That was a narrow squeak!"

When we discussed them at breakfast next morning, I said: "There seem to be so many of them. I don't know where they come from ..."

Anthony said: "It's like this dad. There's a mummy mouse and there's a father mouse ..." He dodged the same slipper that I had thrown at the mouse.

Bloss came into the breakfast room to see another one scurry across the floor. Now, you wouldn't think that mice had a sense of humour would you, but as she jumped up on the chair, they pulled it away!

"Don't stand there laughing," she wailed. "Call the health inspector!"

"Health inspector? These mice are the healthiest mice I've ever seen. They're even using the spring traps as chest expanders!"

"Do something!" she yelled.

I bought a cat. He was doing all right, too, until the mice found some methylated spirit that I'd spilled in the garage. A couple of them came in drunk and roughed the cat up — he's never been the same since. I've seen a queue of mice at his milk saucer, with him right at the back.

I rang up Exterminators Ltd, and they sent a man over. I was really pleased to see him and went down the drive to meet him — me and 1,000 mice.

He said: "Don't worry, sir, leave everything to me!"

When I got home that night he was behind the settee, waving a white flag.

A few nights later, Bloss and I were sitting there talking it all over. We were just sitting there — on the sideboard — and I said: "I think I'll try some poison!"

She said: "That's just like you — take the coward's way out!"

I said: "No, it's not for me — it's for them! Kill 'em all!"

"No! That's un-Christian. There must be good ones as well as bad ones! No, it's not right!"

Honest — 'good and bad' — she says that about everything: pop singers, agents, journalists …and now it's mice!

—oOo—

We sold that house a few years ago and since then it has changed hands 17 times, and do you know, every time it's sold the house agent gets five per cent commission!

Last night I walked my son's dog along the promenade, from Alum Chine to Durley Chine. It's no more than 300 yards, but on that short walk I passed more than 50 other dogs, all pulling at their leads to try to get among the waves, their owners leaning backward to restrain them — me included! I began to wonder why people keep pets. It's to make them feel superior!

This is not a conclusion that I came to overnight. It's what I read this morning in a thick, dusty book at the Westbourne Library — and people don't just write things like that in thick, dusty books because they might be true. In any case, this writer was a professor of something or other, so you can't argue with that can you?

Try the theory on yourself: Why do you keep a dog? "Oh," you say. "I take him for walkies and the exercise does me good." Do you really mean — honestly — that you can't take a good brisk walk in the evening without being on one end of a leather strap? Try again mate!

"My doggie is my best friend!" So, you'd have us believe that half the people in Bournemouth are so short on friends that they have to pop down to the local pet shop and buy one for five quid?

No! That professor was right. We keep old bonzo around the house because, no matter how inferior we may feel, there is always someone who is a little dimmer. I'll bet you that if dogs and cats were as bright as bank managers, or as crafty as theatrical agents, we'd have to go to a museum just to see what they used to look like.

Don't get me wrong. I'm just as involved as the next man, whoever he might be.

Before my work took me to other parts of the world, I had a boxer that we called Butch. When I took him for walks, people would stop and talk to *him* — forgetting entirely to speak to me. I used to return home feeling very underprivileged and depressed. Then one day, Butch attacked a Wallace Arnold coach! He was buried the very next day. It was then that people started talking to me again. "Pity about poor old Butch," they used to say.

Then I got a budgerigar, but I soon got fed-up with people chanting: "Who's a pretty boy then?" I thought that this was the old Butch syndrome all over again, so I opened his cage and let him fly away. A few days later, a lady from further down the road knocked at my door. "I think your budgie is in my garden!"

So I said: "Please don't tell him where I live!" Then I closed the door.

Next I tried goldfish, but they are just not logical. They don't like anything and they don't dislike anything. Out they went — they must be somewhere in Poole harbour by now.

However, what happened next shows that nobody can be an all-time loser, even at keeping pets! It was a cat, a black and white moggie. Most people seeing a strange feline leaning against their dustbin would simply chuck a brick at it, which is exactly what I did. The brick missed by a hair's breadth, but that moggie didn't move an inch. I thought:

"This must be the bravest cat in the world, pity he wasn't here yesterday when there was goldfish on the menu." I discovered that the cat was an idiot. He hasn't got a name because he wouldn't know whose it was anyway. He has been with us for a long time. It took a while and not a little patience to teach him to come in out of the rain and to stop chasing dogs, but he certainly makes a man feel needed.

—oOo—

There is a programme on television called *If I Was Prime Minister* which is quite watchable. It's not that well directed and the programme concludes with little or nothing being achieved. The viewer is left with the thought that the person being interviewed has never been allowed to dwell on any subject for fear of the programme losing its pace.

A viewer can get an idea of the nervousness of the director by watching the speed of the credits at the end. I repeat, it is a good idea — even though badly executed — and the possibilities for similar programmes, such as *If I were a Television Boss*, could be endless. Not the usual drab 'complaints' programme, but a show presented by someone who appreciates good entertainment, and who can suggest alternatives.

All right Max, what ideas have you got?

Space doesn't allow, but one programme that I'm sure would be appreciated by a large audience, would be a programme for the 60 somethings.

The chosen viewer would suggest a programme made up of people, places and events that the elderly would enjoy. There would be no pandering to the young market, no hosts aping Chris Evans, no doubtful language, no rock music where the singers keep the lyrics a secret — and no dark eye-shades.

The BBC archives are filled with film that could be screened for a few minutes. Maybe a sporting event of some 30 years ago and the hero of that event being brought on after the film. The same thing could be done with personalities from the past. Not me of course, I'm far too young!

Such a programme would need to be directed by an established director like Ernest Maxim or John Fisher, not some yuppie direct from university. I feel that with a friendly, mature host to take away 'nerves' from volunteer programme makers, the Beeb would be on its way to a very successful series. Furthermore, I've just given the format without taking a fee. See, savings all round!

It has been suggested that I should 'talk about some of the 'yuks' around me that should have the truth told about them'. If I was a tabloid writer, I guess I would find that quite easy, but I have to say that I find it difficult to 'rubbish' anybody.

A couple of years ago, I took exception to one big star, who had written a book filled with all the names of the girls he'd screwed along the way. He is a hard one to understand. He has never been adored by his fellow artistes but always turns in a professional job of work. I was really surprised by that part of his book, and I reminded him that although most of the girls he'd shared beds with had passed on, they still had relatives who would read these sordid jottings, and I wondered what good it would do him. I didn't get a reply from him, but I got plenty of stick from his agents, publishers and others who could only see cash if the book was a hit, which it was. In my own stupid way, I even added to the sales by stirring up controversy and making the buyers even more eager for the dirt.

A colleague to whom I showed my writings asked me if there was anything in the profession that I feel bitter about. Like many of my vintage — Eric Sykes, Spike Milligan, Norman Wisdom and Charlie Drake — we all think that we have a great deal of entertainment left in us, but the hierarchy of television does not agree. I, for one, cannot figure out why I can go on stage at almost any theatre in the country and play to packed houses, who will applaud my efforts and demand encores, and yet I cannot get a spot on a major TV show. In the theatre we are paid better — much better — than television, so it is not just a question of wages. It matters because television is the best advertisement for our talents. If you are not seen periodically, then you are dead!

Jimmy Tarbuck once asked me why I had never appeared on the LWT show *An Audience With ...* I told him the truth: I had never been asked.

Nigel Lythgoe, a former director at LWT, explained to me that, just supposing Coca Cola are the big advertisers in a certain programme, they are going to back off if Spike, Eric or any of the others that I've mentioned are being featured. Our age group are not going out and buying Coca Cola are they? It has to be the young and that is why so much TV is youth-orientated.

The problem that entertainers like myself have is that we have to keep on proving ourselves, not to the pulic so much as to the ever-changing faces in charge of television. They come off the university production line fresh-faced and technically very capable but with little real knowledge of entertainment or entertainers. It's not their fault, it is the system of training. They should be encouraged to come and see experienced performers, see us in action, talk to us about television. Between us we have hundreds of years of experience, more probably than they will gain in a lifetime. We can tell them and show them how to put real entertainment on television. I could give them one tip right away – the audience the Coca Cola ads are meant for are probably out drinking it!

I heard that Michael Grade was saying goodbye to Channel 4. That's not a bad thing as he filled the TV air with pollution. I like Mike, but he was as much good to television as a BSkyB satellite dish down a coal mine. A couple of times he enthused about some shows that I suggested — then, not a dickie bird. I could imagine Mike in his red braces, puffing on a Havana cigar, wondering what is the best price he can get for a film called 'The Wests Meet Lolita'. I'd better not say any more in case he asks me to play the lead.

The BBC are not so bad. When the chips are down they go to the archives and dig out some *Morecambe and Wise, Hancock* or *Some Mothers Do 'Ave 'Em*, which are always acceptable. This, of course, leads to the question: Why aren't there some new equivalents? You can't say that there are no more

Hancocks or Morecambes.

New comics have to be nurtured and allowed to blossom. Have a look at some of the early Beeb shows with entertainers that became big names and were well-loved before they passed on, and you'll see how they were developed by directors and producers, writers and ideas men. Some of their very early shows were quite awful. Watch Eric Morecambe or Tommy Cooper, who stole his act from the American conjuror Ballantyne, or Hancock, floundering in the early days, and you will realise that someone saw that magic spark that made them all what they eventually became.

I rest my case m'lud.

CHAPTER TWENTY

Stars In My Eyes

ONE OF THE really exciting aspects of being involved in show-business is that you meet and sometimes work with many great people. You not only meet famous people of today, but you also meet legends of yesterday as well as the up-and-coming celebrities of tomorrow. I thought that you might like to meet some of them too.

JIMMY TARBUCK

Jimmy Tarbuck is a good comedian. I have seen him 'on form' and there are few patter comics who can equal his delivery and cheek. See him at a golf dinner, presenting the prizes, and the gags flow as if from a never-ending CD; or see him auctioneering for some charity and he can inveigle several hundred pounds more for each item.

"Sold, to the gentleman sitting next to Dolly Parton. Oh, I'm sorry, it's two bald-headed men sitting together!"

He is fun-loving and will go to great lengths to make a practical joke work. On a couple of occasions I have had to let Jimmy know that I wasn't at all pleased about some gibe he had made about me. I take a lot of stick from impersonators that, at times, gets a bit personal, and in the past Jimmy has occasionally hit below the belt. But I like him and regard him as a friend. His heart is in the right place and I can assure anyone that he would never hurt you intentionally.

He is street-wise and alert and it would be very hard to put one over on him, but I managed it once.

A few years ago, he was in a summer show at Bournemouth. Being a resident of Bournemouth, I met him fairly regularly at Parkstone Golf Club for a game. He is a far better golfer than I could ever hope to be. He gave me a generous stroke advantage and we played for a couple of golf balls. Almost every time he would win and I had to forfeit two new golf balls.

At the time Jim had lost his driving licence for speeding and had to use a driver, who also caddied for him. One day when we played, Jim had won as usual and I had to pay with two new balls. As I passed his Rolls in the car-park, his driver was just putting Jim's clubs in the boot. I noticed that there was a box of new balls. With a wink to the driver, and unseen by Jim, I took two of the balls, walked to the front of the car and gave them to him. He took the balls, gave them to his driver who replaced them in the boot, said cheerio and drove off.

The next time we met I did exactly the same thing — and kept it going for the next half a dozen games. Finally, I took the whole box of 12 balls and said: "Here Jim, you played so well today I want to give you a whole dozen balls." He took them and walked to the boot to put them in with his clubs. A puzzled look came over his face. It was obvious that he was missing something. He turned back to see the driver and me grinning from ear to ear. He looked down at the balls, realised that they were his own and summed me up with three words: "You conniving b******!"

Jim tells this story quite often. I hope that he adds the fact that I did give him a legitimate extra dozen balls as compensation.

GEORGE BURNS

Sadly, George Burns died a little after his 100th birthday, but a few years earlier he had flown over from California to London for a one-off appearance on my Thames Television show. I'll never forget our first meeting which was at the Dorchester Hotel. He had given me his room and floor number. I went straight up and knocked at the door and a small, frail bald-headed man in a burgundy dressing-gown answered it.

"Is Mr George Burns here?" I asked.

"Just a minute," said the little man, and went back into the room.

Twenty seconds later, the same frail, old man returned, but this time he wore a silver toupee, thick glasses, and was smoking a nine-inch cigar.

"What can I do for you?" said George Burns.

The transformation was astounding and I just stood there laughing.

"What are you laughing at? Did you never meet a leprechaun?"

That was exactly what he looked like. So many people must have said so, he decided to get in first. We became friends from that day on and he told me so many stories. It was hard to work out truth from fantasy, but there was never a dull moment with George, who filled every moment. He would talk about Al Jolson: " ...not a great guy as a friend, but a superb entertainer, unashamed schmaltz!"

He'd tell of Fanny Brice, Sophie Tucker, Sam Goldwyn, Ronald Colman and many, many more, all first hand. It was sheer magic to someone like myself, who was content just to sit and listen. It went on for more than two weeks — at rehearsal, at dinner, in the limousine — and, what's more, he never repeated himself!

Many of his stories had macabre pay-offs, like the following. Imagine George telling it, between puffs of his Havana corona:

"You think of fans that adored people like Sinatra and Johnnie Ray? The equivalent in our day was George M. Cohan, the great American songwriter and entertainer. He would give five shows a day and the crowd for the next show would be queued up around the block waiting to get in.

"Between shows, Mr Cohan and the supporting cast would take refreshment in the Green Room, and then get ready for the next performance. It was a great honour to be on the same bill as George M. Cohan. He played all the best dates and the auditorium was always a sell-out. Your date book would be filled for many months.

"At the beginning of a tour that opened in Philadelphia, two hoofers — male dancers — joined the show. They hadn't been in the business long and were a bit wide-eyed at being on the same bill as the great George M. Cohan. One afternoon, between shows in the Green Room, one of the dancers plucked up enough courage to talk to George M, who was deep in thought at one end of the bar.

"He said: 'Mr Cohan, this is the greatest thrill of our lives. We are new to showbusiness and to be an opening act on the George M. Cohan tour is beyond belief. It would give us so much pleasure if we could buy you a drink.'

"George M. then explained that he had just received some bad news. He had just lost his mother and would prefer to be alone, to which the youngest dancer replied: "We know just how you feel — two weeks ago, we lost our suitcases!'"

CLARK GABLE

I had some memorable meetings with some of the Hollywood 'greats' when I was there in 1952. No star was greater then Clark Gable, known world-wide as 'The King'. Although it was only a brief meeting it remains an indelible memory which seems as if it happened only yesterday.

On a visit to my new American agent, I parked my hired Chevrolet in the car-park on the Santa Monica Boulevard. When I came out, I found that someone had parked an MG open roadster at such an angle that it would be impossible to reverse out without scraping either car.

After several minutes of studying the line I needed to take to get out, I turned to see the owner of the MG doing the same thing. It was Clark Gable! My, but he was handsome in the flesh. Dressed in sports jacket with yellow roll-collar pullover, he threw away a cigarette that wasn't half-finished and said: "What d'ye think?" I answered something about using a helicopter to do a lifting job. He smiled and asked if he knew me, saying that my face was familiar.

I remembered that he had been in the audience a few nights before watching Judy Garland. I was a supporting act at the Philharmonic Auditorium in Los Angeles where Judy had introduced him to the audience. Of course she had to sing 'Dear Mr Gable ... 'to the tune of *You Made Me Love You*, as she had done in a movie with Mickey Rooney. The audience had stood up and cheered. Standing ovations were not the fashion of the day at that time, but they certainly stood up that night.

He was complimentary about my performance for which I thanked him. "Let's get back to the car," he said. Having heard my accent and established that I was from England, he handed me the keys to his car. "Here, it's a British car. You'll know more about it than me!"

I got into the car, a young kid from the East End of London, reversing while the world's best-known movie star saw me back. "Slowly back, easy, watch the fender, as you are, easy!" Worried to death about his paintwork, I followed his instructions and managed to get out of a space that would not have accepted a cigarette paper between.

"Come over to the lot and say hello when you have the time," he called

I meant to go to the MGM studios to see him, but I never did. Now, whenever I get into a tight spot in a car-park, where some friendly so-and-so has hemmed me in, I usually think: "Here we go again — another Clark Gable!"

JIMMY DURANTE

"You only had to know him for a minute and, then and there, he'd chase away the gloom. He was no Caruso, but when he sang a song, somehow he'd light up the room."

Those are the lyrics to a song that I once wrote about the great Jimmy Durante. When I was a kid, everybody — and I mean everybody — did an impression of the great Schnozzle, even my mother. Tell her that the soup needed salt, or the porridge was too lumpy, and she'd do a head wobble and say: "Everybody wants to get in on the act".

In 1952, after finishing my spot at the Palace, I put on a smart shirt and got into a cab to New York's famous Copacabana, where Durante was appearing. He was a real favourite with the Big Apple crowd and starred there three or four times a year. All the energy, all the comic timing, the piano playing that he would have you believe was an amateur at work, although it was the work of a very capable professional, had the New Yorkers in fits. It was all clean material and much of it was ad-libbed. I joined in the applause for the encores, which he gladly delivered.

After the show, another legend of American showbusiness came to the table which I was sharing with Jock Jacobsen. Sophie Tucker asked me if I enjoyed Durante's work. I gushed that he was the ultimate. "Would you like to come backstage and meet him?"

Would I? I couldn't finish my Coca Cola quick enough.

"Miss Tucker!" the usher introduced her as we walked into the sumptuous dressing-room, in which stood the great man himself, in a loose fitting singlet and with braces dangling from his roomy trousers.

"Pull your pants up, we've got a gentleman all the way from England come to see yer," she said as she ushered me forward.

"Just a minute Sophe," said Durante. "I need my glasses, where are my glasses?"

Sophie, obviously used to mothering this loveable man, shouted: "They're on top of your head!"

And they were. He pulled them down on to his nose and scrutinised me.

"From England eh! How old are you kid?" I told him that I was 28. "When I was 28," he said sadly. "I was gettin' laid all over New York!"

Sophie quipped: "He was getting laid all over. Now, he can't even make it to Idlewild Airport for a coupla weeks at the London Palladium."

I gathered from their light-hearted banter that Durante had been offered a two-week engagement at the Palladium, but was fighting shy because he wasn't so sure that his humour would travel that well. I tried to assure him that it would, but he still never came.

I listened as he told stories about the times of Prohibition, of meetings with gangster Bugsy Seigal, who would bung him an extra 100 dollars for a couple of encores.

It was all riveting stuff and, when we left, the parting words of Sophie Tucker will stay for ever in my memory: "Jimmy Durante — the man who never had an enemy!"

TERENCE DONOVAN

Hardly a day passes without hearing of some friend, contemporary, or public figure who has passed away. I read the obituary page of the *Daily Telegraph* with trepidation, wondering if I am featured. So far I've been lucky.

I was saddened to hear of the passing of that great photographer Terence Donovan. Once, after seeing him on a chat show, he really won me over with his East End patter and likeable manner, and I decided to have some up-to-date portraits done.

I met him for the first time at his studio, a converted garage in Mayfair. He was a mountain of a man and held a black belt in judo, but he had an easy smile and seemed interested in every word that you said. He banged away at the camera, hardly missing a beat, joking all the time about his East End roots, how it was, and is, and how proud he was to be a survivor.

When he had finished he presented me with an album of his work. This lovely man was responsible for some of the finest portraits of royalty, beautiful models, celebrities and statesmen. I used several of the portraits that he had done of me for quite a few years. They appeared in many theatre programmes, newspapers and record covers, but I never did receive a bill.

"Forget it! On the house!" he chirruped.

When I read that he had been found by a passer-by, hanging from the banisters — a suicide, blamed on depression caused by steroids for a skin complaint — it came as quite a shock. To me, Terence Donovan had always seemed indestructible. The tributes that have poured in have assured his family that he was a man who will be sorely missed.

BILL SHANKLAND

If ever I hear a story about a worm turning, or somebody receiving a come-uppance, I get a glow. I guess most people do. So you can imagine how happy I was to hear this yarn from an old pal of mine, Bill Shankland, whose name may be familiar to some.

He was a professional golfer of some repute in the old days, and even though he is now in his 80s, he still drives a ball from the tee that seems destined to go into outer space. He still has a physique that reminds you of the Berlin Wall that was — and I would still hate to get a clout from those massive hands.

Tony Jacklin was once an assistant to him and speaks of Bill with great affection. In fact, I have yet to meet anyone who has met Bill that doesn't have a great deal of affection for 'Maestro' as he is known at our club in Bournemouth.

Bill is now a senior citizen and, during the week, can be seen walking to the small Post Office in Canford Cliffs to collect his pension. Only a short while ago, he was pounced on by a mugger, who must have thought that Bill would be a pushover. What a mistake! Bill was also a rugby player of fame during his days in New South Wales — and his old skills have never left him.

As he ducked the mugger's jump, Bill threw him. The attacker was surprised, but must have thought that he had timed it badly, so he came back at Bill full throttle. What a mistake again! Eighty-one-year-old Bill gave him a fourpenny one, right on the point of the chin. The incredible part of this true story is that as the dazed mugger lay on the ground, nursing his fractured jaw, he pointed at Bill and cried to the crowd that was gathering: "I want you to witness what this man did to me — 'cos I'm suing him for assault!"

MICHAEL BENTINE

Another friend for whom I had great admiration is no longer with us. I had known Michael Bentine for more than 50 years, from when we were all at the starter's gate for a possible inclusion in showbusiness. At that time we both knew that if we wanted to make progress we would need something that others didn't have. The question was what?

Both in our early 20s, we had finished almost five years with the RAF. We shared the same initials, were almost exactly the same age, and indeed, our

My three children pictured in 1978. From left to right are Anthony, Christine and Maxine. Christine is now living in Australia due to a mix-up at Paddington.

The Queen Mum pays me a compliment as Ronnie Corbett suppresses a giggle.

Quiz Master on *Family Fortunes* in 1980. How I hated that show.

I was once told …if you want to get ahead – get a hat. This was the last straw.

paths were to cross many times. Our first meeting was at the home of Tony Sherwood, my RAF pianist friend who had taught me the ukelele. Tony was a good-looking chap, but Mike, before he went in for a beard, was even more handsome. They had cooked up a double act in which Mike played a mad Russian and Tony provided the accompaniment. The act got them quite a few spots on BBC's *Variety Band Box*. They called themselves Sherwood and Forrest and were in vogue for quite a while.

Later, we were billed on a variety show at Nottingham Empire, where Mike was doing a solo with a prop that was the back of a chair. It was on this date that I received a telegram from the Czar of the entertainment world, Val Parnell. It was to tell me that I had been selected for my very first *Royal Command Performance* — this was in 1950. All the acts that I was appearing with that week came to the dressing-room to offer their congratulations. All of them except one — and he was a very well-known name.

I have never related this story before. I wouldn't now, except for the fact that Mike has gone and so has that well-known name. It happened at the digs we were sharing. About half a dozen of us sat down for supper, including Mike and the 'name'. I could hardly eat, the excitement of the *Command Performance* was too much for me.

The 'name' suddenly said: "You know why you've been chosen? Val Parnell is trying to make or break you!"

Mike put his fork down with a clatter. "What do you mean *break* him? What bloody reason would Mr Parnell have to break him? He wants to *make* him, because talent is a rare commodity and this boy has it. If you don't believe it, go out front one night and listen to the applause — then compare it with your own!"

The meal was finished in silence. A short while later we both shared top billing at the London Palladium with Max Miller and Anne Shelton. Although I never mentioned the episode again, I always looked on Mike as a sort of crusader.

For my 50th anniversary in showbusiness, the Variety Club of Great Britain paid me a tribute with a star-studded lunch at the Savoy Hotel in London. Mike sat next but one to me with his lovely wife, Clementina. After the lunch, my daughter-in-law, Celia, said: "I would have given anything to have been in Blossom's place next to such a wonderful man." I thought she was flattering me — but she was talking about Mike! His speech said too many nice things which makes it hard to be modest, so let's leave it.

Our next meeting was a bit later when we did a thing together at Sotheby's, raising money with some RAF memorabilia for the RAF Benevolent Fund.

When I heard about Mike's death, I was aboard a Qantas flight to Singapore. I found myself offering up a little prayer at 32,000 feet, wondering if he could hear what I was saying. Mike was into the strange world of the spiritual mediums and I thought: "I wonder if he will send me a message at some time, to say that he heard me."

I'm not into mediums and all that stuff, but I swear as I was thinking this, the plane started to shudder. The cabin light came on with the order to fasten seatbelts. It seemed so real that I found myself smiling and saying: "OK Mike, you've made your point."

The aircraft returned to normal and we had one of the smoothest landings that I can remember.

Coincidence? Of course it was, but Mike would have enjoyed the story!

THE ROYAL FAMILY

Sooner or later, at a dinner party or aboard a train, someone will ask: "Have you ever met so-and-so?" If I have, the next question is invariably: "What are they like?"

I have met many so-and-sos, have walked golf's golden fairways with champions of the game — and I do mean champions. I have partnered Seve Ballasteros, Greg Norman, Tony Jacklin, Bobby Locke and Johnny Miller, to name just a few.

I have chatted with every member of the Royal Family, from Her Majesty to Prince Edward, been 'bubbled' over by the Duchess of York — or 'Fergie' as she seems to be better known — and experienced the shy flutter and head tilt that trademarks Diana.

I have also walked the boards with the great Max Miller, Laurence Olivier, Bob Hope and Bing Crosby. Televised with Jack Benny and George Burns. And I've even helped Jackie Gleason recover from staggering when guesting on his TV show. I think I could fill a book just by 'name-dropping'.

The most asked-about are still the Royal Family.

Jennifer — she who I could never do without — held her hand over the phone.

"It's for you — it's Buckingham Palace!"

I thought it has to be Sykes up to one of his games. OK I'll play along with it.

"Yes Your Majesty, what can I do for you?"

A man's voice assured me that I was not speaking to a member of the Royal Family, but that he was phoning on the Queen's behalf. He went on to say that the Queen would like to have lunch with me on May 20th. Was there any food that I was not fond of?

Still thinking that it was Eric doing a very good impression of an equerry, I replied: "I don't like Spam. I had so much Spam during the war that if somebody cracked a whip, I'd probably start to gallop!"

The voice continued unshaken: "I'm sure that we could find something a little better than Spam!"

I became wary. "Is that you Eric?" The 'impression' had gone on a bit too long to be a leg-pull.

"Her Majesty has luncheon with just half a dozen people periodically, and she would like you to be there!"

It was true. The next day the envelope with no stamp arrived — just 'Buckingham Palace' in red lettering on the flap.

On the day I got into the taxi and said: "The Palace!"

Halfway up Piccadilly, I told the driver he was going the wrong way for the Palace.

"Listen mate, I've dropped customers at the Palace Theatre for more than 30 years — this is the right way!"

"I want Buckingham Palace!" I shouted.

"Oh! Why the bleedin' 'eck didn't you say so?"

What is Her Majesty The Queen like? She is a sweetie to whom neither television nor media renders justice. She is both interesting and interested, and enjoys herself when others are enjoying themselves. She has a dazzling smile which comes from the eyes and lingers there, and a joyful little laugh that you remember most of all. Over a two-hour lunch, the only worry I had was when one of the corgis 'jam-tarted'. It was an awful odour and I thought: "Good God! I hope that she doesn't think it's me!"

Prince Philip? I have met him on at least half a dozen occasions, the last time being on his 75th birthday at the Greenwich Naval College. At the time I was the owner of a Daimler that I'd restored. It was a 1950 model and had been owned by King George VI. I was to make a speech preceding the Prince, and sat next-but-one to him at the table. I showed him a photograph of the car, hoping to surprise him.

"Do you recognise the car, sir?" I asked. In his husky voice he replied: "No

I don't, whose is it?"

I told him that when King George VI — the Prince's father-in-law, of course — had died, the car was left to him, and I showed him various pictures with him at the wheel.

"Really! I don't remember it."

Perhaps he was being on guard and not committing himself, which I'm sure the Royal Family have to be doubly careful of doing, but it was the Daimler convertible that, at one time, had to be modified because the Prince's knees were touching the dashboard.

I have a letter from the makers proving that it was the rare 1950s vehicle and His Royal Highness, Prince Philip, was saying that he couldn't remember it!

When the car was finally sold at a Sotheby's auction last year, it was bought by a German and is now in Munich. It was mentioned to the buyer that it used to be driven by His Royal Highness, Prince Philip. All the purchaser said was: "Really!"

The rest of the Royal Family are a mixed bunch. If I had to give marks out of ten for personality, you might be surprised. So I won't.

SEAN CONNERY

I have often said that if you play a man three rounds of golf you'll find out the man's true nature, whether he's polite, a cheat, single-minded, good fun. Almost every quality comes to the surface and, after 18 holes, you will know your partner pretty well.

I have played several times with Sean, seen his eyes blaze at a bad shot, seen him get short-tempered at being held up by a slow game ahead and listened to him wax lyrical about his childhood days in Edinburgh. He's a good bloke.

Today he is a fine amateur golfer, but this story took place when he was like most of us beginners — bloody awful!

It was at Coombe Hill Golf Club, just outside London. Eric Sykes and I took on Sean and actor Stanley Baker. We beat them hands down. Later, in the club house, Sean came up and placed £60 on the bar with: "Here y'are Max, 60 quid. You'll find that's correct!" I asked him what the money was for and he explained that we had a bet of £20 on the first nine holes, £20 on the second, and a further £20 on the game. "That makes 60 quid!" he grinned.

This puzzled me because I had never played for this amount. In fact, the most that I'd ever wagered on a game was a couple of pounds. As Sean left,

Eric Sykes came into the bar. I told him about the money which, by today's standard would be worth a couple of hundred quid.

Eric then said that Stanley Baker had just paid him the same amount.

"Did you make the bet," I asked Eric.

He confessed that Sean had mumbled something in his Scottish accent before the game and Eric, whose hearing is very poor, just nodded his head, so Sean had assumed that the bet was on.

We had a drink and then began to laugh hysterically. We were both thinking the same thing: What a fight there would have been if we had lost!

TOMMY COOPER

Tommy and I started in showbusiness at about the same time. We had both spent about five years in the Forces, him in the Army, me in the RAF. We were both uncertain in which direction to go. Believe it or not, he was quite serious during his act at that time and hardly ever spoke. He let the conjuring earn the applause.

We played the night clubs in London's West End, and if that sounds glamorous, forget it. Most of those clubs were upholstered sewers and catered for the dregs of London's night life. They were the toughest audience that an act could experience and we really earned the standard £15 per week that we were paid, but we were young and enjoyed every minute of it.

Some nights we had to 'double', which means playing two different night clubs on the same evening. We'd perform our spots at about midnight at the Blue Lagoon, then rush to the Panama Club about half a mile away to do it all again for a different audience at around one.

It was quite simple for me to put on a raincoat over my dinner suit and run the distance to the next venue, but much more difficult for Tommy who not only had to carry two large suitcases filled with his props, but also had to 'load' — in other words prepare — his tricks, and that took time.

Tommy would go first at the first club, then follow me at the second. That way he got a little extra time to get his act ready.

One night, at the second club, an irate boss asked if I'd seen Tommy. I knew that he had left well before me and yet there was no sign of him at the Panama Club. The boss told me to do extra and I filled in until I saw the huge shape of Tommy come in and make for the dressing-room, which was the gents' lavatory. When I saw that he was ready, I wound up my stint and introduced him: "Ladies and Gentlemen — The Great Thomas Cooper!"

If you think that his tricks all went wrong when he was at the top of the bill, you should have been at the Panama that night — disaster! I honestly think that was the night he decided to make his living from tricks that went wrong, and the nervous giggle became part of his repertoire. I asked him afterwards what had made him so late.

"I came out of the club and was walking past Garrards the Jewellers in Regent Street when a policeman stepped out of a doorway to ask me what I had in the two cases. I said: 'Magic.' He said: 'Open the cases!' I tried to explain that I did a magic act and that all my tricks were in the cases, but he insisted.

"Of course, when I opened the cases, all the vases and rings were sparkling under the lights and he became suspicious. He thought I was a burglar who had just done a job. At that moment, up came another copper and he happened to be an amateur conjuror so, to prove that I was legitimate, he made me perform one of the tricks. So there I was in the middle of Regent Street at half past midnight, doing bottle-glass, glass-bottle, bottle-glass ..."

Then he said: "Max, I've had a frustrating day. Let's get pissed!" So we did!

TED RAY

Ted Ray was a fine comedian and a practical joker, right up to the end of his life. He had appeared in one of my television shows and was a big hit. We became firm friends.

I visited him at the Middlesex Hospital where he was in a bad way. The car accident in which he was involved left him with a broken leg, a fractured arm and they were having to graft skin to various parts of his anatomy.

I took him smoked salmon, champagne, a cake and lots of tit-bits. In no time we had the sister and nurses in for a small party. After a couple of hours Ted was exhausted and the sister tipped me off that it was time for him to rest. They all left and I was the last to say farewell. Like all comedians from the 'old school' Ted had learned to 'leave 'em with a laugh — that way they remember you the next time you make an entrance'. Ted Ray had been reared in that school. Through glazed eyes he managed to tell me a final story ...

"A few nights ago I needed a bed-pan. It had gone midnight and I was desperate. I rang and rang the bell, but no nurse came, so I attempted to do something about it. I lifted the bed covers off me, slid slowly to the end of the bed and managed to get to the pot with the plant in it. I took the plant out, managed to place the pot on the floor, undid my pyjamas and sat down on it. Just as I relaxed, the door burst open, the lights went on and there stood

Eamonn Andrews who cried: "Ted Ray! Tonight, This Is Your Life!"

Shortly after this, Ted passed on.

ERIC SYKES

We have been pals for more than 40 years. If he or I needed a friend I think we would call on each other first. Eric is a very fine script-writer and a very funny man.

He first learned of this latent comedy when we were both signed up for the BBC show *Educating Archie*, a show that won many awards. Apart from Eric and myself, the show unearthed a wealth of talent: Tony Hancock, Julie Andrews, Beryl Reid, Hattie Jacques and quite a few more.

When we first received the scripts, usually on a Sunday morning to be performed 'live' later that day, we'd read our parts in flat early morning voices. It was the inflection of the delivery that brought Eric's scripts to life. It was how Hancock's "Flippin' kids!" was born, and how I made a national catch phrase of "A good idea, son!"

It was because of this early morning reading that Eric decided to read his own comedy lines. It was usually half an hour of hilarity as he played each part himself. From this he managed to give us laughs that were unseen on the first reading and now we all knew how to attack the script.

From this his confidence grew until the series came to an end. He then entered the film world and his silent movies like *The Plank* and others, plus the long-running television series with Hattie Jacques, endeared him to audiences world-wide.

We became keen golfers together and have become quite competent players, but in the early days, we were like most others that take up the game — hackers!

It was during these 'hacking' days that Eric bought a house for his growing family. He had married a lovely lady who had nursed him when he had ear trouble and was hospitalised in London. Edith nursed him then and has looked after him ever since. They lived in a beautiful home, backing on to St Georges Hill in Weybridge. She also had four lovely children — I am god-father to one.

About that time, the mid-1950s, I was reported to be the highest-paid performer in Great Britain. I was almost resident comedian at the London Palladium, on radio every week, had best selling records, television and my name on billboards all over London — I have to tell you all this because it has a bearing on the story. I thought it would have been impossible to have been British and not to know the name of Max Bygraves.

Back to the 'hacking'. It was Eric's greatest wish to become a member of St Georges Hill Golf Club — his home backed on to the third hole, it would have been so convenient — and so he made an application to join.

On this particular day we were out on the course, having paid our fees and having got permission to play. As we searched for a lost ball on the fourth hole, two golf balls landed quite near to us without a "Fore!", "Lookout!" or "Kiss my foot!"

Soon after, two irate red-faced 'gentlemen' — and I use the word very loosely — humphed their way past, bristling with anger. Later on many more golfers 'came through' and as Eric and I thought that was all part of golf etiquette, we went on looking for our ball. We were that inexperienced.

A couple of days later, Eric received a letter from the club secretary. In essence it read:

> *Dear Mr Sykes*
>
> *You interrupted a competition on this course today — no courtesy was extended to the competitors and your manners leave a lot to be desired. We understand you are desirous of becoming a member of this club; if this is the behaviour we are to expect, we beg you not to bother. This also applies to your partner, Max Hargreaves.*
>
> *Yours etc.*

All this happened more than 35 years ago. Eric, who still lives nearby, and still enjoys golf, is still not a member.

DANNY LA RUE

You would have to travel a long journey to find a more generous person than Danny La Rue. His gifts and kindness to people he likes are legendary. He has survived in a crowded profession on sheer talent. As a female impersonator he has no equal and, although the years are passing many of us by, he still manages to attract audiences at home and abroad and leave 'em laughing.

If he has any fault at all, it is that he loves to 'rabbit'. He really could talk the hind leg off the proverbial donkey. When Danny gets a touch of the verbals it's best to shut up and listen, or else say: "Well, I must be off home 'cos of the baby sitter!" Let me tell you a Danny La Rue story …

Blossom and I went to see his show at the Regent Theatre in Sydney. The show was great. Afterwards we were invited backstage to Danny's dressing-room and we were told by his road manager, Jack Hanson, that Danny was on the other side of the stage talking to some members of the Sydney Ballet Corps, and that he would not be long. Jack gave us a glass of champagne and we waited ...

We were both hungry, having had nothing to eat since breakfast time, and Sydney — like many cities — seems to close down food-wise after 11pm. So we waited ...

Bloss kept looking at her watch. Then, after almost 20 minutes of waiting, she came out with the classic line that Danny dines out on: "We didn't have to wait this long for the real Queen!"

BENNY HILL

If you asked me who was the most famous comedian in the world, I would have to say Benny Hill. The last time that we worked together he told me that his Thames Television shows were being shown in 28 countries, probably more now because they show them and re-run them for ages.

Possibly the richest funny man around, his fame was unbelievable. Once, on a QE2 cruise, we were just leaving Rio de Janeiro, when a young honeymoon couple, hearing my English voice, asked me if I had ever heard of Benny Hill, and I boastfully told them that I actually knew him. They gazed at me as if I were the Messiah and they followed me around the ship for almost a week. On the same trip we made a stop at Tristan De Cunha — population 187 — where a woman who had previously been evacuated to England when the volcano was threatening to erupt, passed me a note to ask me to get a signed picture of Benny when I got back to the UK. I gave him the note later and he was more surprised than I was, that somebody in such a remote place should know of his work.

He was fabulously wealthy but was never bothered too much with money. His stimulant was his work and to make a gag or a funny routine come to life was really all he cared about. The press often tried to make copy from his spartan way of life, but I don't think that Benny even bothered to buy a newspaper.

This particular story isn't too much about Benny, but concerns a friend of mine named Johnny Kelly.

Johnny is retired and lives in Bognor Regis, but he once owned the

Hillingdon Social Club, just a few miles from Central London. This was in the 1940s, just after the war, and people generally were in the mood to be entertained. Johnny kept me going with regular bookings at the club where, for £3 a show, I always went well with the audience.

One particular day in summer I was unable to make a date because of a full week's engagement in Jersey. I wrote to apologise to Johnny and recommended a pal I had met, who was vacant and would do the job for £2.50 — two pounds and ten shillings in those days. I told him that the name was Benny Hill and that he wouldn't let him down.

Johnny still carries that note — held together with Sellotape now — and he will still produce it any time the occasion demands.

Not too long ago, when I was appearing in Bognor Regis, Johnny came to see the show and, sure enough, out came the note. Johnny gazed down at it: "Just imagine, Benny Hill for 50 bob!"

"Did you ever book him?" I asked.

"No fear — he was too bloody expensive!"

FRANKIE HOWERD

I have already mentioned how Frankie and I first met. Like most of us, Frankie had his ups and downs, but always came back. He was always able to capture a new breed of audience when he had exhausted another. He became bigger than ever with the part of the Roman slave in television's *Up Pompeii* He also fancied himself as a clairvoyant, always wanting to read hands, and he was pretty accurate too.

I have never been one for fortune-telling, but Frank would insist on giving a reading at least once a week: "One day you will be a millionaire!" he prophesied. You can imagine my reaction. There I was, living in digs that cost £2.50 a week, one suit and wondering what would happen when the tour was over. No trade and with a wife and baby to support, and there was this amateur fortune-teller telling me that I would one day be a millionaire! All I could say was: "Frank, I think you've got your wires crossed somewhere!"

It was the middle of last year I heard that he had been poorly. I called him to ask if he'd like to have lunch. He said he would and I chose one of the best restaurants in London, just the two of us. We talked mostly nostalgia and I asked him if he still read hands. He said that he did and took my hand and gazed at the palm for a long time.

"Didn't I tell you that one day you'd be a millionaire?" I nodded. "And didn't it come true?" Again I nodded. He gave me back my hand and said: "Well, in that case — pay the bill!" He made a hasty exit and that was the last time that I saw dear Frank alive.

GEOFF LOVE

For the obituary I wrote in the *Guardian* on Geoff Love — July 10th, 1991 — the heading was: 'Love — a many splendoured man'. I tried to put into words the deep affection and respect that I had — and still have — for the lovely Geoff.

We first met in the early 1950s. In those days Geoff was an arranger and I was recording for the HMV label. I was to record a song entitled *Meet Me On The Corner*, a successful Top Ten entry. We actually named a show after the title which had a long run at the London Hippodrome — now known as 'Stringfellows'. The record was a hit because of Geoff's fine arrangement.

We met casually over the years. Then, in 1972, Thames TV asked me to appear in a series called simply *Max*. I was given my choice of orchestras and plumped immediately for Geoff Love. So started a partnership on TV that lasted over 15 years.

Geoff always had trouble rolling his Rs. For our backchat, the writers, unknown to Geoff, would write in lines full of Rs, like: 'The Rolls-Royce is round on the ramp.' When Geoff delivered the line, it came out: "The Wolls-Woyce is wound on the wamp!" Sometimes, to get an extra laugh, I'd say: "Geoff, would you mind repeating that?"

Geoff also recorded as 'Manuel of the Mountains'. His records sold in large numbers down Argentina way. He provided backings for Shirley Bassey, Russ Conway and many more top recording stars. In between, he gave his time to the Stars Organisation for Spastics.

His happiest days were spent in Spain where he was water-skiing up to a short time before his death.

When work permitted, he and his lovely wife, Joyce, would go off in his Jaguar to snatch a few days in Sitges, south of Barcelona. He'd return and show off his sun tan. The grandson of a Cherokee Indian, it was difficult to see, but he assured us that it was there. Even Joyce, a born and bred English lady, would shake her head in disbelief.

On one of his last trips to Spain he was mugged. It happened just outside Lyons in France. He was flagged down by a 'con man' in another car. When Geoff slowed down, the man pointed to the back wheel and Geoff stopped and got out to see what was wrong. An accomplice jumped into the driving seat and was away with the Jaguar, plus all Geoff's belongings, passport and money and so on.

Geoff told me all this over the phone when he got back. "I don't suppose you'll feel like going to Spain again, will you Geoff?" I asked.

"Oh yes," he replied. "I don't feel the same without a sun tan!"

JACK BENNY

During the 1960s I was invited to appear on the *Jack Benny Show* in California, USA. For most of the time that I was there I had dinner with Jack, his wife Mary, and several showbusiness friends at his house in Beverley Hills.

After dinner one evening, Mary put on her coat to take their poodle for a walk round the block before retiring for the night. Jack and I sat in the lounge armchairs, puffing contentedly on two Havana cigars.

On the same block as Jack, lived film star James Stewart. He had recently made the movie *The Glenn Miller Story*. After the filming he liked the idea of the rimless spectacles he used in the film and took to wearing them regularly. Almost every impressionist in America at that time was impersonating James Stewart. It was an easy impression. All one had to do was fish a pair of rimless specs out of your pocket and drawl: "Waal ...er ...just a minute ...er ...hold on ..." to get thunderous applause. He was so recognisable and the drawl became a trade mark.

When Mary arrived back at the house with the poodle she said to Jack: "I just met Jimmy Stewart on the block, he was walking his dog. I asked him how he was and, do you know, you'd have thought he was doing an impression of himself. He said: 'Mary,' then went into the impression: 'Waal ...er ...look ...Mary ...er ...I ...er ...' I said: 'Look Jimmy, it's chilly. I don't want an impersonation, I just want to know how you are!'" And with that, she walked off.

Jack was flabbergasted. He clapped his hands to his face — as he did on most of his shows — and said in disbelief: "Oh Mary, you didn't say that to Jimmy?"

The dog began to bark, she looked at her husband and said: "I told Jimmy to stop doing James Stewart. You can cut out your impression of Jack Benny. And you ..." — she pointed at the barking poodle — "...you can stop your impression of Ethel Merman!"

PETER SELLERS

On my 1997 theatre tour in the UK I have spent some time in the North. Bloss decided, meanwhile, to go to Spain for a short stay with our daughter Maxine.

Bloss figured that it would be a good opportunity to see Maxine and our grandchildren, Oscar and Barnaby. It would also give her a chance to get out of our block in Victoria, which was being refurbished. The drilling, banging and dust, plus all the workmen wandering aimlessly (it seemed) about made it hard to believe that we live in one of London's most luxurious blocks. I keep threatening to move somewhere else, but it is so central and it would cause such upheaval if we did. Not only that, but my office and my wonderful Jennifer is only across the road, a three-minute walk away. This refurbishment has been going on for years. We have lived in the block for more than 25 years and for at least 15 of them have had to endure some of the noisiest and frightful nights imaginable.

We have survived fires, drunks, dope addicts, asbestos removal, thieves and burst pipes during our residence. We had scaffolding on the front of our building for more than *12* years. At varying times we have shared the block with stars like Lord Laurence Olivier, Peter Sellers, Jimmy Edwards, Ingrid Bergman and others, but all of them moved on eventually. I think that we are among the longest residents. Luckily it is not my home — my permanent home is in Bournemouth.

Peter, who lived above us, was the noisiest neighbour. When he moved in, he had the flat redesigned. For almost three months, the drilling and the banging drove us mad. Peter, in the meantime, was away from it all in Hollywood.

Laurence Olivier actually moved out, checked into a hotel and then sent the bill to our landlords, which they paid.

Peter Sellers had a hi-fi system that had a pounding bass. It would go on throughout the night: Peter was nocturnal and played records up until three and four in the morning. I had known Peter for more than 40 years and had often called him to say hello and chew the fat.

One particular night, when the music was going full blast, I picked up the phone at 1.30am and, in my best upper-class English voice, shouted at Peter: "Now look here! If this music does not cease, I will personally have you kicked out of the building!" I slammed the phone down, the music stopped and we never heard it again.

Almost three days later I met Peter in the elevator. Putting on his spiv voice he said: "Ere, this bleedin' Lord Olivier comes on a bit strong don't 'e? 'E phoned me the other night an' told me 'e'd 'ave me kicked aht o' the buildin'!"

I looked at him, one of the game's greatest impressionists, to see if he knew that it was really me who had phoned, but no! Until the day he died, he really thought that it was Olivier who had given him 'a bollocking'.

JUDY GARLAND

If you ever watched the television series *The Untouchables*, you will remember the narration by the staccato-voiced delivery of commentator Walter Winchell, who was probably the most powerful columnist in America during the 1950s. I was awarded a complimentary line in his column whilst appearing at the Palace, New York, with Judy Garland. From that one line alone, my hotel telephone never stopped ringing. Top agents MCA wanted me on their books, so did the William Morris Agency. I was wooed by almost the entire showbusiness scene. Yet all he said was: 'Max Bygraves, the funny man from England, puts paid to the rumour that Englishmen have no sense of humour — don't miss him …'

Winchell started life in vaudeville and was a hoofer. How he gave it up and eventually became the most important showbiz newspaperman in the USA I don't know, but he was, and he remained so for his lifetime. Most people in US showbusiness would have shot their own grandmothers for an inch or two in his column — and Judy Garland was no exception.

We performed two shows daily at the Palace, a matinee at 2.30pm, plus an evening show at 8pm. Most of the theatrical and press people came to the afternoon show, there were no empty seats, every show was a sell-out, and tickets were as difficult to get as for the Men's Final day at Wimbledon.

The show had been running for several weeks when, one Wednesday matinee, the buzz went round backstage: "Winchell's in!" Even the stage-hands moved twice as fast.

Wearing the fedora that he was famed for, he made his entrance into the stalls, removing the hat only when the lights went down for the overture. By now, the entire audience was aware that the Great One was in their midst.

With two or more songs to go, Judy decided to introduce Winchell to the crowd. They cheered, and when those in the upper circle complained loudly that they could not see him, he cheerfully left his seat and walked toward the orchestra pit so that they could get a better view. Judy enticed him on to the stage to thunderous applause. And he was beaming and enjoying every moment as the spotlight picked him out.

Judy Garland told him how thrilled she was to have him on the stage, they threw compliments at each other, then Winchell surprised Judy by telling her that he had actually worked on this stage before as a dancer. She was genuinely surprised and asked what sort of dancing he did. Winchell asked the musical director for a stop chorus of *Bye Bye Blues*, a standard for most dancers. The roof almost fell in when their favourite reporter went into 'a buck and wing'. I stood on the side of the stage watching all this and couldn't believe the standing ovation they gave him for those few simple steps. They cheered him all the way back to his seat. Anything that Judy did after was an anticlimax. It was a case of 'follow that if you can!' Next day there was the glorious review of the *Judy Garland Show* and everyone was happy.

Two days went by and Winchell turned up again, but this time with a couple of friends. He got called on again and the applause was even louder. The spot got longer — he was really stage-struck. The following Monday he came back again. He sent notes backstage for Judy to mention the six friends he had brought along. He also had a couple of questions for her to ask when she called him up on stage. *The Judy Garland Show* was slowly turning into the *Walter Winchell Show* — and Judy wasn't too pleased with the way things seemed to be going. Something needed to be done!

Sid Luft, Judy's manager, who later became her husband, hit on the idea of telling Winchell that members of the Musicians' Union were not allowed to play for any performer who was not a card-carrying union man. He showed Winchell a letter on MU notepaper that testified to this.

The write-ups on Judy stopped from that moment. Judy was sad about that, but relieved.

Years later, when Winchell had passed away, I met Sid Luft in Bond Street and, as we strolled toward Piccadilly, we talked about that Winchell episode.

"It was a good thing that the Musicians' Union sent that letter wasn't it Sid?"

He grinned. "It was a good thing that my brother-in-law was not only the musical director, but was the union representative as well. He had the headed notepaper that we typed up. If we hadn't, Winchell would have been on until the day he died!"

Many great stars I have met, and we all have one thing in common: the need to feel wanted by the real stars of life — YOU!

CHAPTER TWENTY-ONE

The London Palladium

TO DODGE some of the heavy traffic in London's West End, Bert, my driver, tried a few short cuts, but we were finally brought to a standstill at the top of Carnaby Street. For seven or eight minutes I sat in the back of the car, gazing at a door that I must have passed through hundreds of times: the stage door of the London Palladium.

My appearances there in long-running shows, pantomimes and charity performances — not forgetting the many television appearances on *Sunday Night At The London Palladium* — made me a regular performer there for more than 11 years.

Shows with titles like *Wonderful Time*, *Swinging Down The Lane*, *We're Having A Ball*, and pantos like *Mother Goose* and *Cinderella*, kept me busy for most of my time at this tip-top venue that every star — or aspiring star — dreamed of playing.

To many visitors it has no glamour from the outside. It is down a side street near Oxford Circus. Taxis can hardly make it up Argyll Street to the entrance, parking is almost non-existent, and the stage door in Marlborough Street, where I was sitting in a traffic jam, reminds me of a brewery in South London. Yet the 'House Full' boards at this 2,000-plus seater are out most evenings, and it has earned its title of 'The World's Greatest Theatre'.

Apart from my solos on stage, I have walked the boards there with almost every 'name' in the showbiz world. The Crazy Gang, Max Miller, Laurence Olivier, Gigli, Bob Hope, Jack Benny, Lena Horne, Perry Como, Tony Bennett, Dinah Shore, Shirley Bassey, Norman Wisdom, Dorothy Lamour, Count Basie, Judy Garland. I could fill a page about most of these performers who became friends, and every one of them was starry-eyed at the atmosphere that was evoked from just standing on the stage of this most friendly of theatres.

At the turn of the century it started life as Hengler's Circus and some of the greatest circus acts from around the world performed there. For quite a number of years after that it became just another London theatre, off the track of 'Theatre World' which was primarily in The Strand and Shaftesbury Avenue.

During the war years, names like Tommy Trinder, Max Miller and Vera Lynn filled in when the Crazy Gang were not 'at home'. The usual venue for the well-known names was usually the Holborn Empire, two miles away, but the Holborn had been badly bombed, and so the then Czar of entertainment, a gentleman named George Black, transferred the acts to the Palladium.

When George Black died, just after the war, the booking of the theatre was taken over by the new boss of Moss Empires, whose name became even more famous than the acts he booked: Val Parnell! Val, who was a good friend, transformed the Palladium from a 'date up a side street' to the world's No.1. He signed up big American star names to help put it on the world map. One of the first was Mickey Rooney, who was good box-office but had no real act and was a big disappointment to the British theatre-goer, more used to polished performers like Sid Field and Billy Bennett, and big bands led by such personalities as Jack Hylton and Henry Hall.

Later, Val landed a name that won the hearts of the Londoners — Danny Kaye. In those days, the top of the bill act was usually allowed a 15-minute spot. Danny Kaye broke all the rules by staying on stage for almost an hour. The press loved him, Royalty adored him and the queues around Argyll Street lined up in all weathers to see this performer who had the training and ability to win over audiences in a way that had never been witnessed before. In short, he became a sensation. I saw him several times and later we became friends.

British performers were now allowed longer. Instead of eight or nine acts on a variety bill, more time was allowed for the headliner. On one of the last variety bills that I topped at the Palladium there were only two performers: myself, and American dancer, Chita Rivera. We certainly learned a lot from Danny Kaye!

After Val Parnell had used up most of the American performers, he switched to lavish-style shows that usually ran from May until Christmas. Apart from myself, Val built shows around Harry Secombe, Tommy Cooper, Des O'Connor, The Beverley Sisters, Norman Wisdom, George Formby, Ken Dodd and almost any other performer who was 'hot'. Each show was lavishly produced by Bernard Delfont and staged by Robert Nesbitt. It was a great money-spinning format for the box-office which ticked on for many years.

When Yul Brynner decided to come to London with his Broadway hit *The King And I*, he insisted that it must be staged at the Palladium. He rented the theatre then, using his own finance, converted the dressing-room for himself. Later, when he had left, I had the luxury of using the same room that he had refurbished. It was so sumptuous and such a joy after the one that I had used for years, the one that had the fumes of the basement coke-house drifting up during the winter months, the one where the only luxury I was allowed was a life-saving air extractor. Yul Brynner paid £50,000 for the conversion — a gift to the owners!

After *The King And I* production left, the theatre was often rented to show producers. At the time of writing, Lionel Bart's *Oliver* is running, and still performing to sell-outs after more than three years.

There are fewer and fewer entertainers around to go back to the style of entertainment that was. Rentals are a 'no risk' bet for the present owners, who have, alas, become merely landlords.

As a result, the Palladium image has perhaps diminished a little, but it is still a great thrill to stand on that historic stage. Early in the morning, when the place is empty and silent, you can almost hear the ghostly echoes of laughter, and one special voice saying: "Miller's the name — there'll never be another!"

CHAPTER TWENTY-TWO

Finale

MY publisher has warned me that he now has plenty of material for this book and that I must think seriously about ending it — there should be a final chapter. I have enjoyed writing all that has gone before and I will be sorry to have to call a halt.

One person who has mixed feelings about me stopping is Bloss. At the moment she is still holidaying in Spain with our daughter, Maxine. She isn't too bothered about whether I write or not, but I am well aware that I have the habit of going off into 'another world' whenever I try to recall incidents that may possibly be of interest. I am often being told to 'come back down to earth'. She will often say: "Can I get through to you for just one minute?" It is at times like that she will remind me that it is one of the grandchildren's birthday, and would I write 'something nice' on their birthday card?

On the other hand, she knows that I am not bored. I have plenty of dates to fill my time and almost every journey has its funny incident — always perfectly true — which needs recording. For example, last night I was appearing at the Guildhall in Preston, and this morning I discovered that I had not packed a razor. I called the receptionist as they usually keep such items as toothbrushes, toothpaste and razors and so on available for forgetful people like me. I enquired if she could sell me a disposable razor. She said: "Hang on chook …" In a little while she came back to the phone and said: "There's no disposable razors, but we've got these plastic ones that you can use a couple of times and then throw away!"

On the way back to London, the M1 was a constant stream of traffic. At times there were eight lanes filled with cars, all going at 70mph. About 30 miles from the end of this busy, busy motorway, Bert and I both gasped in disbelief at a grey-haired man waiting to cross the eight lanes of traffic — on a push-bike!

I wondered how long he would have to wait. Bert said that he had passed him in February 1987. He added: "He couldn't risk it at night — 'cos he had no bicycle lamp!"

So, I guess it is time to wind up this epistle and hope, dear reader, that this book has entertained you a little. The next thing on my agenda is that when it finally reaches the shops in a few months time, I will have to help the publisher to publicise it. This means 'plugging', chat shows on radio and TV. Interviews in the press, who will be quite unwilling to give any space because it is 'not sordid enough ...not enough skeletons to come out of the cupboards'.

There will be, hopefully, some book signings at bookstores and possibly sales after performances at theatres. Either way, perhaps we'll have the opportunity of meeting in person. We will soon know if the book is a success but, once again dear reader, knowing you have got this far pleases me more than if I had won the Lottery!

Thanks for the interest.
Yours Sincerely
MAX BYGRAVES

Index